Managing
Genius

Master the art of managing people

Denny Long

Published by Franklin Green Publishing
P.O. Box 51
Lebanon, Tennessee 37088
www.franklingreenpublishing.com

Printed in the United States of America

ISBN 9781-936487-318

I have tried to recreate events, work experiences and conversations from my memories of them. Some names and identifying details have been changed to protect the privacy of individuals.

Cover and Interior Design: Bill Kersey, www.kerseygraphics.com

So, my teenage daughter walks by the other day.

"How's the book going Dad?"

"I almost have it done."

*"You know that I'm never going to read that thing.
So, give it to me in a sentence."*

*"OK Katie, Here it is:
I discovered Managing Genius."*

There are only three ways to get work done.

Do it yourself...as an individual contributor.

Share it...by asking willing colleagues and friends to work *with you*. They help based on relationships.

Delegate it...by hiring and managing employees who work *for you*.

Contents

Sarah's Question

Sarah is at the door of my office wondering if I have a minute. She pauses to collect her thoughts. She asks sheepishly, "I realize I should know this, but how do I fire someone?"

Sarah is a senior software manager at our Fortune 100 company. She manages twenty-five employees, with a handful of contractors coming and going. Big job, high visibility and cutting-edge technology.

She came to us from Stanford with an undergraduate EE and masters in computer science. She is a rock star software architect who is extremely bright, quick and innovative.

Sarah previously had a highly successful run as a senior contributor on cutting-edge software development teams. She is a master with the Agile software process. She is highly regarded in our company and well-liked by her colleagues.

Five years ago Sarah's boss unexpectedly left during a major project. This gave her the big break to move into the management ranks. She embraced her new managing role with enthusiasm. She was full of ideas.

At the time she gushed, "I want my employees to love their jobs." She dove into a pile of leadership books and signed up for the suite of leadership classes that the company offers. She called her parents to share her exciting career milestone.

However, as Sarah sits down in my office today, her demeanor tells me that the bloom is off the rose.

She says she loves the daily interaction with her employees but she feels bogged down with the administrative side of managing people—explaining policy, approving time off, signing expense statements and dealing with individual requests. There is always some new policy or program coming to her from HR.

She shares that at the end of the day she shuffles through emails and texts where people want her to make difficult decisions. It is not easy to find simple answers that make everyone happy and keep the project on schedule.

Sarah shares, "This weekend I could be at Whistler skiing with my friends. Instead, I'll be stuck at home filling out performance appraisals."

In private moments she wonders if she made the right decision moving into management. She misses writing code and being part of the software development team.

Because I am a senior HR leader for the organization, managers like Sarah regularly come by my office to decompress and ask for advice. I have been coaching her on how she can be more assertive in giving feedback, how to lead meetings and a dozen other practical skills seldom taught when someone moves from individual contributor into management.

Sarah continues, "Where do you go to learn how to fire people? Is there a 'firing range' where I practice, LOL?"

Sarah's pressing problem today is Zachary, an employee she inherited in the last reorganization. He is a highly talented but cocky software architect who designed a big revenue-generating product. Now he acts like he is entitled to special treatment as the resident expert.

Sarah shares that Zachary thinks he can come and go as it suits his fancy. He is perpetually late for meetings. When he finally gets there, he fills the room and expects the last word.

Sarah shares, "Sometimes I think he's listening to me but later I find he was just nodding his head."

"Then I hear that Zachary is 'dissing me' behind my back. How can I get him to respect me as his manager?"

Sarah has more to share if we have the time.

Sarah drifts into a couple more personnel challenges. "You won't believe this. I gave Sanjay a big chance to present his work to senior management. He totally embarrassed himself with his lack of preparation."

Without taking a breath, she continues, "Then Natalie assured me that she was on schedule but then she surprised me by dropping the ball. Tyler and Blake still refuse to get along, forcing me to work around their personal drama."

As we talk, Sarah scans my bookshelf and ticks off the popular leadership books that she has already read.

She picks up the classic book on leadership, *Good To Great.* She quotes the oft-repeated business maxim, "You've got to get the right people on the bus."

As she flips through the book, she points out her dilemma. "Sounds great in theory but how do I actually get Zachary *off* the bus?"

The reality is that any manager, below CEO, sees the prospects of getting people "off the bus" as arduous, if not virtually impossible. So managers like Sarah often feel like they are not actually driving the bus.

As managers try to deal with employee issues, they become increasingly aware that anything they do and say is under a microscope. Senior leaders and HR are averse to messy people situations, so they hold good managers to a high standard for maintaining peace in the neighborhood.

"TGOD for human resources," she says with a laugh. Sarah tells me that Zachary has found a sympathetic ear with one of the HR reps. He has cheerfully offered to mediate our next meeting to ensure that "everyone gets listened to." Sarah calls him "Jeffrey Weinerslav" after the HR guy on *30 Rock.*

Sadly true, HR can feel like the live-in grandmother who meddles in our parenting style, while taking no responsibility for the sick child in the middle of the night.

Sarah will need to follow a well-choreographed script to hold this difficult conversation with Zachary. She will have to jump through hoops when people chime in with an opinion. When employee issues become complicated, managers may take the easy way out and wait for the next reorganization. "The company made me do it."

We have run out of time and Sarah jumps up to fly to her next meeting. No immediate solution on Zachary but she seems to have brightened a bit. As she runs out the door she says, "To be continued."

I know Sarah appreciates the opportunity to vent her fears and frustrations, even if there are no easy answers. It feels like Sarah will leave carrying the same backpack of managing burdens that she came in with, albeit repacked.

As I reflect on our meeting, I think that the most important advice I can give Sarah is something that is difficult to apply. She needs to stop looking over her shoulder and trust her best judgment. However, I do not believe Sarah can do this without ignoring the sting of criticism that is wearing her down.

As I watch her run down the hallway, I wonder where she would go, outside of my office, to let down her guard and share her managing struggles? Where does Sarah go to learn how to manage people?

This is a great mystery to me.

We should all be top management experts by now with all the books, training and HR staff hovering around at our disposal.

Later, I am walking through the dark parking lot. I see Sarah in the office of a trusted colleague where she is, quite possibly, getting a second opinion on her personnel dilemmas.

The office window frames Sarah. In the picture is the typical good manager that I have worked with over the years. Sarah has all the right stuff—professional abilities, initiative and ability to deliver results. She is an effective communicator with endearing people skills.

As I look at the picture, I can see that Sarah is not confident as a people manager. She is struggling to keep her many plates spinning and it is difficult to imagine a time when she will feel successful.

As I drive home, I wonder. . . How can a good manager like Sarah step-up to become an exceptional manager?

A Meeting with Emily

The next morning, Emily strides into my office with a huge smile. She is juggling two Starbucks lattes and her iPad. Emily is the director of a large software test group. Simply stated, her group finds the bugs in the software before you do.

She walks in with a purpose. It is clear that she has already thought through why she is here. Her preparation gives her confidence and poise; she seems ready for anything.

Emily was first promoted into management four years ago as a test manager. Within eighteen months she was promoted to director for the entire thirty-employee test group and several offshore groups.

Emily is a geek with social skills. She has an engineering degree from Michigan State. She has a self-effacing style that draws people in. She often says, "I'm a Big Ten kind of girl."

She likes to remind me that so far she has avoided all the training where they "mold good leaders," as she says it. However, she has embraced her management role with a passion.

I thankfully accept her coffee bribe. She begins to apprise me of what is happening in her work group, referring to notes on her iPad.

She has recently made some decisions that she wants to run by me. Emily methodically talks me through her rationale for what is happening and what she intends to do.

During her discourse, she mentions a mistake that she made. With a laugh she says, "Remind me not to do that again."

Emily occasionally takes a breath to see if I have any "wisdom to add." Her eyes light up with a couple ideas that I share.

I ask her about a couple past issues and I am pleased that she has already "put them to rest."

She asks me a specific question that fills a hole in her logic. However, she is not hunting for answers. Emily is clearly not a leader who is lost or acting helpless.

There is one matter for which she has several alternative solutions. She wonders which way I lean.

I explain my rationale and she brightens at my feedback. "Precisely, Watson," she says, which is one of her favorite retorts. It makes me feel like we are working collaboratively.

We are talking about solutions, not positions. I never feel Emily is trying to cover herself.

There was a recent issue with one of her employees running an end around on her and her team. She was quick to correct this without acting out against the personal affront.

She says with a smile, "I reminded Devin that I'm willing to talk further about this, but we need to remember why we are here." Emily has the presence of mind to come back to the big picture and not get pulled into side skirmishes. She seems to be steering the entire group in one direction and not just catering to a series of individual whims.

We talk about Reyna, who is her latest employee challenge. She explains, "She is all thrust and no rudder. But I have found ways to bring out her best." She steps up to the white board to draw out where she fits into the flow of work and how she has realigned Reyna's job to best use her skills.

Emily has a knack for getting to the heart of complex issues. This gives people good reason to want to listen to her.

Last week, I sat in Emily's Monday morning strategy session waiting for my turn in the agenda. During the meeting she was called into the hallway to answer a pressing budget question for the controller.

Without a word from her, one of her employees jumped in to lead the meeting and keep everyone on agenda. He was as good as Emily leading meetings. The group smoothly moved forward and stayed on task.

When she returned, the team dove into an organized approach to get to the root of a sticky technical problem. For a while, people were bouncing off the walls with ideas and opinions. Emily participated both as a team member and discussion leader.

Eventually, Emily pulled the group back together to give closure so that everyone knew what would happen next. People left looking engaged and energized.

Back to our meeting, Emily's face brightens as she tells me about a couple people on her team who have recently accomplished noteworthy work. What I like about Emily is that she sees her people as capable, as if they are the reason we are here. She mentions people by name and understands their work. Emily shows a high public opinion of her employees.

Emily gives me a heads-up on Christopher, who is an under-performing software team leader. Emily has been coaching Christopher and it is clear to her that managing teams is not his strong suit. Emily has given Christopher clear feedback that she sees him as an individual contributor for his next assignment.

I do not have much to add. The whole process has moved ahead efficiently without drama or third-party involvement.

I get the feeling Emily takes ownership for whatever is happening within her group. She does not complain about roadblocks. She does not act as if senior management is against her. Policies may be just speed bumps and she makes it sound like HR is working for her.

Meeting with Emily feels like conversing with a skilled cook who is able to carry on a detailed conversation while cooking a gourmet dinner. Skilled chefs have mastered the core essentials to smoothly move through a series of complex steps without pause or worry. They never seem scattered or distracted with what they are doing next.

This allows them to maintain a personal connection with the people in the room, while at the same time creating an impressive meal.

In the same way, Emily knows what managers do to keep moving their teams forward. She is relaxed and able to bring out the best in her employees because she is not worried about what she will say or do next.

My phone rings and Emily is off to another meeting.

Later that day, I walk by a meeting room and see Emily at a white board discussing a work project with a small group of her employees.

I pause to reflect on the scene.

It is a picture of a confident and effective people manager. Emily seems to be able to put her hand in the fast-moving stream and guide the water in different directions without making huge waves.

Emily is a wonder to me.

Where did she learn to lead groups? How did Emily master the everyday mechanics of managing people? Why do people willingly listen to her and follow her lead?

As I walk away, I am reminded that exceptional managers like Emily are the secret ingredient for our business' success.

Emily is a Managing Genius.

Finding Managing Genius

I set out on a five-year quest to find what is behind the uncommon quality of Managing Genius. I sought to answer the question, "What do great managers like Emily do?"

I decided that the best way to research Managing Genius was to study the exceptional managers whom I have personally worked with in my career. I identified fifty of the best of the best people managers. I call this list the Managing Genius 50 (see Appendix).

Our shared work experiences became the framework for this book. I went back through my work journals and wrote real life examples that capture their composite actions and collective mastery.

I started my career in engineering and production operations. The last twenty years I have been a senior HR leader.

I have worked in Fortune 100 companies like McCaw Cellular Communication, AT&T Wireless Services and Weyerhauser. In addition, I have worked in numerous technology startups and other mid-sized businesses in Seattle. This has allowed me to work in the trenches with hundreds of people managers at all levels of the organization— CEOs, senior executives, group directors, senior managers, mid-managers and team leaders.

What I Did

I have hands-on experience working within the bowels of the business. I have helped build business units and entire org charts. This allows me to draw on knowledge and understanding of how the business enterprise works. Been there, done that.

Interestingly, professors and pundits often study leadership from a distance where they characterize what is happening "over there in that building." However, you see things much differently when you work with leaders inside the meeting room where they make real decisions concerning real people doing real work.

Another requirement for this study was the sweep of time. Management decisions play out across business changes, budget cycles and the whims and fancies of senior leadership. The cast of players is in flux, the budget is a moving target and the script gets rewritten often.

This book is not a study of flash leadership where you rearrange the deck chairs. I believe that seeing work through and achieving sustained results will always be an attribute of a Managing Genius. So the researcher needs to hang around to see how the story ends.

I also decided to focus on the leaders, like Emily, who take ownership for current events and pressing business decisions. Managing people is not a hobby where we have the flexibility to step away to perfect the craft. *Right now,* we carry responsibility and the clock is running.

There is an amazing difference in people managers who embrace the urgency of the business. Great managers understand that customers are counting on their teams. Deadlines are there for a reason and money is being spent.

Another attribute that I esteem in any Managing Genius is their amazing ability to improvise in the moment to find what I call imperfect solutions. We read books that focus on the lofty success formulas of popular CEOs but the real experiences that managers face are more like off-road driving. We are managing people, right?

I sought to capture the Managing Genius mindset that allows them to make do and play through. They seemingly have an internal compass that keeps them moving forward when facing sticky problems. They can weather mistakes, miscues and the occasional gaffe. Why does their work group seem more resilient to bumpy roads and dust?

Finally, I decided that it is essential to look at the whole picture of the managing role. Leaders cannot be exceptional at anything unless they take ownership for all components of the job.

Our bookshelves are filled with new ideas on some "shiny part of leadership." However, a Managing Genius like Emily must succeed at hiring, firing and everything in between, all before lunch. Great managers have a knack for multitasking across the whole board.

I set out to create a model of Managing Genius that captures the whole picture of what great managers do. From my everyday work experiences with the 50 top managers, I boiled down their common genius to a framework with ten essential elements.

This book is organized to give you a one-stop total resource for each of these elements. You get ten chapters that are "mini-books" which give you everything you need to master that essential.

Take a quick tour through the book so you can get to know the neighborhood. You can read the chapters in any order. I suggest you start with Chapter Six, *Captain of the Ship*. Once you have read it, you will think differently about your managing role.

Important to note, these ten elements are not independent steps to be followed in sequence. They are strands of the rope which are braided together in order to combine them into a stronger form. See them woven together as a *single action* that makes the Managing Genius.

I stop to say, *remember to be you*. There were not two identical Managing Geniuses in this study. If you met them, you would find fifty personalities with their own unique managing style.

However, all master the ten elements that make the Managing Genius.

What I Discovered

5	5
Things you do	Things you think about

5 THINGS TO DO

Your goal: Master the five irreducible minimums for managing the people who work for you. This brings clarity and mutual understanding of what to expect from my manager. Infuse your personality and communication style into how you use these core elements.

Do you like to be in a relationship where you are continually "left hanging" with unresolved issues and dangling conversations?

People will eventually step back from ambiguity and uncertainty. If your manager is scattered and random, employees may feel the need to fend for themselves. You may sense emotional detachment or mistrust.

Understand that your employees have a pragmatic side that needs feeding first. They may not have the ability to articulate them in the moment, but they have simple questions that simmer below the surface: What do you want from me? Why is this important? What happens next?

Your employees also care that everyone around them share the same clarity and even-handed treatment. It bothers people to see that their team members are not treated well. We want to see that someone is steering the ship to create consistency, order and a sense of closure.

From this study, Managing Geniuses will always master the following five tactical areas. These work together to provide welcome clarity for everyone at the table. This is what great managers do as an everyday way of doing business.

Teach and discuss these so everyone understands your managing approach. Embed these within the fabric of everyday team operations.

Plan and Set Up Work (Chapter 1)

It is easy to fall into firefighting mode, slapping together a plan. It is Managing Genius to think before you delegate work. Earn respect for your understanding of the business and become knowledgeable about what you are asking people to do. Take the lead to create a culture of planning and preparation. Turn this into a group practice so everyone plans and prepares as a way of doing business.

▒ Set Expectations and Delegate Responsibility (Chapter 2)

People would love to work for you, if only they knew what you wanted. Master the art of delegating in clear and unambiguous ways. Great Managers guide workplace conversations, meetings and hand-offs to ensure that everyone knows what they are supposed to do. It is clear across your group why each and everyone is here. This becomes embedded in the work culture as everyone seeks clarity and works together to weed out ambiguity.

▒ Recognize and Champion (Chapter 3)

It is pure Managing Genius to use positive affirmation to encourage and guide people. When you succeed at this, you rise to a higher level of leadership. Recognizing great performance builds awareness of what is important to you and the team. People can proactively align their actions and behavior. This will establish a spirit of optimism and encouragement.

▒ Feedback (Chapter 4)

Giving and receiving feedback is a business essential for any successful manager. Regular and honest feedback will forge relation-ships based on shared expectations and trust. Master the art of sharing feedback through your intentional words, delivery and timing. Not all feedback comes from the manager—you ensure that your employees get the feedback they need, when they need it. You set the tone through your openness to receiving personal feedback and embracing change.

▒ Guideback (Chapter 5)

Every manager will face individual employee problems sooner or later. You prefer to *guide people back* to harmony with the business, the team and you. When needed, you can confidently step in to resolve performance or behavior issues without fanfare and drama. You take the lead and get to the heart of the matter to ensure that everyone concerned reaches closure. If needed, you can move the issue forward through progressive steps, including taking ownership for the firing process.

5 THINGS TO THINK ABOUT

Your goal: These five essentials are foundational for a high-performing team. These create a shared mindset for how your people connect and interact with you and the team. It creates a powerful team culture when you weave all five into one.

From my study, these essentials lay the groundwork for effective working relationships between managers and team members. For the manager, these five essentials are "do-it-yourself team building."

This is how you interact with your employees and how they, in turn, interact with you and one another. This is how you want people to think when they walk into work. "Work with me in this way and this is what you can expect from me."

These are the "operating system" of your team.

Accordingly, they run in the background to direct and guide the team's way of doing business. Like your computer, occasionally your team will need a reset or even a new install.

These build respect for your leadership as you establish a consistent way of doing work.

You may not see the value of these qualities at first glance, but in time you will see the *absence* of corresponding undesirable attitudes and behaviors. For example, adult attitudes are one of the team essentials; non-adult attitudes become visible in undesired drama and entitlement.

For all five of these areas, a chapter in this book will teach you everything you need to know and only what you need.

▧ Captain of the Ship (Chapter 6)

Why should your employees pay attention to you? This is your team and you have responsibility for the people who do the work. You will need to establish respect for your managing role and find effective ways to ensure that people are listening. Learn the art of combining authority, power and influence to delegate work and directing people. Teach your people how you intend to manage so they know what to expect.

Value People (Chapter 7)

Do you value people or are they just cogs in a machine? It is pure Managing Genius to show respect and value for every member of your team independent of their job title or current performance. This builds long-lasting commitment beyond today's work. Consider how this one element compliments the other elements. Role model this group norm and pump it into the air at work.

The Adult Way (Chapter 8)

Everyone searches for the magic key for team culture. Actually it is quite simple: adult behavior is the one ingredient that drives every aspect of the work culture. A Managing Genius builds and leads an adult-minded work culture based on maturity and personal responsibility. When you foster The Adult Way, you are leading your work group onto the high road.

Individual Approach (Chapter 9)

It is Managing Genius to see your employees as individuals. Recognize their unique desires and abilities so you can manage how to bring out their best. This insight allows you to fine-tune your managing approach to the situation and individual. In turn, this creates a culture based on performance versus entitlement. You cannot have a high performance culture without allowing individuals to shine. "We are a group and a team, but I am unique."

Workplace Relationships (Chapter 10)

People come to work expecting a colleague-friendly work community. Social connections at work are a strong indicator of job satisfaction. However, community does not just happen. It is Managing Genius to shape and guide the work culture to create ways to build rapport and affinity. You set the tone and establish the right balance. Manage this as you would any team essential.

Discover Your Managing Genius

- From the research, a Managing Genius will always master ten key areas.

- In this book there is a chapter for each of the ten key areas. Read each chapter like a mini-book for that core essential. You get everything you need and only what you can use.

- See the big picture. First scan the bold headers and summaries so you learn how the parts work together.

- The magic is in how the whole system works together. Managing people is like a decathlon. Master all ten elements.

- The best learning comes when you can fine-tune your managing approach while on the job. This book is organized for easy access when you need inspiration or specific guidance. For example, before giving feedback look through the feedback chapter.

- Do you manage managers? Now you have a book to train, coach and set expectations for your direct reports who also manage people. Use this framework to assess and problem-solve struggling managers.

- Invest in the future: Use this book as a discussion guide to mentor select individuals who show promise for leading and managing in the future.

- Be sure to read this book slowly. Managing Genius is a one-year quest.

Plan and Set Up Work

Everyone comes planned,
prepared and ready

Big Idea

Make work organized and efficient. Think and plan before passing work to others and avoid tossing work over the wall or firefighting the latest issue. Earn respect for your knowledge of the business and how work gets done. Make it an everyday practice that everyone on your team comes prepared and ready.

This is some rescue. You came in here, and you didn't have a plan for getting out?
　　　　—Princess Leia to Luke Skywalker on the Death Star in *Star Wars*

Indiana Jones: *Get back to Cairo. Get us some transport to England ... boat, plane, anything. Meet me at Omar's. Be ready for me. I'm going after that truck.*
Sallah: *How?*
Indiana Jones: *I don't know ... I'm making this up as I go.*
　　　　　　　　　　　　　　　　　　—From *Raiders of the Lost Ark*

Jack: *Six Sigma says that a manager must understand every aspect of the business that he or she oversees.*
Liz: *Which means?*
Jack: *I'll be here everyday. Soaking it up.*
　　　　　　　　　　　　　　　　　　　　　　　　　　—*30 Rock*

Oh, this is a refined operation, son, and I've got it timed down to the last wave of the brakeman's hand on the last train outta town.
　　　　　　　　　　　　　—Professor Harold Hill, *The Music Man*

I know you can fight, but it's our wits that make us men.
　　　　　　　　　　　　—William Wallace's father, *Braveheart*

Important to Know

To get one's ducks in a row essentially means to ensure all of the small details or elements are taken into consideration before embarking on a new endeavor, like a new work initiative or product launch.

The most popular theory suggests that the phrase get *one's ducks in a row* came from early bowling alleys that used shorter and thicker pins than are used today, which led to the nickname *ducks*. Before the advent of automatic resetting machines, bowling pins would have to be manually placed between bowling rounds.

Get your Ducks in a Row

1 Before starting the work

2 A goal is not a plan

3 Is the work possible?

4 Focus on "real work"

So "having one's ducks in a row" is metaphor for having all of the bowling pins organized and properly placed before sending the next ball down the lane.

How does it feel to work for a scattered, reactive manager? You race to complete the work, only to find out later that goals are still in motion. So you do rework to see if you can hit the new target this time. You wonder, *Is my boss just making things up as he goes?*

It's easy to fall into response mode—firefighting problems, slapdash planning and assigning work without thinking things through. This is how you lose confidence and respect in the eyes of your employees.

Discover a better way—get your ducks in a row before you delegate work. Master the art of planning and setting up work. Make it the way of doing business for your entire team.

1 BEFORE STARTING THE WORK

I had a memorable job experience that reinforced the importance of thinking before jumping into the work.

My first career was in mining engineering. To get experience during college, I worked a summer job as an underground miner near Wallace,

Idaho. I was assigned to the hot, humid, and very dark 7300 ft. level. In other words, I worked a mile and a half below the ground.

I was often assigned to operate a small underground train. As the miners advanced farther underground, they needed support beams—medium-sized tree trunks cut into six-foot lengths—to shore up the roof and walls. I would drive the train through a labyrinth of tunnels and deliver the logs.

Once they were unloaded, I would switch the cars to load up the ore laden with silver and haul it up to the hoist, where it was transferred into bins that lifted it up to the surface for processing.

> We earn respect when we think before starting the work.

Over time, logs would sometimes spill off the railcars and become mired in the drainage ditch along the tracks. Over time, these logs became water-soaked and embedded into the wet muck and sand in the ditch.

One shift, the foreman told me to clean out ditches. Manually removing the logs was a very dirty job that was perfect for the summer college kid. I knew this task could take my whole shift to complete and I would be coated in muck at shift change.

The foreman assigned another crusty miner to assist me who seemed eager to put me at the muck side of the work. He had arms of steel and muttered several choice words as he gingerly picked his steps down into the ditch. We each had a large pry bar in hand and we prepared to muscle out the saturated logs.

I paused to think. There had to be a better way.

I told my coworker to grab a smoke and went down to the crew station to rummage through the shop. Eventually, I jury-rigged a chain and harness to create a system where I could use the train to pull out the logs. My coworker smoked and watched as I did the heavy lifting for both of us. Later, my boss came back and silently watched the "new kid's" system.

This was the turning point for me on the work crew. I graduated from "Hey, stupid shit head" to "smart college kid." In fact, the Operations Manager apparently heard the story. He came down to 7300 to ask for a demo and offer me a plum day shift job in the mine if I wanted to quit college. (No thanks.)

2 A GOAL IS NOT A PLAN

One CEO of a Seattle Dot-com launched the fiscal year with a stated goal to increase annual sales revenue by 5 percent each quarter. It was a rah-rah speech designed to infuse enthusiasm and commitment. He talked the goal up at every opportunity. In the end, as with many top-down initiatives, the results widely missed the mark.

Later, the CEO expressed his disappointment and wondered what had gone wrong. Was it lack of commitment to the goal? I asked him, "Is a goal a plan?"

The five percent sales goal was an aspiration floating in the air waiting for someone—the CEO or his delegate—to lay out a plan to achieve it. The tires need to hit the road after the GPS gives the clear directions to the final destination.

It is Managing Genius to pull together the plan to achieve the goal.

We need to guide people and make sure that everyone—including you—completes the necessary planning and preparation steps to get from aspiration to results. Teach this and make it a group practice.

During the Seattle Dotcom era, two ex-Microsoft Techies met with me for business advice on their vision for a new software product. Their vision was lofty and cutting edge. Once I got to speak, I asked if they had given thought to what it takes to bring a physical product to the market. For example, did they consider the product design process, off-shore manufacturing, and supply chain, inventory and customer service.

Their faces showed their impatience. Their reply, "Hey dude, you are getting way too detailed here. Focus on that the amazing things this product can do. Customers will love it." Like many other Dotcoms that failed to get off the ground, their product idea fizzled with no investors.

Go back and watch the classic movie *Back To The Future*. The character Dr. Emmett Brown has a goal to get Marty McFly back to the future using a time machine built from a modified DeLorean. It was not just a grand idea—Dr. Brown put together a detailed plan to make it happen. He builds a model of the town to explain his plan to Marty, "Let me show you my *plan* for sending you home."

3 IS THE WORK POSSIBLE?

You make a positive reputation for yourself when you understand the work and the time and effort it takes to get things done. You generate respect from your employees when you demonstrate that you understand exactly what you are asking of them.

The flip side is that managers will frustrate their employees if they throw work their way without understanding what it takes to do the work.

You won't always create smooth sailing. There will always be the occasional unexpected crisis where you will need to ask for flexibility and extra effort to power through the change.

A Managing Genius links aspirations with reality.

Nevertheless, you cannot keep coming back with last-minute changes and new deadlines and then expect your employees to stay committed to you. You cannot always solve today's problems by asking people to work faster and harder.

As an everyday expectation, we want our employees and teams to look ahead and think before they start working; they will not do that unless we communicate that expectation to them; they will not do it unless they see *us* do it.

Rather than seeing logs in the ditch and instantly applying heavy lifting, we want them to step back and think through the steps it will take to get the job done. We want them to see that the work is possible.

4 FOCUS ON "REAL WORK"

In the classic movie *Office Space*, the movie character Peter Gibbons is speaking to an organizational consultant who is interviewing employees to learn what they do in their job. This is all part of a reorganization with a special name, "Is This Good for the Company?".

Peter Gibbons explains, "Well, I generally come in at least fifteen minutes late...I use the side door—that way Lumbergh can't see me...after that I just sorta space out for about an hour. Yeah, I just stare at my desk; but it looks like I'm working. I do that for probably another hour after lunch, too. I'd say in a given week I probably only do about fifteen minutes of real, actual work."

So you walk about the workplace and what you may see at first glance is people staring at monitors, using smart phones and talking with coworkers. There is hustle and bustle giving the sense of motion and activities. You need to stop to ask how much of what you see is adding value.

Jon Stewart once said on *The Daily Show*, "The Internet is just a world passing around notes in a classroom." Our computers and smart-phones are amazing tools but we too easily slip into a slapdash culture where people talk about it, look at it, analyze it and then email the report. We know how to fill the boss's in-box with status updates, questions and activity. Then we reward the people who facilitate the meetings and create process charts.

It is Managing Genius to dive into team business and develop a working knowledge of what each person does and how it all fits together. Become the most knowledgeable person in the room to talk about how "real work" gets completed in your work group.

You should serve as an "expert witness" on why we are here, why it is important and what is happening next. A Managing Genius is always in a leadership role concerning how work gets done.

> Become an expert on how your group adds value through real work.

This is a management paradigm shift. Instead of only telling people what you want done, teach and discuss the work. Ask insightful questions and help people see for themselves the work and technology. Sometimes it is as simple as standing at a whiteboard and drawing out boxes and arrows to get a picture of how work gets done, showing the process steps, hand-offs and interdependencies.

The goal is that everyone understands the work and then as an everyday way of doing business they "get their ducks in a row."

This Is Managing Genius

Managing Genius is written for you. I want you to be confident and effective. Being totally in the know concerning how work gets done in

Everyone Comes Prepared and Ready

1 How work gets done

2 Must-haves for an effective work culture

3 A simple planning guide

your group and the business puts you into a leadership position. You are a real player with value to add because of your expertise and preparation, not just because of your position.

You must have a systematic way to get your own "ducks in a row" before talking about and delegating work. Become the most knowledgeable person in the room.

Create an amazing sense of "why we are here." Everyone knows how work gets done and we feel like owners, not renters. When something needs to happen, there is an organized way to think about and approach the work. This becomes embedded as the way of doing business.

Scan ahead—you may already know some of this chapter. The key is to teach it and build it into the fabric of your work group. Establish the new norm: everyone comes planned, prepared and ready for work.

But first, understand how work gets done in your organization.

1 HOW WORK GETS DONE

Beth walks into the crowded meeting room to participate in a senior level business planning session. People are finding their seats and chatting about everyday business.

She casts a nervous glance around the room and all she sees are highly competent people senior to her on the org chart.

She starts to panic and wonders why she was invited. These people are big players in the company and she sees herself as the least qualified person to participate in a such a high level strategy meeting.

Then, from across the room, the senior vice president calls a greeting to her and introduces her to the group. "I am so glad Beth is here. Beth is a top expert in the signal processing industry and I have never met someone with such a complete technical understanding of our core business. I learn from her every time we talk technology."

Earn respect through preparation and planning.

With that said, the meeting starts and Beth claims her seat at the table.

Know your business

At the advent of the Internet in 1995, I became the first HR manager for a skunk works product development group. We were charged with building a fixed wireless communication system, which was a pioneering step toward what has become today's wireless broadband.

Just for some perspective, in that job I used a cell phone and email for the first time. We had built a world-class advanced engineering organization and went on to develop the first wireless broadband system. I was charged with hiring three hundred engineers and software developers with specific technology expertise who would build the system. This was a smart, talented, cutting-edge engineering group.

Later, I was interviewing a potential chief technology officer candidate from a major competitor; a leading expert in the industry. At the end of the interview, he commented to me, "I'm surprised to meet an HR person who understands the technology."

People love to talk about their jobs. Just ask.

His words were a great compliment and they caused me to consider how important it was that I was able to master the business, the technology and the industry.

Now it seems amazingly simple—I learned from the smart, experienced people around me. The trick is to know that *people love to talk about their jobs*. I walked the halls and had dozens of informal whiteboard chats with managers and engineers who were each subject-matter experts for some component of the system.

For example, one brilliant PhD from China labored to explain to me the open system interconnection model that defines a networking framework to implement protocols in seven layers. He explained that control passes from one layer to the next, starting at the application layer in one station and proceeding to the bottom layer, over the channel to the next station, and back up the hierarchy. This engineer was proud to explain that he was working on the third layer.

During interviews, I would ask candidates to explain details on their resumes, taking the opportunity to learn new technology or what the competition was doing. This is actually a valuable interviewing technique, as it allows you to see if people have the ability to communicate their ideas to team members in a simple fashion. The side benefit of my inquisitiveness was that I learned a great deal about the technology, business, competitors and overall industry.

Thus, I became a "student of the business," and the investment paid off: I had a good working knowledge of fixed wireless engineering systems. Even though I was "HR," I could participate in business discussions with a sense of reality and perspective. I was included in business meetings and strategy sessions.

Knowing about your business will enhance your standing within your organization and give you a platform of respect. People will seek you out and include you in important planning and business decisions.

The adjacent Quick Guide is a learning to-do list. Stay in a learning mode to track down this background information and ask questions when the moment feels right. It all seems so real when you can connect the dots and understand the technical side of the business.

Learn about general business operations

Wei stops by my office for advice on his team operations. He shares his exasperation with how much time he spends "blathering over stupid corporate stuff, red tape and logistical details."

Wei has a PhD in engineering from Cal-Poly, and he has authored or coauthored seven patents. Unfortunately, he believes that he spends

Get to Know the Business

1 **Org chart:** Understand the players and playing field. Know names and responsibilities; how the business enterprise lives and breaths.

2 **Key players:** Know the key business leaders and influencers in the company. Follow the movers and shakers who are on the leading edge of new products and services.

3 **Customers:** Identify them, get to know them, and fully understand what pleases them. This counts for Internal customers as well.

4 **Lingo and Biz Speak:** Understand the terms and how to read reports so you can talk like an "insider." Stick around to ask about the biz, technology or new stuff.

5 **How things work:** Understand the nuts-and-bolts of your company's core product and services. Be able to give a 30-second explanation of anything your company does.

6 **Supply Chain:** Know what happens between Point A and Point B. Learn what's "inside the package." Gain perspective of knowing unit costs. Know about the vendors and suppliers.

7 **Cost of doing business:** This is what the senior team is focusing on. Become fluent with the budget and monthly operational reports. Pay attention to the numbers that drive the business.

8 **Technology:** Have a working knowledge of company shared applications. Know the network, accessing reports and how IT works.

too much time and energy on what he calls insignificant noise—things not directly related to product strategy and design.

These business items "only bog him down"—tasks like budget, hiring, purchasing, office space, IT and HR rules and policy.

Wei shares that these kinds of admin issues do not interest him and trying to obtain staff cooperation does not come naturally to him. He wonders where he can learn to navigate the maze.

As I reflect on Wei and hundreds of managers like him, I'm reminded that there is really no opportunity in our college education or career development process to learn the everyday basics of business management. If you do not master these essentials for getting work done in any organization, they just keep tripping you up.

It is Managing Genius to take *ownership* for anything important for team operations. In fact, these kinds of issues, seemingly nonessential to the technology or core product of any business, are often the point of failure for entrepreneurs who move into a new business start-up.

> Manage staff and service providers as you would any business need. They work for you.

Successful business leaders know how to pull together the business operations backbone. They know what they want, they know what is needed and they know how the different staff functions work.

Not only do you need this business acumen to advance in your career, your employees need to see you in a leadership role for anything important to the team's success. Your employees need to feel confident that these details will not get in the way of the group's success. If not, they will by-pass you and fend for themselves.

There is no alternative: Act like you own the business. Walk down the hall and ask questions to learn all you can about the essential functions of the company, like accounting, HR, purchasing and legal. Meet the people and find out what they do. Understand how they help and ask them to whiteboard their process.

In every company there are certain people who are go-to people who have a special knack for weaving through traffic to get things done. Find these people and build bridges.

Successful managers always have a grasp of key financial, reports and the budget. You cannot delegate this because it is in the frontal lobe of everyone above you on the org chart. The budget is the engine of the business and do not think you can just turn on the ignition and drive. Become fluent in understanding what the numbers say and why it is important.

It is doubtful that managers like Wei will advance without understanding how important these "peripheral details" are to his success. Managing Geniuses always take ownership of their corner of the business and it is more than just what is listed in their deliverables. Take the lead for anything important for the success of team operations.

> Top managers always have a grasp of key financials and the budget.

Create a learning environment

You cannot own something unless you fully understand the whole job. Too often, we assume that our employees have somehow acquired the ability to do a job, when in fact there are gaps that have a way of springing up later.

First, identify core competencies that you want everyone to know. For example, not everyone can build and schedule a project plan. Your willingness to teach and share know-how becomes evident and people will ask questions from you and share with one another.

Look for natural segues to teach different subjects. For example, "I've been asked a few questions about the budget. Would anyone want a quick flyover?"

On the other hand, be careful not to "monologue." I once had a CEO who loved to share lengthy technical explanations for everything. He

> This is your company. Go see what people are doing. Talk to people.

came across like an elderly uncle at the Thanksgiving dinner table. Not everyone wants every detail of how the business works. Focus on what people need for their jobs and answer their specific questions.

Success is when you see people sharing expertise and knowledge with each other on the team. Shared learning and common knowledge creates a closer-knit work culture where everyone feels in the know.

2 MUST-HAVES FOR AN EFFECTIVE WORK CULTURE

Managing Geniuses are always striving to build an effective and efficient work culture. People want to work for them because they cut through the clutter, make things efficient and simplify everything.

I was asked to attend a weekly planning meeting for an engineering group and as we were preparing to get started, the group director called in to say that he would be delayed due to a customer call.

> **The simple basics for an effective work culture**
>
> 1. Action planning
> 2. Process design
> 3. Continuous improvement
> 4. Proficiency and competence
> 5. Attention to Detail

The meeting started on time without him. Different people spoke up according to some unspoken, well-oiled plan that everyone present seemed to understand. There was a shared system for approaching the work.

I could see that this group had established an operating system that was commonly understood. People just stepped up to make it happen.

But this has to happen at the front end. The group director had established group norms for how people interact to get work done. He taught and role modeled these shared expectations.

Then, rather than guide and coax employees through what happens *between* Point A and Point B, spend more time *at* Point A or *at* Point B where the group starts or finishes work. This can only happen if everyone understands at the starting line how to run the race.

It is like visiting a neighbor's house and watching as everyone in the family gets up from the dinner table and without a word the family works together to clean up the kitchen according to a well-understood system. A house guest would see that sharing family chores is how this house is run. It is an embedded practice for how we handle the after-dinner stuff—"the way of doing family."

These actions do not happen accidentally. These are embedded practices.

Early on, you need to set group goals for incorporating these practices, just as you would a sales initiative or product development plan. Teach and make them a part of the everyday routine for team business. Talk about these five basics so your team understands that they are important to you. They are not just a special program from your boss or HR. This is the team "way of doing business."

1. Action Planning

Goal: Create a sense of closure and completion through action planning.

Tom Peters, the quality guru, taught, "Good managers have a bias for action." We know that we have responsibility for goals and plans but Managing Genius is in the follow-through.

Take the lead to create a sense of closure and completion to whatever is discussed or agreed to. It sounds so simple but make sure that everyone leaves the room with clarity around what happens next. Ask for agreements and promises. This always includes the who, what and when.

Someone should be responsible to track and email progress so team members can stay attuned to what is going on.

There is a method to the work. We are in a move-forward mode of operation.

Do not get yourself into a position where team members depend on you to juggle to-do lists and act like the nagging parent. In fact, you may have an action item on their to-do list. The person holding responsibility manages the action planning.

2. Process Design

Goal: See the whole process that shows the steps that get us to the finish.

It is Managing Genius to make work organized and efficient. To effectively get work done, make sure process steps are clearly communicated and understood. Effective processes are simple, repeatable, broadly understood and readily owned.

Designing repetitive work systems takes a different mind-set. For example, when deciding what business is going to get your takeout pizza order, you probably use these three factors: quality, price and delivery history. Pizza only arrives at your door after a series of successful steps, from phone call to cooking to pizza box to delivery.

That last great pizza experience didn't happen by chance. There was a clear process to make and deliver perfect pizzas every time. It was a great experience because a manager had clearly communicated a "proven" process for getting a pizza to your doorstep.

Not many pick a supply chain course in college, but it is the heart of how business gets done, always using the same three factors for getting great pizza to your door: quality, price and delivery. Managing Geniuses understand how the work happens. They see the steps and underlying process. They also understand that the process will be repeated continuously.

> Move everyday repetition and routine into the background through well-designed processes.

Dennis was the senior vice president for a product realization organization for a complex mega-million-dollar business. He believed that success was when everyone in his organization could understand the business as well as he could. He developed a simple, one-page document that he used to teach every employee. He often referred back to this document in meetings. He wanted everyone on the team to see where they stood in the process and how their work flowed toward closure.

By designing the process and deliverables, Dennis was able to closely manage third-party staff and vendors. Even when you do not have direct authority, you can still establish the process and make certain suppliers know where they fit in the overall flow of the work.

3. Continuous Improvement

Goal: Improved process through continuous improvement. This will infuse a spirit of optimism. People love to work where things get better.

Liz Lemon on *30 Rock* spouts a lofty goal, "Well, believe in yourself and you'll reach your goals." But she adds with chagrin, "I read that on a bottle of women's exercise water." When we talk about improvement goals, it can sound trite and rah-rah.

How well can you relate to the employee experience in your work group? Could your employees be wondering, why do we keep repeating the same mistake? Can we stop wasting time and money? Can we get the product quality right? Can we take a new look at this?

A Managing Genius is always looking to improve processes and find ways to streamline the work. Efficiency and effectiveness trump status quo. You make continuous improvement a driving force in the group that gets discussed at every opportunity.

I have observed that a Managing Genius is always in the middle of improvements for the work group. You earn respect when you show your employees that you care about the overall employee experience. Take the lead to make the work easier.

> Show you care about the employee experience. Remove frustrations, fill potholes and make the work easier.

While continuous improvement is your responsibility, you don't accomplish it in a vacuum. Even if you could initiate every opportunity, it is critical that your team is involved to feel like owners, not renters.

Remember, your employees are the subject matter experts in their jobs. They likely know the process better than you do. You will waste a tremendous opportunity for team building by not allowing employee participation in the process-improvement arena. Become a master at asking thought provoking questions that help people see their work differently.

4. Proficiency and Competence

Goal: Build a culture that has respect for mastery and competence.

We think we can click for anything we need, so why invest time and energy into acquiring competence? This attitude can create a culture where we throw it all together on the fly and then work it out as we go. There is no need to master how to sail the ship when you can Google this information, assuming of course you can get WiFi in the middle of the Pacific Ocean.

Important to note, a minimally competent work style may work for individual contributors or in small groups where everyone is familiar with each other and the work. Jeff Bezos, the founder and CEO of Amazon, calls this his "two pizza" secret to productive meetings. His philosophy: Fewer people makes for faster decisions. (I think the *right* people in the room make for better decisions.)

However, large groups of people are not so nimble. It is Managing Genius to take the lead and set up the group for success. Create value for the discipline of skill and knowledge acquisition—the orchestra masters the material through practice and rehearsals. Recognize the musicians who have practiced and are prepared to play key roles in the orchestra. They are there because they invested time and energy to master their craft.

Example: You catch Adam after the meeting, "I am amazed at how proficient you have become with simplifying complex IT systems. You have emerged within our group as a technology leader."

5. Attention to Detail

Goal: Everyone knows when it is important to sweat the details.

High-performing team cultures always have a mind-set for paying attention to the right details. The small stuff can make a big difference, especially when it affects the whole team.

The key is for people to know details are important and then turn that understanding into a everyday way of doing business. The goal is to decide as a team what will make us better together as a group. As we walk through the workplace, these details are well understood by everybody. This is how the neighborhood works.

Through my experience, the following team norms are must-haves for a high-performing work culture.

Prepared and ready: I was inspired by my daughter's middle school when they added a new category to the class grading scheme. Students get a daily check for coming to class "prepared and ready", worth five percent of their total grade. What a concept.

How many times have you heard: "My bad, forgot that report at my desk. Want me to go get it?" "I brought most of the numbers you asked for and I can email the rest by tomorrow." "I thought the budgets were due next Tuesday."

Value people's time: Expecting people to follow a schedule or arrive on time at meetings may seem trivial but it impacts other people and should becomes a team norm.

Not every Managing Genius is on time for every meeting—realistically they operate within a demanding management circle with multiple priorities vying for their time. But they always have a respect for people's time and a sense of urgency. They speak openly about how to best manage everyone's time.

Smart spending: Similar to how we use time, how we spend corporate resources is a huge reflection of the respect we have for our business. Everyone should act like entrepreneur-owners who pay the bills and spend money like it is their own. Your people will quickly pick up on this and mimic your words and actions.

Keep promises: Your team members should feel a sense of obligation to their team members and coworkers—and you. One way to implement this is to have people *verbalize* agreements in the light of day within team meetings. It then becomes a public statement, an implicit promise and something tangible to discuss again.

Facilitate the discussion to get people to use direct communication. Everyone should work to weed out ambiguity.

No-excuses: In Managing Genius work cultures, I have observed that there is always openness to taking responsibility and learning from mistakes. They do not allow whining and drama that distracts from results, nor do they just blow things off or sweep them under the carpet.

Checking work: One of my engineering professors would often say, *"To err is human, to forgive is divine, but to check your work is engineering."*

Important work needs a second set of eyes—you should establish this as a group practice and the second eyes should not always be yours. People should seek out their own "editors" to check their work so that you receive a finished copy.

When a mistake surfaces, it is not *who made this mistake* but *who checked this?* How can we prevent this from happening again?

3 A SIMPLE PLANNING GUIDE

Planning checklist

1. Outcome
2. Estimate
3. Forecast
4. Measure
5. Group schedule
6. People and players

It is Managing Genius to develop a consistent system to plan and set up work.

You do not do all the planning for your team. Rather, you teach and share expectations for *how* you want your people to plan and prepare using this simple planning checklist.

Make this feel like an everyday part of the fabric of your team. Schedule time for planning and model what it looks like to be prepared.

This is not some special corporate program—this comes from you. This is simply how you take the lead to get everyone asking the right questions and closing on next steps.

1. Outcome

There is nothing more important for a Managing Genius than to be able to clearly define the desired outcome of a project or work task. You need to nail down the desired outcomes.

Without a clear destination, your work group may waste time worrying about non-essential side issues. In addition, they may loop back or reopen issues for more discussion. It is Managing Genius to lock in on why are we here and keep people focused on the main event.

2. Estimate

A popular interviewing tactic in the Seattle high-tech community is to ask impossible questions in order to see if the candidate knows how to think things through. So you ask, "How many windows do you think there are in downtown Seattle?" Or, "How many cows are there in Canada?" Of course, the exact answer is not important, but the idea is to see if people can think on their feet and come up with a reasonable estimate based on logic.

The Internet gives us more information but it has not made us better thinkers. Estimation is a lost art because we can depend on technology tools and electronics, and the Internet always gives us a quick answer, right? When I need the answer, I will just go hunt for it. We manage projects in real time versus planning based on well-founded thinking and complete analysis of all options.

Think about how you make educated guesses as to what you need for a home improvement project before driving to Home Depot. It is not just a shopping list, but you piece together an estimate of what you will need by stepping through the job and drawing on available experience. Like a building contractor, learn how to do rough calculations—"I know it takes sixteen hours to do this, and twenty-two to do this."

Involve your team and you will find that you collectively know more than you realize. This will heighten a feeling of ownership when you have shared in the original estimates and you see it all come together.

> Dig in to understand the business and you will grow in your ability to estimate.

How much detail is needed? It always depends on the job at hand. A quick envelope calculation in the hallway may suffice for some jobs, while for a lunar space mission one would obviously need more detailed project plans with precise calendars and supply chain management. The trick is to teach your people in advance when, where and how much planning detail is appropriate for the mission.

It is important to know when and where to micromanage—anticipate the issues that need your attention—and know how to pull back.

One of the biggest "demotivaters" in the work world is a manager who gives an employee a task and then takes it back. Make sure your employee has the right skill set, decision-making ability and necessary tools and resources. Then get out of the way and let him or her do the job.

Identify business issues up front that you cannot afford to let flounder: core mission, critical path work that affects the entire group or high visibility, big-ticket items. Become adept at moving in and out as needed to keep the work moving.

3. Forecast

Anticipate and plan for contingencies to minimize later surprises and crises. Ask "what if" questions and seek input from others. Identify future events and decision points. Planning is 80 percent anticipation so that you can minimize stops and starts. That means putting in sufficient thinking to anticipate future needs, and what might stop or alter work.

The words *goals* and *planning* are not theoretical exercises. They are a means to an end result; they have a destination in mind; they show us how to get there. You will develop a skill for planning by asking *what if* questions.

> Learn forecasting. Think about what is down the road and around corners.

A key element of forecasting is *staging* for future needs. During the hectic Dot-com days, we were growing our organization so fast that at one point our hiring outstripped our computers and desks. This was a bonehead forecasting mistake, as we had information on budgeted headcount, open requisitions, offers made and accepted and even people's future start dates. Plan what is needed for the next round; the alternative is to miss the incredibly obvious.

4. Measure

You don't set audacious goals and wait six months for the grand finale; you measure progress along the way at established frequent milestones to measure as work progresses through the process, thus preventing later surprises. Communication of progress to the team is paramount.

Think about any family board game. You can look down at the playing board and clearly measure *progress*. It would be a frustrating experience to not know the score while the game was being played.

5. Group Schedule

For a group to work effectively together, everyone involved needs to have access to a common group calendar with activities, events and milestone reviews. However, the real issue is how to keep the shared calendar current and relevant. The trick is have team members own the process for keeping the shared calendar updated.

6. People and Players

The goal is to clarify project roles (the cast list) and responsibilities (deliverables and decision-making authority). There are three items for special attention: services and support, shared responsibility and management controls.

Services and support: You must manage corporate staff as if these employees are working for you. Too often, we tightly manage the work of our own employees but then allow staff providers more leeway.

First, if it's business critical it should be a line-item in your plan. An HR outsourcing example would be, "Final sales manager candidate identified by May 1." Then form service agreements to agree on the deliverable and schedule from staff who work outside of our direct supervision. Build a collaborative relationship, but expect to be treated like a customer.

Shared responsibility: Clearly identify third party roles and responsibilities. Be sure those players understand what you expect from them.

The trick is to *actively manage* corporate staff and other non-direct reports that you carry in your budget and depend on for specific services. Those staff have multiple customers and your specific needs can become lost in the weeds. Give extra attention at the front end for outcomes and deliverables. Define shared responsibility where you work together.

Management controls: Work bogs down and frustrations build when management roles and work assignments are not well-defined. Some managers seem to give responsibility freely, only to take it back by stepping in and taking over at unexpected times. At the front-end, define the scope of authority:

- Decisions: What decisions do team members make and where do you depend on others for review or final sign-off?
- Access to information: Can team members independently access key people and ask for needed information?
- Your role as manager: Your level of involvement will never be the same on any two work initiatives. For some work you will need to stay involved and engaged, say for a big-budget item, while others you can pass the ball and step back. Just be sure to explain this up front.

Discover Your Managing Genius

- Think and plan before passing work to your team. Make "how we do work" an everyday part of the fabric of your work culture.

- See the magic in the system: When you start with well-established plans, there will be less need for corrective feedback or rework.

- First, gain respect for your business knowledge and for your understanding of how the work fits within the business enterprise.

- Second, earn respect for your organized and thoughtful approach to delegating work. People love to work for a leader who has thought it through. No one likes it when work gets tossed over the wall or when they constantly have to fight fires.

- Third, become passionate about how your team gets work done:
    - Build a team culture where people come prepared and ready.
    - Use the five basics for an effective work culture (page 36) to make your team more efficient. This will result in a short list of common work practices that creates unity.
    - Use a simple planning checklist (page 42) for how to plan work. Make this a natural part of everyday business.

- Team leadership should come from you. Translate and explain things in your own words.

Expectations and Responsibility

Everyone has clear expectations, assignments and direction

 Big Idea

Master the art of delegating work in clear and unambiguous ways. Take the lead to guide workplace conversations and meetings to ensure that everyone leaves knowing what they are supposed to do. This becomes embedded in the work culture as everyone seeks clarity and works together to weed out ambiguity.

Jack: *True enough, this compass does not point true north.*
Elizabeth: *Where does it point?*
Jack: *It points to the thing you want most in this world.*
                                        —*Pirates of the Caribbean*

Find me that piece of paper I had in my hand yesterday morning.
        —Miranda Priestly, character in movie *The Devil Wears Prada*

Six Sigma values direct and honest communication between coworkers, so uh ... thank you, Liz."
                                        —Jack Donagy in *30 Rock*

They just were not prepared. They were arrogant thinking they were just going to wing it."
                                        —Mark Cuban on *Shark Tank*

Years ago, I was reading a story to my daughter and I was doing voices and everything, and she turned to me and said, "Just read the story. And stick to the main points."
                                        —Robin Williams

Important to Know

Christy is a senior manager of the West Coast sales group. She comes by my office to debrief after meeting with Lucas, one of her regional sales employees. I ask the usual question: "So how did it go?" She rolls her eyes and replies with a smile that it started well, but once again she felt like she rode across the Lake Washington Bridge.

Christy knows that this is my metaphor for holding an employee meeting where you think you are driving. However, then you find yourself as the rider going to some unintended destination. Managers often get caught up with "Lake Washington conversations" where we are not sure who is driving.

Stay in the Driver's Seat

1 A simple guide for clarity and control

2 Mucking up our message

Christy shares that today the meeting started out well. They were engaging in a pressing problem that Lucas actually owned. However, after Lucas left she realized the discussion had drifted to side issues that were important to Lucas. She was left with unresolved items.

So as she tells me, she realizes the other person was driving the car across the Lake Washington Bridge. "How did I let this happen?"

This chapter is about how a Managing Genius leads and guides the swirling cloud of a workplace discussion—the words in the air, on the white board, or in an email—so that it all comes together with amazing clarity that moves people forward in your desired direction.

1 A SIMPLE GUIDE FOR CLARITY AND CONTROL

If you get work done through others, you need to find a way to share what you want them to do. It is Managing Genius to lead and guide workplace discussions and meetings to make sure they know what the business needs.

I have boiled it down to three simple questions that should be running in the back of your mind throughout the work day. This is how you make sure you are driving the workplace conversation.

1. Why are we here?

A Managing Genius stays in control of workplace conversations by establishing amazing clarity around the reason for being there. They guide people away from a random "Let's talk" mode.

Imagine going to a meeting where everyone in the room is working on the same issue.

This is a paradigm shift: *You do not try to control what people say or do. Instead, you make the reason we are here clear*

Take the lead by asking the right questions:

1. Why are we here?
2. Why is this important?
3. What happens next?

You take control when you bring into the room a sense of plan preparation and intentionality. You set the tone at the start, then guide the discussion to keep everyone focused on the agenda. For example:

"Today our first priority is to nail down the quarterly sales projections. But first, does anyone have updates to share?" Starting the meeting in this way establishes why we are here, while leaving room for input, involvement and team connections.

The key is to be prepared to state at the front end, "Why are we here?"

- ○ We are here to brainstorm ideas for cutting the budget.
- ○ We are here to problem solve a manufacturing quality issue.
- ○ I just wanted to meet for coffee to wind down from a tough week. Anything you would like to share?

2. Why is this important?

The anchorperson who does the evening news is probably talking at two hundred words per minute. If we estimate that people normally talk at half that speed, there were about three thousand words floating in the air during today's thirty-minute employee meeting.

Which words were most important? What words do you want remembered and what words can be ignored?

People will remember what is important to them, so an element of any workplace conversation is to take what is important to the business and make that personally important to your employees.

You also establish *unimportance*.

Usually the issues are mutually understood, if not obvious. As you develop a higher level of trust and everyday communication with your employees, people will connect the dots for themselves.

3. What happens next?

In C. S. Lewis's classic *Chronicles of Narnia: The Silver Chair*, my favorite character, Lucy, gets lost while trying to find her destination. Finally, in a fit of exhaustion and exasperation, she sits down to have a good cry. Then we read how she finally pulls herself together with this amazing self-realization:

> *Crying is all right in its own way while it lasts.*
> *But you have to stop sooner or later,*
> *and then you still have to decide what to do.*

This is an amazing principle. It's OK for Lucy to cry but eventually she will have to do something. *Something always happens next.*

For example, if you have had a difficult workweek and you go out with a few colleagues after work to vent and unwind, you may feel better—it is "all right in its own way while it lasts"—but actually *nothing has changed*. When you leave, "you still need to decide to do something."

If one of your employees feels the need to vent frustrations to you, it is "all right in its own way while it lasts," but the individual will need to get his or her bearings and decide on what to do next.

What happens after you leave the room?

People need someone to whom they can blow off steam, ask questions and ask for directions. Empathy, advice and encouragement are "all right." But eventually people must reset and *decide what to do next*. It is Managing Genius to guide and nudge people to keep moving forward.

2 MUCKING UP YOUR MESSAGE

I am meeting with Alina, a senior executive in our organization. While we are working together in her office, Benjamin stops by and Alina asks me for five minutes so she can pass on a time-sensitive assignment. This allows me to watch Alina in action.

She is pretty clear on the desired outcome and she remembers to stress why this is important to the customer. I do not think she could be clearer that she needs Benjamin to get this completed by next Friday.

Benjamin does the classic push back. He feels that he will struggle to get this done on time and he feels like he is an awkward position. He has more excuses if you care to hear them.

Mitigate: To lessen in force or intensity. To make milder or gentler.

Alina pauses and looks out her window as if she is thinking. In her gracious voice, she shares, "We need this wrapped up by July 1 but do your best and we will see how it goes. I realize this is a tough project but I will help you."

Oops. Alina has just mitigated her words.

Alina was clear with why we are here, why it is important and what happens next. But then she allowed mitigated communication to muck up her message. Now she is holding the bag for this work as Benjamin walks away.

I have boiled down the top ten ways we muck up the message:

Watering Down

Alina is mixing in support and encouragement, perhaps to appear as both a reasonable and supportive manager. "You absolutely need to come in under budget for this project but yes, we do have some wiggle room if something unexpected happens." Are you delegating work or giving wiggle room?

It is easy to turn empathy into leniency. Remember, if you step in to bail someone out, someone else will have to do the work. One Managing Genius I reported to would often say, "Don't put the monkey on my back." In saying that, he was making me aware that someone needs to own the responsibility and it was not him.

Telling Stories

One senior executive I worked for seemed to have a story for every business situation. The problem was that I was never sure if he was conveying an expectation to me through the story or coaching me in general. Then again, maybe he was just reminiscing.

For example, one day we were discussing the need to cut the budget by five percent. Then he slipped into the story of a manufacturing plant in Atlanta and how they eliminated jobs and increased production. Was he trying to give me direction without being direct?

Telling stories can come across that you are all-knowing based on your amazing career experience. It does not leave room for folks to participate in the conversation. Of course, they lack your superior knowledge, skills and experience.

Indirect Communication

My first engineering boss was casually talking about his own boss, Joe, who was the general manager of the operation. He proudly shared that he had received positive feedback from Joe, "I can always trust your numbers."

I was left wondering, *Is he indirectly telling me he didn't trust my numbers?* He had that look on his face.

Of course, you're thinking I should have asked for clarification, but indirect communication does not call for a direct reply and it was only many years later that I learned this.

> A Managing Genius can balance empathy with straight talk.

Hard Sell

Much to our chagrin, parents often use three tactics on their kids: 1. Raise their voice; 2. Slowly enunciate words; and 3. Repeat their words.

Hopefully, we are smart enough to forego the first two options with our employees but I see good managers often repeating their words to make the "hard sell."

Did you get that? You often repeat yourself to make sure you get listened to. *Like what I just did.*

You press people to reach acquiescence through the repetition of your words. "Let me explain it a different way." But repetition makes you come across as a nagging parent. Then later you stop by their cubes to ask "How's it going?" This is when people begin to tune you out.

Wrapping Paper

There are all sorts of formulas, like it is best to package three positives with one negative. Therefore, Alina should share a few well-dones as she leads up to the really important news.

Actually, when you use this tactic, you forget that people like Benjamin are smart enough to know how this works. Benjamin's mind drifts into "ignore mode" while he's thinking like Robin Williams' daughter, *"Just read the story and stick to the main points."*

It is OK to be nice but this is a tricky zone of mixed motives. Disingenuous compliments, social conversations or family talk can become wrapping paper that blurs why we are here.

Actually, employees for whom you have to obsess about the wrapping paper may be the wrong people to invest in.

Side Deals

When we are hesitant to ask people to do difficult or unsavory work assignments, we may make promises to sweeten the tea to help them choke down the pill. Side deals are one-off individual arrangements that must be finessed and carefully applied.

"If you get this done by July 30, I can give you a couple days off to catch up."

Once you start making side deals, you have trained your employee—and anyone else within earshot—to ask for an accommodation on future projects. If you want to make a side deal, bring the deal into the mainstream of your work group at a team meeting.

Why not? Everyone is going to hear about it through back channels anyway.

You will earn respect when you share the accommodation as a thoughtful decision. "We will all notice Sarah working weird hours to upgrade our sales tool, so later she'll get some well-deserved time off."

Asking Questions

Thoughtful questions will stimulate critical thinking and serve as an activator for good workplace discussions. But ask yourself, do you want an answer or are you filling air space with "happy dialogue"?

Sometimes we ask questions when we should be making clear, well-formulated statements.

For example, you may ask your team, "What do you think we should do next?" You should say, "We are here to plan next week's schedule."

We have all worked for a boss who asks questions when he or she already has the answer. The boss might ask what you think about shifting the schedule, when someone else has already revealed that it is a done deal. He or she might ask you for an opinion on a hiring decision, even though the top candidate has already been picked.

> We may act like we want input, but we are just looking to sell the idea and collect fans.

These questions cause people to pay *less* attention to you.

"Bully Pulpit"

President Teddy Roosevelt coined this term,[1] which means using a higher position as an opportunity to share your views with an audience.

One of my early engineering managers used his position to pontificate on politics, social causes, child-raising and anything he was thinking that day. Of course, we were forced to suffer through his monologues. I am sure he did this to impress us but soon enough any respect we held for him evaporated.

If people can tune you out on one subject, they will start to tune you out on everything.

---

1 Doris Kearns Goodwin, *The Bully Pulpit: Theodore Roosevelt, William Howard Taft, and the Golden Age of Journalism* (New York: Simon & Schuster, 2013).

Open Mic Syndrome

Nowadays we hear that good managers should give everyone a chance to speak. The best ideas come from the wisdom of the group.

But even the flattest of today's organizations can become a hierarchy in disguise. Who said everyone should speak? Should we listen to everyone, when in fact your top performer took the initiative to lay out three alternatives after detailed analysis? If we have "Open Mic," anyone can stand up first to start talking.

> Lt. Bailey: *We have phasers. I vote we blast 'em!*
> Capt. James T. Kirk: *Thank you, Mr. Bailey. I'll consider that when this becomes a democracy.*
>
> —Original *Star Trek* TV series

If we allow unfocused discussion, private agendas can spring up. These can turn into voting blocks as we make alliances. Then people may freeze into a position to oppose an idea.

If you want to share leadership or allow people to speak on your behalf, you want to plan for an "organized transfer of power." Frame the discussion and you control the outcome.

Blather and Bull$*#!

There is tendency to alleviate stress and anxiety by filling the airspace with words. You share a few nuggets within the mitigating speech.

Corporate speak uses jargon and lofty talk to take on the superior mode and put distance between you and your employee.

Formality or *rules* are a fall-back position when feeling out of control. "I'll check with HR." "Let me check with the COO."

My favorite is *anonymity*. This is when we use company reports and electronic media to take off the names of the people who did the work and talk about the information as if it is a third party in and of itself.

> *"The monthly report points out that our production is down."*
> *"The budget is telling me that we need to cut travel."*
> *"I'd love to do this but HR policy is holding me back."*

This Is Managing Genius

Leaders always start with a vision of the outcome. Imagine Steve Jobs turning to his staff and asking "Anyone have some ideas on what we should do?"

A Managing Genius gives welcome clarity so team members know why we are here, why it is important and where we are going.

Managing Geniuses have mastered the art of speaking "in the moment." They can focus on bringing out the best in their people because they are not so worried about what they will say and do next.

So how do they do it? What is the secret of their success? I have cut through the clutter and found five strategies that make the Managing Genius.

Sharing Expectations and Responsibility

1 Know what you want

2 Leading large groups

3 A simple guide for delegating

4 How jobs get built

5 Plan to finish

1 KNOW WHAT YOU WANT

Think about your past jobs. How much time did you spend trying to figure out what your boss wanted? No one likes to work for a manager who is randomly slapping things together, shooting from the hip and always changing his or her mind.

Know what you want to communicate before speaking

Your employees deserve well-planned, well-thought-out assignments, as opposed to knee-jerk reactions to today's latest crisis.

That means you do your homework so you can clearly explain why we are here and where each individual fits into the big picture. Actually, going into an employee meeting armed with talking points will give you a tremendous feeling of confidence and position you as a leader.

Know that your personal communication style (concise, scattered, random, whatever) can get passed down to your employees. I observed this one day when William met with one his direct reports, Hannah, to review her design of the new company home page.

William paused as if reflecting deeply and then asked, "Have you thought about putting the mission statement in a more prominent spot?"

Hannah paused and replied thoughtfully, "Well, we considered that but it just didn't work out."

Interestingly, William shared his concern in a vague, indirect manner and Hannah's response was delivered in like fashion. Not a whole lot of productive information was passed in either direction.

> We pay attention to people who come to a meeting prepared and ready.

Free your people to work autonomously

How can people take responsibility for sailing a ship if you have not shared with them the destination? When you clearly communicate the destination, your employees can sail off by themselves and not need your hand on the rudder.

> Front-end delegation frees people to run with the ball.

Autonomy is only possible when you give clear expectations at the start. In fact, if they have clear direction and know where they are bound for, your employees will need much less oversight from you.

Managers who wander off track or change their minds too frequently often create dependent team members who must wait around to catch today's new idea or direction. People will need to check back with you frequently, and you will stay entangled in the work. Do you like people depending on you?

Both your words and your approach matter

How we pass on expectations and responsibilities can either empower people or quench initiative. Tossing out urgent, last-minute tasks just starts people scrambling to react. Sharing your impatience and disrespect or thinking out loud just multiplies this fire-drill response.

In one organization, different team members would take turns leading the group meetings. One day, I observed the group director starting a meeting by saying, "I'm not sure Dave is ready to lead our meetings, but I'm going to give him a chance."

You may think you would never do that but you also may inadvertently send the same signals through your body language and tone of voice. Do you start playing with your phone when Jennifer is presenting but pay closer attention to William?

People will respond to your signals differently

I walked with Robert on the production floor, where forty of his employees were assembling electronic devices. He stopped and turned toward Ahn's work station and proceeded to correct her on eliminating excess scrap. Later, we learned that Anh felt deep humiliation for receiving what she perceived as a rebuke in front of her coworkers.

> Build respect for your thoughtful and methodical approach to handing off work.

As we walked back to Robert's office, he stopped in the hallway to talk with Bucky, one of the cost accountants, to discuss a discrepancy in the budget numbers. This direct interaction passed without a hitch.

My advice to Robert was to adapt his communication style to the listener and the situation. Some individuals are OK with quick communication in the hallway, while others may prefer a private, one-on-one discussion. Some people love in-your-face confrontation, while others prefer to give a careful reply after analyzing both sides.

Here is the trick: Get the time and place right. Create the right space where the listener has no need to feel defensive or guarded.

Making assumptions

Most leaders wrongly assume that their staff members will act exactly the way they act, enjoy what they enjoy and love their jobs.

In passing goals to a subordinate, recognize that you are on a different playing field than your staff members. You have a greater ability to deal with ambiguity because you make the goals, own the budget and can move around people and resources. This gives you a greater ability to improvise.

2 LEADING LARGE GROUPS

Amanda is a manager of a large product engineering group. She has asked me to sit through her weekly group product planning meeting and give her feedback on the effectiveness of the group forum. Afterwards we debriefed in her office.

We look up to see Sheila standing at her door asking for "just one minute for a quick question." Actually, it is not a quick question because Sheila disagrees with one of the action items that the group decided on thirty minutes ago. She was afraid to speak out for fear of what the others would say but can Amanda get coffee with her later to discuss?

Groups with shared work need a different managing style

- Share more with the whole group
- More front-end leadership
- Shared goals and accountability
- Excel at all-team communication
- Run very effective meetings

A few minutes later, Victor sticks his head in her door to give her the budget. He would also like a minute to share his opinion about how the meetings seem to drag on.

After he leaves, Amanda begins to complain to me. Victor was supposed to come to the meeting prepared with that information and now Amanda will have to email everyone with the new numbers. This new information will likely open up additional email discussion.

Sanjay follows through the door to provide more information on an issue that the group just spent thirty minutes hashing over. When he leaves, Amanda looks at me in frustration as she holds up her phone showing two texts and one email from meeting participants who want to share follow-up ideas.

Amanda is a good manager, but she is spending too much time holding private briefings and personal coaching sessions. Great managers become more effective by sharing clear expectations at the group level. This establishes a work culture where we feel accountable to the group.

Share more with the whole group

We aspire to build a great team culture and an effective work system, yet somehow we find ourselves spending most of our managing time in one-on-one sessions. Why is this our default?

First, managers naturally think that work goals, performance appraisals and feedback have to be private and confidential. Second, it can seem easier to take on employees one at a time, where you can focus on them and their problems.

Employees have a default predisposition to take issues and questions straight to their boss. You are in the judgment seat that decides, tweaks goals, alters priorities and controls spending. So it makes sense to ask the judge to meet with you in private chambers.

Employees are also eager to please their manager and present their case in the best light possible. Getting you alone is their chance to toot their horn and play a solo without the orchestra there to drown them out.

> Getting work done at the group level requires more upfront communication and coordination.

To share more common messages at the group level, you need to understand the main reason why we default to talking at the individual level: simply, *we let it happen.*

Good managers unknowingly get sidetracked by whatever presents itself at that moment—the ringing phone, the latest email, or the individual wanting to chat. The rabbit runs, the hound chases. Great managers stay focused on the task at hand. When a potential interruptions appears, they politely but directly do not let it interrupt them.

You have to make a conscious effort to *push* discussion to the group level. "Hold off on that discussion, I want the whole group to hear about you changing that date." "Let me put that on Friday's agenda." "I'll send a group email."

Good managers are over at Starbucks talking with their individual employees, while a Managing Genius is back in a conference room working with his or her intact group to make complex plans, share decisions and butt heads over overlapping issues.

More front-end leadership

If you and I are working alone, it is easier for us to throw together a plan and improvise as we go. It is easier to jury-rig solutions and shoot from the hip with fewer people, especially people with whom you are familiar and friendly.

Getting work done through groups calls for more front-end planning. Everything you do and say at the start has a ripple effect, affecting the trajectories of many people as they begin their work assignments. That's why it's so important to have your group meeting objectives and assignments thought out in advance.

Groups need clarity up front so they know who is doing what and how they will work together in an organized and coordinated fashion. The larger the group, the more likely your thoughtful, well-planned, hands-on management efforts at the front end will make a positive difference.

> Groups requires more front-end forming and organizing to get everyone coordinated.

Individual conversations an ineffective use of your time.

It is also more likely that the issues that get raised in the individual meetings will not get the benefit of feedback and scrutiny from the whole group.

You will multiply your effectiveness when you share more direction at the group level. You communicate the message once, everyone hears the same message and everyone gets the chance to speak up.

Shared goals and accountability

I had an insider's view as a new department head was hired to turn around a product development group. Under the previous vice president, the group had worked in a scattered and unplanned fashion and now the program was at risk.

The new leader made an amazing turnaround by pulling people together using shared goals and accountability.

First, he created one uncommonly large management team consisting of all the key players. This gave him the chance to establish common goals and project reviews that were held around the team table. It erased internal silos and competition and allowed the senior leader to get to know the capability of team members in the glaring light of group inter-action and peer pressure.

He shared the big picture and key issues he was worrying about— locking in on the product design, budget and product delivery dates. Then he asked us for help.

This led the group to lock in on the final business goals. This was important because if the team shared goals, individuals would not be able to independently change things without the review of the group.

> Master the art of facilitating group discussions. This is an essential skill.

With everything on the table, the group made key decisions together as one management team. What a feeling of teamwork when they had one set of shared goals, schedule and budget.

Not everyone liked this mutual accountability, visibility and peer pressure. Some people chose to leave but the people who stayed thrived.

The concept of sharing goals and accountability with the larger group will build a stronger team bond. You will see your team get more and more proficient as they begin to sense they are all in this together.

Excel at all-team communication

A misused concept in American business is the idea that "my door is always open." How this offer usually plays out is that any individual can ring your bell and take up your time with what they deem important. People should be bringing these issues to the team table as group busi-ness. Do they respect the group forum?

Amanda's employees are circling back to her to get personal briefings. It feels good to be an insider and know more than others, so employees may stop by to surreptitiously squeeze more information from you.

- **Build respect for the group forum**

One Managing Genius I worked for would always carry a future agenda list close at hand. He would take out this list and add late-breaking topics to it, saying, "We need to cover that at the next meeting so everyone can hear." You could use the Notes App on your smart phone. Whatever you do, create a visible action where you signal to people that this issue is for the next all-group meeting.

If the question was barn-burning urgent, he would send a group email and follow up at the next meeting. Usually he would just add it to the list of agenda items for the next meeting where he would ask the person to present the question for group discussion.

Meetings are inefficient when people do not bring everything to the table. This experience caused me to *respect the group forum.*

- **Run effective meetings**

To share more at the group level, you will need a way to bring people together to coordinate activities, share progress and keep everyone in sync. A Managing Genius always excels at leading meetings.

This chart is a simple guide that contains everything you need to know. You should be investing at least as much time into planning a meeting as you do into holding the meeting itself.

Take this to heart. Meeting leadership is the one skill that broadly showcases your personal leadership abilities across the organization. In my experience, few business leaders shine at running meetings and facilitating group decision-making. Do this well and your reputation for leadership will rise within your organization.

Meeting Leadership

1. Invite the right people
2. Send out agenda—Why we're here?
3. Everyone comes prepared
4. Stay on course
5. Track agreements, action items and open items
6. Closure—what happens next?
7. End on time

- **Manage everyday team business**

Remember, you have many employees and there is only one of you. For the sake of efficiency, decide how and when you want to handle the nuts-and-bolts administrative questions.

One trick is to figure out and resolve what burns up your managing time. Look to eliminate repeat conversations by saying it once to all.

Some items are just not worth rehashing for everyone who comes to your door.

For example, I observed a national sales director who surprisingly took the time to teach his preferred process for employee expense statements. I wondered at the time why he was going through this "administrative detail" with all of his senior sales team. I later saw the wisdom in his ways. Assemble your team and say it once. This frees you up for bigger concerns by eliminating repeated instructions.

Urgent business: Your door is always open. *Everyday admin stuff:* Say it once to the whole group.

Give people full access to you, but *keep it within the group forum.*

3 A SIMPLE GUIDE FOR DELEGATION

Scott was my first boss and he gave me my first look at Managing Genius. Today he is a senior executive for an international nonprofit organization.

To appreciate Scott's managing style, you need to know that Scott pitched for his college baseball team. Scott could throw a baseball ninety feet, applying the right speed, spin and roll to cause the ball to cross the plate according to his intent.

Scott shares that his pure pitching skill was not enough to win games in college. So he learned how to be a *smart* pitcher—to think ahead and make pitching decisions based on his careful reading of the situation.

Master the art of delegating and assigning work.

He studied the proclivities of the batters he would face and prior to each pitch, he would scrutinize the batter's stance and behavior.

Make pitching natural at work

It is Managing Genius to have a systematic way to share with your employees. This will communicate competence and control. You will bring out the best in the people who are working for you.

Here are three simple questions that are the foundation for how you delegate and direct the work of others. Everything you do as a manager hinges on how clearly these three questions are communicated.

This applies for any employee, whether working down the hall or virtually across the city or in India.

This clarity creates a powerful connection with your employees. You build trust by eliminating open questions and ambiguity. You allow people to take the initiative by giving them a complete "hand-off".

It is fair game for your employees to expect you to be able to answer these three questions. Teach people to ask these of you and of one another. This should become a common, everyday way of discussing work.

Step 1 **Why are we here?**

Think differently: Instead of telling people what to do, first reach agreement on why we are here.

Amazing GPS tools tell us Where are we? Take the lead to make sure everyone understands *Why are we here?* :

- *What you say:* Take aim and pitch across the plate. You want your communication to be specific, measurable, actionable and outcome-based. Show how, listen or sometimes tell. Mutual discussion and understanding is the goal but remember that your direction is what matters most. Do not be the "great mentioner" who leaves people hanging with unformed ideas or vague directions.

- *When and how you say it:* Actually, getting the time and place right is 80% of sharing clear expectations. People are more apt to open up when they feel comfortable and safe. Get people in the right space.

> Never assume people know why they showed up for this meeting.

Consider the message, the person, timing and situation. Talk things through, ask questions and leave space for self-discovery and initiative.

Prepare your team for quicker decisions when facing pressing needs. Not every workplace conversation is a relaxed meeting over coffee. The key is to become skilled at cutting through the clutter to highlight what is the chief concern. Great leaders are simplifiers.

Step 2 **Why is it important?**

Think differently: Inspire self-initiative by sharing why it is important to you and what it means to the business.

Team members need to understand the importance of the work that you are passing to them. This enables them to commit to and identify with the work. Establishing the importance and priorities will minimize getting sidetracked or chasing rabbits.

Your words and demeanor should match the importance of the work. Lean in and give eye contact to show this is important to you. Most people only need a reminder without you having do a hard sale.

> People will commit to things that matter and make a difference.

Discussing the importance of an issue is a great conversation starter. First, discuss the importance of the issue including "who asked for this." Use one or more of the four "attention getters"—customer, cost, context, consequences.

You should also establish what is *unimportant*. Pull sidebars off the table to keep people focused.

Step 3 **What happens next?**

Think differently: You get the "last word" by making sure everyone in the room has a clear understanding of what happens next.

During a baseball game, you will occasionally see a timeout during which the pitcher and catcher hold a discussion on the field. When the meeting is over, watch that someone always takes the ball and something always happens next. Remember, "nothing is something."

You want whoever is responsible to leave with clear sense of ownership. Ask people to verbalize their promises.

> What happens after you leave the room?

This is not a top-down command system where you assign the mission and then report back at 0900. Instead, you are taking the lead to make sure that everyone leaves with a shared understanding of *what happens next*.

Later, if your boss pokes her head into your office for a status update, you will earn respect when you can rattle off the next steps.

Managing Genius
QUICK GUIDE

Share Expectations

Step 1

Why are we here:
Clearly delegate expectations. Both your words and approach matter.

Step 2

Why is it important:
Set priorities and apply the right weight and focus. Connect on who wants this.

Step 3

What happens next:
Everyone leaves with closure on next steps: who, what, when. Give responsibility.

Perfecting your delegating skills

The above three-step process will help you organize your thinking as you lead workplace conversations and meetings.

To take this to a higher level, I sought to capture the best practices that I have observed in great managers meeting with their employees. What do they do to bring out the best in their people as they delegate work? Here is a fly-over of what has stood out to me:

Speak less, say more. Plainly said, some advance into leadership positions and then think that their words now carry more weight. A leader gains power and respect with fewer, well-chosen words. If you apply one thing, do this: Speak less and say more. In the abundance of words, people may stop listening and mentally disengage. Ask yourself after any workplace discussion, who talked most?

Personalize the meeting. You are talking to real people. Make real connections by using your unique personality to customize your approach. Understand that people have different ways of receiving new information, dealing with change and juggling priorities.

For example, Michael is acting like he wants to go back to his office to think things through before he commits to next steps, while Hannah has already made up her mind. Kimberly is not at her best when facing last-minute deadlines, while Katie feeds on last-minute adrenaline.

All will deliver equally on outcomes. Delegate work in the most effective manner for individual employees. (Go ask them.)

Shared discussion. Leave space for people to discover things for themselves. It is not your job to tell people every nuance about the work you are delegating. Most people will get the picture without you painting an oil landscape. Questions stimulate thinking. Give people the opportunity to ask questions and fill in their own knowledge gaps.

Self-initiative. Individuals are more likely to keep promises for which they take personal ownership. Let people figure things out and work out the details. People love to solve problems. Too often we dump solutions on people when a trained monkey would know what to do. If your goal is to delegate work that someone owns, then share problems and not solutions. Follow-up only as needed; leave space; do not corner people.

For example, compare these two requests: "I have talked with our customer and here is what she wants," versus "Here is the latest customer feedback. I would like you analyze the numbers and come back with possible solutions."

> Give people problems that they can wrestle with and solve.

Sharing autonomy. Where you can, give choices and options so people can make their own decisions and feel ownership. But make this a decision based on the people and work at hand. Not everyone handles autonomy in the same way and not every employee wants it.

Remember that serving as a "hands-off" manager is moving power and authority across the table to an individual. Is that what you want to do? There are some potential pitfalls to giving autonomy in the wrong circumstance. It may slow down decisions. It may cause confusion. Talk this through at the front end.

Define follow-up before people start running. Autonomy sounds wonderful but we are beholden to customers and business needs. A big part of setting expectations is in how we will measure the work, how we'll close on feedback and how we will decide the work is finished.

Turn individual goals into team promises. People are more apt to own their words and responsibilities once they verbalize the goals in a group forum. People will show more ownership for promises made explicitly, verbally and publicly.

Talking openly at a group forum has a way of forcing you to cut through the blather. The added scrutiny will encourage you to talk about your work in a clear and unambiguous manner. Naturally, if people can wallow in vague discussions in private meetings with their boss, they can cast shadows and create wiggle room for later.

Everyone knows when to sweat the details. Sometimes a quick review or status check will suffice. On the other hand, if you have dele-gated a very complex and detailed task, you need more details on the employees' planning and prepa-ration. The trick is to make sure everyone understands when and where to sweat the details.

> A Managing Genius is always a great simplifier. They can get to the heart of things.

Micromanaging. The word "micromanage" is used to describe watching every step your employee takes. You stand ready to jump in to take over. But in fact, there can be business reasons that call for closer management controls. The trick is to identify this up front, "This project is straight from the top, so bear with me, I'll need to stay more involved." This alerts team members so they know what to expect.

Surveillance mode. You may ask for something but then become frustrated when you do not see the outward signs of action. This can put you into surveillance mode. Grrr, why are they sitting at Starbucks? Why are they not doing what we discussed?

But wait, who likes to be watched?

You just make yourself look weak and worried when you chase the kids. People may pay lip-service to show you a good attitude. Step back and focus on outcomes, not actions or attitudes. It is reasonable to ask for scheduled check-ins and you can also ask, "What will you do first?" Seeing people get started can allay your fears.

Everyone raises questions to weed out ambiguity. Encourage people to ask for clarity and raise concerns early in the process. They should raise their hands if they don't understand something. Do not let people passively hang back to "lie in the tall grass," only to pop out later and act surprised: "Whoa, Dude, you never said that."

Set limits and boundaries. We may pass on clear expectations but then we leave people hanging on what are they *able* to do. Explain what choices and authority people have. If not, they have to keep coming back to you. Is that what you want?

Clarify up front if there are choices to be made or immovable objects to work around. Be sure to discuss schedule and budget. Where do we have wiggle room for decisions? What are must-haves?

Everyone has work that must be done—just spell it out. It frees people to run with the ball if they know the playing field.

Look for issues that need a "last word." You may need to exercise your responsibility and authority to close the discussion or move certain people on their way. Watch for repetition of the same pitch or looping back over decisions. Not everything requires group discussion and a committee decision. In fact, it is good for your group to regularly see you make a decision that closes an issue.

> Delegation means you do not do some of the work. You are passing responsibility.

Simplify. What does not calm us? The Internet and smart phones, which can create more loose ends, dangling conversations and open issues. Ambiguity and uncertainty can undermine your work group. What does calm us? Fewer variables. A feeling of control over what we are facing. A clear sense of what happens next. Clarify how decisions are made.

People need the power and ability to do the work. What decisions can they make? What spending guidelines do they have? When do they need to check in on their status? When you hand-off responsibility you should also give them the required power and ability to do the work. If not, they may need to come back to you for answers or assistance.

4 HOW JOBS GET BUILT

It is Managing Genius to have a thorough grasp of your entire organization and a deep knowledge of the jobs that people do.

See jobs as something you craft intentionally and then fine-tune to best deploy your people according to current business needs. Keep the org chart relevant to the current business and team needs. Design jobs like a skilled architect with a mind to cultivating a stronger team and giving people opportunity to grow.

It is important to understand the nature of jobs

When you create a job, you are combining a list of expectations into a "boxed set" of delegated responsibility.

You are assembling expectations when you create and assign jobs. You do this so you do not have to start each workday making the same routine assignments, such as, "Yesterday I asked you to manage petty cash and again today, I want you to manage petty cash."

The problem is that we often let job content slip and slide. People move in and out of your group and jobs can become undefined. As the group manager, you can choose to not get involved in the details. You may decide to take a hands-off approach where you hope people just work it out for themselves.

Often what happens is the Type A extroverts will take over and grab the most desirable parts of the job. The less vocal people may get ignored. This can create a free-range mentality where people learn ways to stake out their own territory, grab the shiny parts or hold onto status quo.

Wait, no need to worry. Eventually senior management or HR pulls off another reorganization to redesign your jobs for you. Of course, your people see you as the administrative care taker.

It is Managing Genius to continuously align individual jobs to best use your team to meet business and customer needs. Make this a part of a roll-out of annual goals or changes that affect the whole group.

Seek group input to fine-tune the distribution of work

This is one area to bring all discussion to the group table versus private lobbying sessions. This is an important step toward avoiding an informal hierarchy or status quo. Review in a team meeting, as the topic arises, to clarify boundary issues, overlap and missed or open items.

Avoid entitlement and status quo

It is important to build a team ethos where people are willing to do whatever is necessary to meet customer and business needs.

Everyone understands that job requirements may change. They will trust the system when they can participate in changes that affect their jobs. Avoid surprises or special assignments for a favored few.

> The true art of a Managing Genius is displayed in how you craft jobs and finesse the org chart.

Look for windows of opportunity such as natural breaks in the work, new budget cycles or when people come or go. See yourself in a position where you can decide on job assignments to optimize team performance and develop your people.

Develop your people

Sports coaches study their players and are constantly trying different lineups to use people's strengths and abilities. They are developing future players with multiple skills to optimize the team and create flexibility.

It is Managing Genius to facilitate new experiences to allow your people opportunity to learn and grow. People love to work where they can try new things and expand their abilities. Give people a chance to discover their potential. Make them feel respected for all that they bring to the team.

It is not as easy to swap out whole jobs but see yourself in a position to tweak job responsibilities to give new experiences. Often the opportunity presents itself through filling in for extended absences or vacation relief.

5 PLAN TO FINISH

Anthony, a software director, has asked me to join him in interviewing a software development manager candidate. This manager will lead a new initiative—a cutting-edge software feature with a senior sponsor.

Anthony is torn, as this new open position would be a good career opportunity for Emma, who is managing a software team that has been working on a software development project for nine months. This is Emma's first management experience and she has shown great promise. Her team is nearing the midpoint on this project, ahead of schedule of course. The team has really jelled through Emma's leadership.

There will be other opportunities for Emma but Anthony wonders if he owes it to her to give her this opportunity. However, in doing so he would break up her team and also keep her from finishing the project.

As we discuss the options, Anthony reflects that in his own career he has made a move every eighteen to twenty-four months. It seems there is no great reward for finishing work. In fact, this has been the way to move up the ladder and the only way to get a pay increase.

Our candidate is seated and ready to go and so I ask the first interview question:

> *"Tell me about a project you have*
> *successfully taken from start to finish."*

Value finishing

It is pure Managing Genius to finish what you set out to do. You give everyone a feeling of closure and completion. However, it is unique in today's business world to see leaders with experience taking responsibility for the full cycle, start to finish.

Have you wondered why your employees may not take you seriously? A work culture of half-done creates a mentality that says *do not take seriously anything that management says*. This affects employee attitudes and motivation in so many ways.

Why spend so much effort planning if we always change things later? We come to meetings to talk about activity, not progress toward the goals. Then we fall into a trial-and-error work style where we make things up as we go. If we are falling short on a goal, we learn to pull the cord to stop the train so we can rethink.

Look up; someone is at your door with that look, "We need to talk."

There is always learning and course corrections after the ship sails, but the Managing Geniuses I have worked with have an amazing ability to keep everyone focused on the destination in spite of what is happening around them. Even within the business whirlwind, they keep their team moving forward toward the stated goals.

Lock in Expectations

We know that a Managing Genius starts with clear, unambiguous goals and expectations. Everyone concerned should know what the finish line looks like.

Leeway is the problem. Leeway is the sideways drift of a ship that slowly, even imperceptibly, moves the ship sideways. Unless you manage the leeway of your ship, you will slowly move off the desired course.

> We love to drive home from work with a feeling of closure and completion.

So your group meets for hours to hammer out a detailed plan. Then people go their separate ways where they rethink things, see the road blocks or develop alliances. We often leave the meeting room as a team, and then start the "What about me?" Individual processing.

However, the biggest reason for business leeway is that it is too easy for individuals to shift the ship' direction whenever. Email and texting allows people to act spontaneously, if not impulsively. We move from face-to-face accountability and allow unfettered electronic banter.

Take the lead to set expectations so that everyone on the team will mutually respect goals and promises. You set the team work culture. Here are talking points to discuss and teach:

- Do not discard agreements and plans at the first hint of resistance. In fact, it should not be too easy to stop the train.

- If we do open up an issue, we will refer back to the original plans to connect to the previous thinking and planning.
- We should be learning and adjusting as we go but nail down what we just learned. There should be a compelling case for this change.
- Set up a practice where the team will review proposed changes together for mutual accountability.
- Email and texting is to exchange facts, data and information—not debate, sell ideas or make key business decisions.
- The person carrying this responsibility should *sign off* on revisions.
- This applies to you as well, of course. You should avoid tweaking your own goals or unpacking plans at every stop. This managing style sends the wrong message to your employees.

We certainly will face work that has a high potential to get changed midstream. There could be special customer demands, budget pressures or business risk at play. You will earn respect when you identify these potential changes *up-front* so people can stay tuned in and not be surprised later. Make "forks in the road" a line item in the project plan.

Plan for the End

The French philosopher Jean de la Fontaine wrote, "In everything one must consider the end." *Planning* for the finish is a skill that few master. A Managing Genius can find the finish line.

At the start, create an expectation that we will finish. Build in a mutual expectation and commitment that team members, including you, will work through the entire cycle.

Big-picture road maps. Seeing the big picture at one glance will highlight the end point. This is also a skill to develop in your team—when you can simply and succinctly layout the project, you prove that you understand it. This will increase ownership in the whole job, start to finish.

Shorter managing cycles. You are not managing like your Dad. Technology advancements have resulted in new products and services coming out at breakneck speeds. Today's millennial generation likes to work on shorter/faster projects.

With this in mind, plan assignments to allow people to work in shorter segments and establish milestones so people get to finish.

Sweat the details in how you will plan to start and finish. Eighty percent of your management time should be spent at the start and finish of any project. A finish is a transition into another start, so expect the same planning for both the start and the finish.

Finding the finish line. Even with clear goals, teams may need help closing down the work. We can circle around the airport not knowing if this is the time and place to land. It is human nature to let inertia keep current events in motion.

Baseball teams bring in a "closer" to finish the game.

There is also managerial strategy wrapped up in keeping things as they are to try to maintain budget and headcount.

Someone needs to say, "We are done."

Building a Team Culture that Finishes

Show value for the people who stick it out and finish. It is easy to reward the people who invent new things and get things started. Always consider the people who persist to the end. Make finishing a highly valuable achievement, worthy of top recognition.

Avoid pulling people away to cover today's trending topic. Let people stay to gain experience with finishing what they started. Sometimes we pull people off to the latest crisis, which of course is called fire-fighting. Make finishing things a topic to discuss with senior management when they throw out the latest "Let's go this direction now."

When you need a change in the lineup. The needs of the business and customers will sometimes force you to switch the players. Make an orderly, well-communicated decision that speaks to less slap-dash and a more well-founded business decision.

Manage by the seat of your pants and your team will never get the feeling of finishing.

Expect people to exit professionally and respectfully. Informally teach people how to hand off work responsibly. Communicate your expectation that an orderly hand-off will be the norm for your team. Seek an orderly transfer of responsibility.

Discover Your Managing Genius

- Master the art of delegating work in clear and unambiguous ways. Make sure everyone has clear expectations and responsibilities.

- This is a new approach—instead of telling people what to do, clarify and reach mutual understanding on three key questions:
    1. Why are we here?
    2. Why is it important?
    3. What happens next?

- You will feel confidence and poise if you know in advance what you intend to do and say. When you are free from worry over today's meeting agenda, you can focus more on bringing out the best in the people who are in the room.

- Best practices for Managing Genius:
    - Clear front-end delegation frees your people to work autonomously.
    - Manage more at the group level.
    - Lock in expectations from the start and your team will experience closure and completion at the finish line.
    - Make "planning for the finish" one of your team's core competencies.

Recognize and Champion

Use positive affirmation
to encourage and guide

> ## 💡 Big Idea
>
> The art of giving positive affirmation and encouragement is not a skill that comes naturally. When you succeed at this, it is pure Managing Genius. Recognizing great performance points people to what is important to you and the team. People can proactively align their actions and behavior. This will establish a spirit of optimism and appreciation.

Well! I'm actually feeling rather good about this. I think we all arrived at a very special place eh?

—Jack Sparrow in *Pirates of the Caribbean*

I have been salesman of the month for thirteen of the last twelve months. You heard me right. I did so well last February that corporate gave me two plaques in lieu of a pay raise.

—Dwight Shrute, *The Office*

They keep creating new ways to celebrate mediocrity.

—Bob Parr, alter ego of Mr. Incredible, *The Incredibles*

What if I send it in and they don't like it? What if they say, "Get out of here, kid. You got no future?" I just don't think I can take that kind of rejection.

—Michael J. Fox playing Marty McFly in *Back to the Future*

It isn't about the words you say. It's about the energetic message you send.

—Pete Carroll, Coach of the Seattle Seahawks

💡 Important to Know

I could feel the difference when I walked into the meeting room. Team members gave one another eye contact and talked with enthusiasm and encouragement. No one was staring at a phone. Everyone was totally present in the moment. They wanted to be there to fully engage and connect.

Encourage and Inspire

1 Think differently

2 You want to hear it from your boss

3 Positive affirmation is a learned art

4 Build positive connections

5 Inspire your people

In the center of the buzz, I saw Jennifer, the group director, interacting with various individuals and pulling together the group to get started. As she began, I sensed in her voice a spirit of optimism and encouragement.

She started the meeting with words of appreciation for individual and team contributions. She pointed to what people do best and even mistakes had a way of becoming shining lessons and valuable experience. She talked about work as if there are more good things to come.

Jennifer is demonstrating the essence of managing people through a spirit of positive affirmation and encouragement. She has tapped into what they are doing right and what they do best.

1 THINK DIFFERENTLY

If you look under the hood of the business enterprise, people are paid in exchange for specific work performed. This sounds formal and stuffy but the company is a system that operates to convert people's contributions into value. It is in fact a business relationship.

Don Draper: *It's your job. I give you money. You give me ideas.*
Peggy Olson: *But you never thank me.*
Don Draper: *That's what the money is for!*

—*Mad Men*

However, you do not need to treat people like cogs in the machine or use a cookie-cutter managing system. Given, there are appraisal forms, rating systems, policies and other admin aspects that must be accomplished.

However, these do not need to describe your managing approach or define the everyday working relationship with your employees.

Managing Geniuses I have worked with create a working relationship based on affirmation and appreciation. They cultivate a team culture that is optimistic and encouraging. They take ownership for this, choosing to manage in ways that brings out the best in people.

I pause to note that this is often not a shining skill of managers. It often becomes the responsibility of HR to create the rah-rah team spirit for managers through corporate awards, t-shirts and programs like employee of the month. However, it is important to note that these programs do not come from you and they do nothing to strengthen working relationship with your employees.

This chapter is written for you as the manager. There are simple ways to recognize people and create a powerful connection with your employees through your positive words and actions.

2 YOU WANT TO HEAR IT FROM YOUR BOSS

My first experience as a manager was at an open-pit mining operation in the Upper Peninsula of Michigan.

Don was one of the hourly workers I was supervising. He was the solitary bulldozer operator on the top of the waste rock dump. If you were there, you would see what looks like a small mountain with a flat top. The heavy equipment operator worked alone to maintain a roadway for the trucks, create drainage and make it possible to keep adding more material as the waste mountain got bigger and bigger.

> Recognition: Thanks, gratitude, acknowledgment and appreciation.

One day on my rounds of the mining operation, I climbed out of my pickup and climbed up on his dozer to chat with him. He was glad for someone to talk with and offered me coffee from his Stanley stainless steel thermos. As we talked, I commented to him what a good job he was doing that day. I pointed out that the area was at the right pitch for drainage and that it looked like a work of art compared with some of the other waste rock dumps I had supervised.

I was surprised to see how touched he was by my words. He shared, "That's the first time in twenty years' working here that someone in management has said something good to me."

The next day he thanked me again for my kind words and handed me a brownie wrapped in cellophane from his wife. He had shared my words with her and they had made her happy as well.

3 POSITIVE AFFIRMATION IS A LEARNED ART

Soon after your child learns to talk, he or she will begin to repeat the phrase, "Watch me!" It seems everyone wants someone to see what they are doing.

Look at my art project. Watch me ski down the half pipe. Take a look at this marketing report. Can you come to my presentation?

Make a mental shift to look for what people are doing right.

Positive affirmation also serves to give valuable feedback that tells us when we are doing something right. It assures us that we are on the right path. "That is exactly what we wanted; keep going."

Corrective feedback is more often a private conversation. Recognition can be a public message. When others listen in, it doubles the effect of the affirmation. It indicates to other team members that this is what you and the team value.

However, this is not a managing style that comes naturally. We struggle for the right words and often fall into general statements like "Thanks," "Good work, Sanjay" or "Appreciate you, Katie."

Also, managers may not even know what they wanted in the first place. They may be out of touch with the everyday happenings of the team. So we miss exceptional work when it occurs. Then our words of praise stumble out haphazardly as if we are surprised or relieved that it all worked out.

Some managers are shy to give to give people affirmation because it can feel "personal," since it is coming directly from you. You are expressing what you think and even what you feel.

As with any communication, both words and approach are important. Our words can rush out at the wrong time and place or we may miss our chance to thank our employee in the moment. Later, we might wonder if our words sounded genuine. Was the recognition received in the spirit we intended?

Giving positive feedback is an art that needs to be practiced and refined. When you succeed, it is pure Managing Genius.

4 BUILD POSITIVE CONNECTIONS

One summer, I had a stint working as a logger. The foreman was a grizzly man of many skills and talents and his instructions to me, the "college kid," were simple. "Here is your chainsaw and oil can. Now work your way across this tract of state forest land (mostly twenty-foot-tall pine trees) and drop (cut down) the taller Alder trees that are not supposed to be growing here." It was extremely hard work, a bit dangerous, with enough thrill to keep me going. I must say I got pretty good at dropping trees with a chain saw.

After several weeks on this job, I was at the road one evening putting away my equipment and I saw the foreman standing on a stump and gazing across the pine forest. He commented, "That is GD amazing. You did exactly what I wanted. You did a perfect job."

Then he jumped off the stump, got in his truck, and drove off. That moment is a memory that I can still share with pride.

Personal recognition is a form of feedback where we give people closure on their work performance and behavior. You can help them feel successful in their jobs, which will in turn give people a connection with the workplace, their team and you. They see your words of affirmation as a confirmation that they are doing the right things.

"Yes, that is exactly what I wanted" inspires me to do it again tomorrow.

5 INSPIRE YOUR PEOPLE

During World War II, there was a race to be the first country to develop the atomic bomb. It was a different time and place but someone was going to develop the bomb first. Imagine our world today if another nation had developed the bomb before the Allies.

The special, top-secret team that developed the atom bomb was part of the Manhattan Project. It was a race to solve the complex technology that involved the brightest scientists congregated at the Los Alamos Laboratory in New Mexico. Physicist Robert Oppenheimer was the leader of this cutting-edge, scientific team racing to be the first in the world with this weapon.

At one heated moment in the project, a key scientist, George Kistiakowsky, threatened to leave the program because he could not get along with a colleague. When Kistiakowsky came forward to quit, Oppenheimer told him, *"George, how can you leave this project? The free world hangs in the balance"*.[1]

Your employees walk through the doors to start work, wondering, "Why is it important that I work here?" The best managers I have worked with have a way of inspiring the people who do even the simple, routine work. Their words and actions communicate to employees that they want them here and why they think they should stay here today . . . and next month.

Unfortunately, we often wait until they submit their two-week notice before we think about what we may be losing. Then we lavish praise and appreciation; we share the bright future. Please stay.

---

1   Warren G. Bennis, *Managing the Dream: Reflections on Leadership and Change* (New York: Basic Books, 2000).

This Is Managing Genius

Encourage and guide through positive affirmation

1 Master the art of giving recognition

2 Set the bar high

3 Celebrate group success

4 Champion and support

5 Be a generous leader

It is Managing Genius to focus on positive affirmation and recognition as a communication strategy with your employees. Exceptional managers demonstrate a skill and affinity for using positive words with their employees.

This chapter is for you, putting you in the driver's seat for creating a team culture of optimism and encouragement. This is not a skill that comes naturally to most managers and you need to decide that you want to excel at it.

Here are five essential action steps that will lead you toward Managing Genius.

1 MASTER THE ART OF GIVING RECOGNITION

My father drove a ready-mix concrete truck for thirty-five years. His daily routine when he got home was to sit at the kitchen table in his work clothes and drink a beer before going downstairs to get cleaned up. He would talk with my mother about adult things that are now long lost to my memory. It is interesting that I only remember my father talking about his job on days when he had received praise from his boss.

My kid ears probably picked up on this because his voice became happy and animated. For that moment, he did not seem so tired. It almost seemed that whatever his manager said counted double.

Take the lead for recognition of your employees

Genuine recognition and attention from your manager really does matter. We love to hear praise from people who know us personally. My boss and team may be the only ones in the company who really know what I do.

My boss should have the best idea of what I had to do to get this work done, what obstacles I faced and how tough it was to reach the finish line on time. Your manager has the best grasp of current events pertinent to your work. It matters more when you get genuine, positive affirmation from your boss.

Your employees may flow in and out of the consciousness of senior management and staff. They can get lost in programs and become a box on the org chart. It is too easy to feel lost in a company and sense that no one knows what you did today.

Any other praise or mention of your name in the company is welcome but we will take those words back to our boss and our teammates to receive validation. Managers are in the best position to give meaningful affirmation that is genuine, targeted, personal and timely. You know your team's work, so you have a unique ability to recognize what is important and relevant to your people.

Moreover, as the manager, you hold the keys. You can link an employee's effort and commitment to future assignments, autonomy and rewards.

From my observation, Managing Geniuses take all this to heart, bringing individual contributions into the light of day, so people can take pride in their work. Positive affirmation is a "way of doing business." Find yourself naturally stepping in at the right time and place to give positive affirmation and encouragement.

Give clear communication

The Managing Geniuses I have observed speak in adult language using words that link actual behavior and outcomes to the business's needs and current events.

"You ran the meeting today masterfully."

"I like how you worked through that problem. You were efficient and kept us all focused on finding a solution."

"I was amazed with how smoothly you transitioned to a closing during the sales meetings."

The phrases *Good job* and *Thank you* are fine, but they do not tell me what I have done right. I once had a manager tell me, "Wow, you've been a busy beaver." You get the picture.

Remember to be aware of your body language and facial cues. This is positive affirmation—you should be happy. Make what you say important and memorable by your words and actions.

It is important to decide up-front that you want to personally recognize your own employees. Start looking for opportunities to speak up.

Right time and place

One senior manager taught me that his personal goal was to "never let a good opportunity to say a positive word pass by without acting." The trick is to stay in the moment and act when you see something that deserves the attention. The right time and place is everything…and that moment will not be back again.

In fact, in my experience, do not worry about what you say, just get the right time and place.

> Catch the right time and place. People will be more open to your message.

Most times people have an idea that they just did something good, so you catching the moment will speak for itself. Just the act of turning around and walking up shows you caught what just happened.

Stay close to your people and the action so you can manage in the moment. If you are in tune with what is happening, you can step in to provide encouragement at a timely moment. On the other hand, if you are distant and unaware of what is happening on your team, anything you say may sound shallow. As a result, your people may start to disregard what you think and your words will come as disingenuous.

There is one key element that cannot be ignored as you stop to share in that moment. Make sure your words and body language clearly show that this moment is the most important thing going on right now.

In this world of multi-tasking and over-scheduled calendars, you can really connect with people if you can step back from the frenzy and make them feel like this moment is all about them. This is a "turn-off the phone" moment that says this is important.

I can remember a planning meeting that I facilitated for a senior leadership team. As I gathered up my things, my boss was standing at the back of the room to tell me great work and to share several well-dones. It was sweet music. You just had to be there.

Catch specific work

The best employee recognition is work-related. Speak to people about what you like about their contributions to the business. Too often, we do not have a clear view of the plan or desired results. Getting closer to the work allows you to be better able to give specific feedback.

People often *do not* have jobs that speak to clear feedback for a job well done. We are not building straight brick walls or laying smooth concrete walkways that allow us to step back with pride and see our work. People's contributions can be embedded in group project or in the complex spreadsheet that spits out key numbers that people notice.

See what people do and be as specific as you can. Rather than praising someone for a "good job with your sales numbers this month," use numbers and actual results, like "I was impressed that you brought in three new major clients that added $200,000 to our quarterly revenue."

Praising employee motivation and attitude *(I can see that you really care about the company)*, or good effort *(I can see that you are really trying)* is subjective and can sound paternal.

Ask people to *show you* their best work

Tucker would stay around after a presentation to ask the presenter what went well from his or her own perspective. There's no need to have all recognition come from you or put yourself in a position where you need to find what people did best.

Why not ask them? Give artists the opportunity to reflect on their painting under your attentive listening and reflective questions.

Give them time to verbalize what happened and what they felt went well. What did they do that made them feel particularly proud? What did they learn? What would they do differently? What would he or she do again next time?

You create a powerful connection when you pause and let people unwind and self-reflect.

Mixing praise with feedback

When you connect a screwdriver to both the positive and negative terminals of your car battery, you create sparks. If you have accidentally done this, you can correlate the results of that action with trying to give affirmation and feedback at the same time. Not a good idea.

It is conventional wisdom to begin improvement feedback sessions with some kudos. The instinct is to soften the blow by mixing some sugar with the oatmeal.

The problem is that people are usually quick to spot this tactic and in their minds they think, "OK, I know it is coming, so get to the point." Later, we think that it feels manipulative.

Imagine giving applause to a performer while at the same time saying, "You do know that you're tuned a bit sharp."

Back to what we learned in Chapter 2, always ask, *Why are we here?* So if you are there to generally discuss the project and there are some positives as well as improvement suggestions, just say up front that your agenda includes a mixed bag of feedback. You can still mix in varied feedback but you need to say it up front: "Here is what is coming."

Praise work

Build a work culture that is focused on performance and outcomes. Everything you say should be connected to what people actually do.

Any positive feedback will be personal: "You did a masterful job of running that meeting." The praise should be something that they did personally and done in the context of the business.

"Sarah, our customers are pleased that you do what you promise."

"Thanks, Jennifer, for going the extra mile with this customer."

"Just a special word of thanks to Vijay for completion of the software feature on time and under budget."

You can also give recognition and positive affirmation for career development or job development. "I can see that you've grown in your project-management skills; let's look for opportunities for you in the future."

Praise the right person

Most of us can share a story about a coworker who took credit for our project or idea and reported it to the company as if it was his or her own work. It is frustrating when your manager gets it wrong and praises the wrong people or doesn't realize who did what.

Imagine a movie that dramatizes your work group. Run through the credits: Who did what work? Who contributed in what way? Whose idea was this?

People love to hear their names. Do the right thing and give credit where credit is due for work done, ideas or anything you can link to a personal name or team effort.

One size does not fit all

Julie was one of the best employees I ever managed and there were hundreds of times that she deserved recognition for extra effort. She would always go the extra mile.

Once I gave her public recognition at a meeting that included the entire company: "A special thanks to Julie for her extra effort." The full story was followed by hearty applause. Later, she shared with me that she preferred one-on-one feedback and that the recognition in front of a group embarrassed her.

Everyone is different. Understand that some people do not desire the limelight or personal attention. The trick is to know your people and find the right way to share heart-felt appreciation.

Individuals deserve individual attention. This is exactly why the company programs fall flat. Your team deserves personalized attention that means something to them, delivered by someone who knows what they do.

Although she was unassuming and quiet, Julie very much enjoyed lattes delivered to her desk.

Keep it proportional

Make sure your words fit the moment. I listened to a sales manager once as he praised one of his sales reps for the way he handled a sales call. Later, I asked for the details and learned that it was actually a small sale that brought an insignificant profit for the company. In fact, it looked like the sales rep spent an inordinate amount of time on such a small job for the purpose of showing off.

I think that praising people who "ask for it" just feeds them to keep doing so. "C'mon Tom, if we give out rewards for every minor sales we'll be here all day."

In another situation, the manager gave recognition to an employee who served on a company committee to plan the summer picnic. There's nothing wrong with this but there were employees in the room who had worked for months and who received no recognition for deliverables.

When we focus too much attention on trivial things that are not part of the mainstream business plan or desired outcomes, we water down the real work that focused employees are doing.

People may get cynical when praise is over the top, so save some of your words for that big bang moment. If you feel like you're trying to prop people up emotionally to do a better job, you might be parenting them.

Using words of praise to curry favor or friendships

The recognition we are talking about in this chapter is job related, not a personal compliment like "You sure look nice today" or "I like that color on you." There is nothing wrong with sharing those kind words but you may say these and think you have done your "recognition duty."

Flattering words or praise are more friendship oriented. Sometimes we preface difficult feedback or bad news with superfluous words that may water down our message. Quite often, our desire to seek approval from our employees leads us to share positive comments or compliments aimed at the *person* instead of at the *work*.

Self-evident praise

It sometimes seems like we send our employees through a tunnel and when they come out successfully at the other end, then we look for something good to say.

Spend some of your managing energy at the *start* of the tunnel. Explain what would constitute a great result at the other end. Let the praise come to your people in a self-evident fashion that is clear, unambiguous and self-explanatory.

In a basketball game the players know that when you shoot from outside the line, you score three points. A track sprinter knows the feeling of the breaking the string at the finish line.

Create systems where people can automatically feel successful without looking to you for affirmation.

2 SET THE BAR HIGH

I was working as a staff engineer at a large research organization with hundreds of ongoing projects. In a quarterly recognition program that was touted to recognize superior performance, several top performers received cash awards and special recognition.

One of the researchers, Jon, seemed to be a favorite among senior management and over the past few years he had been selected for multiple awards. Management would give heart-filled praise for his extra effort that was demonstrated by staying late and working weekends.

> It is Managing Genius to decide in advance what behaviors and actions you want to highlight.

However, the truth was that Jon was a chronic last-minute person. He would wait until the last minute and then power through fueled by an adrenaline rush. But this always involved Jon expecting others to respond to his urgent needs.

Rachel, another employee who was honored was the group training officer; she was cited for exceptional team spirit. But she also had a very annoying habit of drawing out stories in vivid detail. Her team members knew enough to avoid her if they wanted to get something done that day.

People left the recognition meeting wondering whether it was performance or politics. What is interesting is that the company invested time and money in this recognition program. However, the net result to team morale was negative.

Group praise shows what you deem as important

Your words and actions, especially in a group or public forum, communicate what's really important to you. You build your team culture based on what you highlight. Also, you speak for the company and people will assume that what you say is what the company values.

It is all about "airtime"—what gets talked about the most. Without someone deliberately steering the ship, the most talented group of employees will turn into a social club, political party or group therapy session. It's like composing a tweet—you only get 140 characters, so what is the most important message you want people to hear?

Be proactive and decide in advance what behaviors, actions and team conduct you want to encourage. Set the bar for your own team. Keep this simple; you do not need a special program with a fancy name.

Mainstream goals and deliverables

Recognize the people who do the real work in your group—the ones who make sales, solve problems, handle customers and do the "heavy lifting." Too often, company recognition programs favor people with social skills and gloss over the people who work under the radar but carry the true loads.

You do not hear someone going home to tell his or her spouse "Isn't it great—my boss thinks I have a good attitude" or "I won the good neighbor award at my company."

We would rather go home and share some highlight about professional advancement, business decisions or real results. "I really nailed that quality project" or "My boss complimented me at coming in under budget at the meeting with all of the top brass" or "My sales numbers were top in the region."

Talk more about the focus of your group's work and the core competencies. Too often, we communicate a wrong message that the way to get ahead in this organization is through the special stuff, the heroic actions off the grid or sucking up to senior management with their personal request. Talk about the people who work at the heart of the action.

Personal values

Decide in advance what values you will reinforce with your group's success. Some examples of values to emphasize include customer service, innovation and teamwork.

If you lead people at Nordstrom, you would make sure that praising customer service gets sufficient airtime. If you work at an electronics manufacturing group you might want attention on process detail and quality as part of a Six Sigma program.

Make sure you reinforce what is important to your group.

Competence and learning

Recognize when people attain a new level of performance or mastery. Take a moment to acknowledge the fact that they have attained a higher level status. Praise people when they acquire skills and abilities.

Always praise learning and educational achievement when your employees invest sweat equity and show the initiative to improve. "I want to take a minute to commend Claire, who just finished her evening MBA program."

Decide what will not get undue airtime

Early in the history of Apple Computers, Steve Jobs constantly reminded his group that bringing products to market was everything. In fact, his motto was "real artists ship." In other words, the work meant nothing unless the group was able to produce a tangible outcome.

Be careful not to overly commend certain behaviors

At today's staff meeting you led people through a review of the budget, checking off action items and talking about a sticky customer problem. Eventually, you got to the team items, at which point your face brightened. It was time to talk about the fun stuff.

There was an award to Jeremy for his ten years' of service and thanks to Ahn and Trisha for putting together today's team lunch. Then you commended Jose for his work on the quality committee. You spoke of his ability to quickly get the team to a correct root cause for the issue by his skill at using the "5 Times Why" technique.

We often praise and give non verbals that show we like the soft, subjective stuff like loyalty or team spirit. While everyone loves it when an employee brings in baked goods every week, it's important to recognize the employee who is handling six Tier 2 service calls a day and is beloved by the customers.

Be intentional about the people who deserve recognition

In any group, there are people who are highly skilled at seeking out attention. There are people in your group who are very good at drawing in recognition; you might even think they are skilled at "sucking up" to management.

These people generally find their way to the right committee or wind up working on the hottest new project that gets visibility at the top. The slick Power Point presentation or the full-color report on customer retention wows us. On the other hand, there are the quiet introverts who plug along without fanfare and drama. These people may not volunteer for certain committees, nor do they hang around your desk seeking attention.

Recognizing the right people shows you know what is actually happening on your team.

Remember: the person raising his or her hand in a classroom may not be the most knowledgeable person in the room. Become more deliberate with your team recognition and make sure you recognize and reward the right people.

3 CELEBRATE GROUP SUCCESS

Affirmation means more when it comes from people you know and work with daily. People will work extra hard to win recognition and respect from their teammates. Make it your strategy to use group forums to bring more recognition into the light of day.

It is true that people love to hear their names, so the "Go team, good job" collective message may get lost. Find creative ways to bring your team together with your words of affirmation.

Find individual contribution in group work

Most work in the business world is shared in some fashion. It is important to understand how work gets done and how the pieces all come together. Thanking only the person who passed you the final report without acknowledging the people who contributed to the effort is an unfortunate error that will make you appear to be out of the loop.

It takes greater effort on your part to pull together pertinent and relevant recognition for a group effort because you need to sort through the layers of differing participation. Often we see that something happened but we do not understand the nature of the team effort. It is easier to see individual effort but you have to look more carefully to see the people who contributed the most to the team effort.

Stay in touch with the group work so you know who is doing what. This is tough for some managers who may have a tendency to meddle or give unsolicited advice when they get close to the work.

We also tend to overstate individual heroes and miss the collective effort. It is easier to greet one individual and focus on specific things he or she has done. Some people have a way of drawing undue attention and pointing the light on themselves. Find and reward the most worthy contributors, not the most visible.

Half of the world are introverts (thank God) so it easy for some people to get forgotten. Go out of your way to look behind the scenes. Too often we overstate the so-called heroes and miss the collective effort.

Promote an adult-minded team culture

When your employees are together in a group, find ways to reinforce desired actions and behavior through what you choose to recognize and reinforce. As you start giving positive affirmation, your team members will follow suit.

By bringing desired actions to light, you can encourage people to forego selfishness and their own personal agendas. People will take a higher road when surrounded by adult-minded peers who are moving together in a common direction. It gives a healthy dose of peer pressure and this will reinforce desired actions and behavior.

This is not as easy as it sounds. Group consensus is not easy to win and what you choose to highlight may not play with popular sentiment. For a potential hire, your team may voice preferences for friendly, socially skilled people. But as manager who carries responsibility for the work, you know the team needs to increase its technical skill base. You make a business decision for the hire that best benefits the organization.

Celebrate completion of milestones and achievements

If you have done a good job planning and setting goals, you should have a wealth of great work accomplishments to recognize and celebrate. The trick is to not miss these opportunities.

You have the project schedule, so put on your calendar points where you should be there to recognize the contributors.

Let people talk about what they did

I was once in a large group meeting where our CEO praised a staff person for a job well done. Unfortunately, I was sitting next to the person who had actually completed the work and just about everyone in the room knew the real story. It was an honest mistake but it can make the CEO look like he or she is out of touch. It embarrasses the wrong person and takes away the moment for the right person to shine. Try these ideas for employee recognition:

- Who knows better who helped than the people who were actually there doing the work? Introduce people at the group level and give them the opportunity to share their own achievements. One Managing Genius I worked with would bring people forward at group meetings and interview them about the work they did.

- Do not make everything about you. I have seen managers give offhanded praise to their employees while keeping the spotlight on their own achievements. "I was able to solve the final hurdle and get the work done but I have to say that I could not have done it without Susan's help." Let *your* praise and recognition come from someone other than yourself.

- Make the extra effort to know and correctly pronounce each individual's name. This is a growing challenge but if the newscasters on CNN can do it, so can we.

Post self-scoring systems

During a basketball game, players can track the game and see their status. This is "self-evident achievement."

Let your people measure themselves and feel the sense of accomplishment that comes from their own knowledge and understanding of the work. It is difficult to feel ownership without seeing progress and feeling successful.

It takes extra work for a manager to think about and create a self-reporting scoreboard. It is even harder to maintain it. Keep things simple and make it a group effort. Make sure the connection is clear between the score on the wall and how the individual (or team) impacts that score. Daily results are more effective at driving tomorrow's output than last year's performance.

> Allow people to see for themselves how we are doing.

This visibility gives people the chance to see real-time results on how your team is doing, creating a mutually supportive, "fist-bumping" team culture where people can stay tuned to what is happening around them. Not all recognition comes from you. You make sure people can access what they need and that it is relevant.

Stay in the lead

Many employees believe the term *recognition* in the work environment is synonymous with a corporate program run by HR on behalf of the company and managers. For example, we get an "Employee of the Month" who gets a special parking spot. There is a special achievement award on your desk with a balloon attached. There are gifts for ten years of service.

These company recognition programs are often irrelevant and uninteresting. They usually emphasize cooperation or some HR initiative and they are not part of current events within your team.

But the main rub is that these company programs come from HR or senior management. I want managers at the center of team operations where they are the leader. Only you can make recognition meaningful and relevant to your team.

The best recognition comes from inside your group—from you and the people on your team. As manager, you can validate any award or company praise and put it into the context of what is happening on your team. It's all about stepping in as an active sponsor for your team and the individuals who report to you.

Put yourself into a leadership role with Company programs.

Act like the owner and note that you have the power to use your words and actions to give timely appreciation and recognition. Your words are the secret sauce that makes people feel valued and keeps people committed through tough times and challenges.

Stay apprised of corporate programs that are coming down the road. Then you can take ownership as it rolls out to your group. Fine-tune anything that needs changing and make sure that the right people are recognized. Link corporate awards to the individual's work performance.

Integrate company awards and events within the context of your own group. For example, if the company has an employee appreciation picnic, you can announce it like it is a group event. "Our team needs to have some fun and good food. So next Friday we are having a team picnic. I've invited the rest of the company to come as well but I look forward to hanging out with you all."

4 CHAMPION AND SUPPORT

Amanda was one of those rare managers everyone wants to work for. She had a reputation as a leader who looks out for her employees and gets behind them.

As I watched Amanda, I saw that it was more than just words. With her actions she demonstrated she was on their side and wanted them to succeed. She wanted people to feel that "my boss has my back."

It is more than just saying thank you

Amanda would keep a watchful eye to see that work got started well and give that extra word of encouragement when people needed it. She would advocate for her people around the company and defend them where needed. She would speak out to build up the reputation of her people among senior management and her colleagues. Amanda showed, by her actions, that she believed in her people. She had a knack for stepping in at the right time to advocate for them.

> A champion supports and advocates for your success.

Access to your manager

It is a powerful affirmation to show up where employees are working. See if they want help or pointers; be available for questions or complaints or just show up. This is also a way to show that you want people to succeed.

Rather than waiting until the end of a project to thank people, give them positive affirmation early in their process so they can feel confident and assured. This is something that gets scheduled even if it's a quick message to follow up.

Also, show that you want people to succeed by supplying what they need to do the job: budget, people, resources, tools and time. This demonstrates that you are advocating for your people; you want them to succeed. Making things easier and removing frustrations is a great way to show that you want people to do well.

Believe in your people and have faith in them

Give confidence: point out why you believe they can do it and why you think they have the skills and abilities to accomplish the work. "I know you can handle this customer call. I have faith in you."

It is Managing Genius to show them that you trust and respect them: Amanda makes her employees feel like they are something special. She gives them true responsibility and the power to make decisions. She allows them to fail and learn from their mistakes.

Advocate for your people in the company

Your team should come first ... not your status in the company or your relationships with top management. The latter is called "Managing up" and your team will be quick to pick this up.

Run point on navigating company policy and turf issues. Step in to defend your people and stick up for them in the company. You should fight internal turf battles and navigate politics for your people. Do not let corporate bullies shove your people around and share mean-spirited words. Be ready to advocate for them.

If you do not, then they will have to fend for themselves. Some things have to come from you.

Be an active supporter across the company to teach others about the role of your team. Highlight who is doing significant work. The great managers I have worked with have shown a high public regard for their own employees and routinely speak up to send positive messages in the company. This attitude infuses a spirit of optimism and provides less opportunity for anxiety or fear of the future.

Of course, to accomplish this you need to take the time to get to know your people. Discover two key items: What they do best and what they love doing the most.

"You need to talk with Jennie; she is a spreadsheet genius." "Marcus is an excellent people manager." "Maya is an amazing project manager ."

Standing behind your people will engender trust in your leadership. You can remove that feeling of uncertainty coming from outside the group knowing you are actively engaged with your employees.

Give that extra push

Living in Minneapolis for ten years gave me more than a few snow stories—usually the story involves pushing my car or having someone else push it while I steer. You could tell when a car is stuck in snow by the very distinctive sound the wheels make as they spin in the snow. Hearing this noise was the signal to get your coat and go help. Strangers would come out of their homes when they heard the sound. One helpful and well-timed push would usually get the car moving again.

Often, people just need you to come alongside of them and give them that little nudge with a thoughtful question or quick bit of advice. It is important to learn the art of giving a push when people need help. The key concept to know is when to step in and when to step back out. Make note of what people are asking for.

Show recognition in tangible ways

Amanda is going back to corporate for a planning meeting and she decides to invite one of her top performers, Matt, to join her at the meeting. She does this to communicate to Matt appreciation for his extra effort at work and give him an opportunity to broaden his learning.

Later she calls Kanaye to her office and invites her to work on a special committee to streamline the purchasing process. Kanaye is a top performer who works in the background, often unseen in the group.

As a result of an employee leaving, there is a window cube open that is considered prime real estate in the group. She decides to give the space to Valerie. Valerie is a relative newcomer in the group but clearly a star performer. This is a good chance to show that performance counts.

What Amanda is doing is looking for tangible ways to give perks and privileges to the people who are most deserving. There are actually more opportunities than you realize to reinforce and affirm good work behavior and performance.

You may not have the power to use compensation for current events. However, you can use everyday management decisions to show positive affirmation, for example, assigning office space, training, vacation relief or special assignments for committees or task forces.

5 BE A GENEROUS LEADER

You want your people to see you as a giving person, not just someone who takes. The reason for your success is the combined contribution of the people who work for you. They are sharing your responsibilities and you succeed because of their contributions. When you are promoted or receive accolades, be sure to thank the people who have contributed to your success.

Try this exercise: Make a list of all of your previous managers. By each one's name, put either a G for giver or a T for taker.

Of course, you then have to ask the tough question, what letter goes by your name? What's interesting to note is that your employees have already figured that out about you.

Make the decision that you will give of yourself personally.

Find ways to give back to your team

Aaron Rodgers, the quarterback for the Green Bay Packers, expressed a huge thank you to his offensive linemen in December 2014—including the reserves, practice-squad players, and backup quarterbacks. When they showed up at the stadium, they found fifty-five-inch smart TVs, tablets, and headphones in each of their lockers.

In comparison, Brett Favre, his predecessor at quarterback, was a horrible Christmas gift giver. He was known as "Alligator Arms," for his inability to reach for his wallet.

Yet Brett Favre's leadership style gave to his players in other ways. His down-home style and backwoods sensibility grounded younger players during a time when they couldn't possibly deflect all the attention they received. He made people believe in themselves.[2]

Appreciation for your employees should come from you personally. Find your own style for achieving this. It does not need to include lavish gifts but in the end you want your employees to see you as a giver, not a taker.

---

2   Read the interesting story by Conor Orr, "A Very Brett Favre Christmas" at www.nfl.com.

Serve and share from your own pocket. Remember that your people serve you in their contributions so that you can succeed and advance.

I remember one year my company was making deep spending cuts at year's end. They canceled all company-sponsored holiday parties. Undeterred, a software director decided to hold a party for his group at his home, at his own expense. It made quite an impact—his commitment and good will were paid back many times over.

> A Managing Genius is always a giver, not a taker.

We cannot all afford to host large events but there are many smaller opportunities to give from your own pocket. Have a Starbucks card loaded and ready for your direct reports to share a break. Bring in a pizza, donuts or sponsor a Friday post-work social hour.

Sharpen the saw

Back to my north woods experience. My foreman, Charlie, was a unique model for managing people. He was a grizzly guy with a big beard and dirt under his fingernails. He did not have polished social skills but Charlie had the knack for reaching out to make connections with me at the right moment. He was a memorable manager.

One day, Charlie stopped me in the woods and took my chainsaw to sharpen the chain for me. As I sat watching him, he shared stories of the woods that had messages of safety built in. He taught me how to service the saw myself, then he oiled and cleaned the chainsaw. I really appreciated it and this made my work easier.

That 15 minutes gave me a wealth of wisdom and confidence.

This would be like showing your employees how to use a technology application to make their presentations more attractive or showing how lookup tables can make a spreadsheet more efficient.

You are not just doing something for your people. You are using the time to make a lasting connection.

The gift of time and access

Look at your schedule to see if you tend to give your direct reports the best part of your day. Do you push things aside to find time for a team member?

We can fall into a trap where we invest more on managing *up* in the organization. That's where we spend more time with colleagues and powerful people who can do things for you.

In would be interesting to get honest feedback from your people. If asked, can your people get to you when they need you? Are you consistently on time and prepared for meetings? Do you give your direct reports your undivided attention? Do they feel like you want to meet with them?

The very best thing you can offer your people is access to you. Make space in your schedule and provide a listening ear when needed. Turn off your phone and give them your undivided attention. Talk about what is important to them or what they worry about.

I once worked with a peer who showed me a powerful way to acknowledge someone's value. Whenever anyone walked into his office, he would immediately make eye contact, push back in his chair, remove his glasses and set them on his desk. The message was clear: whatever I am in the middle of doing, your presence is of more value.

Personal touch

See your people as individuals and find unique ways to give a personal touch and make appreciation meaningful and memorable. Just watch, listen and see what is important to them.

For example, I shared a love for great coffee with one of my employees and we often met for one-on-one meetings over a latte. Another employee loved technology and just giving him an occasional listening ear over his latest acquisition was an opportunity to make a connection. It's a positive thing for all involved when you can relate to all of your team members in a unique and meaningful way.

Your actions speak loudly

Stan had a great stage presence. When he stood up at the quarterly all-team meeting for his eighty-person work group, his words of praise and affirmation seemed like they should warm everyone's hearts and convey to his team that he loved and valued each of them.

However, Stan's employees were winking and rolling their eyes during his speech. Stan was a classic over-reactor who was well known for his screaming fits. The previous week he had vented his rage at three of his employees for coming in below sales projections, even using the word *idiot* several times. When employees come to Stan's office with a question, he tends to continue typing emails or scroll through his smart phone as they speak to him.

Nevertheless, Stan really does appreciate his people. Note the difference between group communication and individual treatment. Senior managers at Stan's level know to speak warmly and professionally to their entire group. However, when they interact at the individual level their true character emerges.

Watch how you react to problems and stress. As managers, we do not always have the right to share our feelings and react to every situation that crosses our desk. We need to remember that "he rules who rules in calmness."

As the words of affirmation come out of your mouth, ask yourself if your actions and attitudes are supporting your words. Make sure you balance both positive and corrective feedback and that you walk the talk.

Discover Your Managing Genius

- The art of giving positive affirmation and encouragement is not a skill that comes naturally. When you succeed at this, it is pure Managing Genius.

- You are recognizing job performance and work outcomes. You are giving positive affirmation that is job-related.

- Managers are in the best position to give meaningful recognition to encourage and guide their team.

- Recognizing great performance points people to what is important. People can proactively align their actions and behavior.

- Take an intentional view of recognition. You build your team culture by what you praise and highlight.

- Recognition will infuse a spirit of optimism and appreciation in your team. This gives people the ability to work without fear.

- Celebrate group success. People work extra hard to win recognition and affirmation from their coworkers.

Feedback

Ensure that your people
know how they are doing

Big Idea

Giving and receiving feedback is a business essential for any successful organization. Master the art of sharing feedback through your intentional words, delivery and timing. Not all feedback comes from the manager—you ensure that your employees get the feedback they need, when they need it. You set the tone through your openness to receiving personal feedback and embracing change.

The problem is not the problem; the problem is your attitude about the problem. Do you understand?

—Jack Sparrow, *Pirates of the Caribbean*

When I make a mistake, I have eight different people coming by to tell me about it.

—Peter Gibbons, character in the movie *Office Space*

Carson: *William, are you aware the seam at your shoulder is coming apart?*
William: *I felt it go a bit earlier. I'll mend it when we turn in.*
Carson: *You will mend it now, and you will never again appear in public in a similar state of undress.*

—*Downton Abbey*

I can promise that my performance will improve, especially if you're a little more flexible on your end.

—Jack Donaghy, *30 Rock*

Important to Know

Talia is hovering outside my office waiting for me to get off the phone. I wave her in and she announces that she just has a "quick one." She plops down in a chair and explains that she had received feedback from Claire, her Group Director. Now she is trying to "make sense" of the message. She wants help to understand it and read between the lines.

As I talk with Talia, I know she is asking herself, "Am I in trouble? Is there something *else* I should know? Are people talking about me?"

Personal feedback has a way of stirring up further analysis, introspection and defensiveness.

On the other side of the table, I can guess that Claire is trying to smooth things over to restore the working relationship. Managers often leave a feedback discussion without that satisfying feeling of closure. Did they hear me? Will they respond? Will they quit?

Staying Connected

1 Feedback keeps us in tune
2 People overestimate themselves
3 Feedback is a good thing
4 We want to hear it from our boss

Claire asks why giving feedback makes her feel like she is walking on eggshells. *She wishes she could just push reset or download the updated version of the employee.*

1 FEEDBACK KEEPS US IN TUNE

Every musician in the orchestra has responsibility for tuning his or her instrument to the lead violin. During the performance, there is a continuous flow of guidance and feedback that allows the individual musicians to play as contributing members of the orchestra.

If you are the director, you need to find ways for your players to stay in tune with everyone in the orchestra. Musicians are responsible to self-tune their instruments but they can only do this through outside feedback. Only if needed do you reach out to instruct someone to tell them to get back in tune.

We cannot be part of an enterprise without a way to stay in harmony with the group. The orchestra masters the material through practice and rehearsals that are filled with comments, opinions, judgment, criticism and coaching.

When you play in the orchestra, you are always aware that you are part of the larger entity. You need to stay in tune to continue as a fully performing participant. We are interconnected within the group and our performance is part of the whole.

Feedback comes from outside our personal sphere. It is the connection that allows us to continue as a contributing member.

2 PEOPLE OVERESTIMATE THEMSELVES

Three psychologists did a study on the difference between what people believe they are capable of doing and their actual performance. The results showed that in every situation people overestimated their ability—and sometimes by a great deal.[1]

How accurately we self-access our own performance	
Athletes	47%
College students	35%
Employees	20%
Managers	4%

They studied all kinds of situations including college students' view of test performance, athletes' view of their sports performance, managers' view of their management effectiveness, and employees' view of their work.

The difference between perception and reality was reported as a percentage (inset box). Athletes apparently have the best perspective of their performance, yet even they get it right less than half of the time. From this study, it is clear we need to get feedback about our own performance from an outside source.

---

1 Dunning, David, Health, Chip and Suls, Jerry M. "Picture Imperfect" *Scientific American Mind*, November 4, 2005, 20-27.

3 FEEDBACK IS A GOOD THING

If we choose to get work done through employees who work for pay, we will need to find effective ways to tell them how they are doing. You will need to share whether their work is satisfactory or not. Giving feedback is a core skill for your success as a manager.

However, just say the word *feedback* and people get tense.

"Here it comes—I screwed up again." We think of feedback as mostly criticism that comes from somewhere above us. It has the potential to upset our position in the organization. It is often given at the wrong time, so we find things out too late to make a difference.

It is Managing Genius to turn this around and give feedback a positive spin through your words and example. "Feedback is a good thing."

Imagine a world without feedback. Try driving your car without a speedometer. Attend a university without grades and you would never know if you had a chance of graduating. Have you experienced a relationship where you never knew what the other person was thinking? You were left hanging, wondering where you stood.

> Feedback turns experience into learning and growth.

It is unfair to leave people guessing. We will stop at the point where we lose perception and withdraw at the next convenient point. We often do not know something is wrong but we do feel disconnected.

This is about you—bring yourself to the point where you see the concept of feedback as a good thing. We need to promote a positive way of thinking about the concept of giving and receiving feedback.

Feedback calibrates us so we know our status in the company. We need a way to stay accountable to the enterprise that is paying for our services. If there are no strings attached, there is no reason to do the work or get paid.

Feedback provides welcome closure so we are not left hanging and wondering where we stand in the relationship.

Every human being is responsible for his or her actions. Behaviors have consequences and we need outside help to see the relationship between effort and reward. Everyone needs a way to check his or her work and it should not be the final customer or consumer. Without feedback, everything stays the same. Feedback is the basis of self-learning and growth. It turns experience into competency.

Feedback should feel everyday and welcome, like reading the news.

Someone needs to "sign off" on our work and seal the deal. "Yes, this is exactly what we wanted."

Accountability means, "I'll see you tomorrow." We have good reason to stick around and continue to play a role on this team. Feedback ensures that we keep adding value to the business, customers and our team. With effective feedback we stay connected and vital to the enterprise.

4 WE WANT TO HEAR IT FROM OUR BOSS

The world of work has become increasingly complex and fast-moving. Actually, we are swimming in messages and information that come at us from all directions in the company. Anyone can talk with our employees.

However, feedback from the boss provides a continued assurance that we are on course and diminishes the uncertainty that we face.

People want a sense of control and will "act out" if ambiguity and uncertainty rise to unbearable levels. At that point, they will reach out to the closest person who understands what is happening and has more control of the situation than they do.

My manager has the best seat in the house to give relevant and useful feedback.

You are in a key role to provide feedback. In fact, feedback from the boss is the only thing that really counts. You are in control of so many aspects of the job and team dynamics. You have responsibility to make decisions and judgments about how your employees are performing and if they are doing the right things. *It matters what you think.*

In any event, it's unfair to leave people guessing or to allow the working relationship to meander or lose its way. Absent of a clear view of status for individuals and your team, people may seek their own feedback from colleagues with whom they have alliances.

People may respond by seeking out their own feedback from an ally. They may lose perception of the right path and pull back. They may start defending themselves.

All this contributes to a loss of connection with you and the team. It zaps people and they lose the energy to take initiative. This is the conversation the boss does not hear during discussions after work.

You are in a unique role to provide feedback. It is important to note, *you have the best seat in the house:*

- You have the best vantage point for the work within your work group. In fact, you may be the only person who knows exactly what each employee contributes to the team and the company.
- You have a vested interest—you want to see your employees do well in their jobs because they are sharing your responsibility.
- You know what is relevant and how to make feedback meaningful.
- You can explain and validate what others are saying.
- You can help screen out extraneous or irrelevant feedback.
- Feedback from colleagues and senior management is often scattered and random, coming after the fact. You can meet the need of the moment and speak to the questions that matter to people today.
- You hold the keys—you can connect outcomes to future assignments, pay and perks.

Your goal: Make sure that your employees get the feedback and information that they need to stay as a fully-performing team member. Serve as a first point of contact to validate and discuss feedback from the company and peers to make sure it is relevant. Be ready to step in and defend your people. Build trust that you are on their side.

Make feedback as everyday and commonplace as reading the news.

This Is Managing Genius

When I watch a highly effective manager, I always see a smooth, skilled provider of feedback. There is nothing haphazard or tossed together at the last minute. The secret behind confidence and poise comes from mastering all aspects of Managing Geniuses.

Manage the Feedback Process:

1 Create an environment of feedback

2 Give more feedback to the whole group

3 A simple feedback guide

4 Holding difficult conversations

5 Formal performance appraisals

But nothing changes without you embracing feedback as a good thing and deciding that feedback is not some administrative task that is required by HR. Feedback is a business essential that you manage and master. You take the lead in how you value feedback and build a team culture that makes feedback feel positive and everyday.

What follows is a boiled down summary of everything you need to know about feedback. Use it, show it, teach it.

1 CREATE AN ENVIRONMENT OF FEEDBACK

Do you see what I see?

You want team members to stay open to new information and become more observant of people and situations. By doing this they are able to take more personal initiative and responsibility.

This will not just happen; it takes a new mindset and plenty of practice to get people to observe what is important within the swirling events of their work environment.

To take one interesting example, the famous writer Ernest Hemingway taught aspiring writers to watch people and become skilled at describing what they do and say. He was noted for one exercise where he would assign writing novices to sit in a Paris sidewalk café and describe how people got in and out of taxicabs.

I had a similar experience with my first boss, Scott, who taught me the importance of collecting pertinent feedback. He shared that you cannot give feedback unless you first become observant. Keen observation leads to effective feedback.

To teach me this, he would often ask me unusual questions that caught me off guard. One day after we left a business meeting he asked, "What was the color of that guy's tie?"

Scott explained that he wanted me to become more observant at work so I would not need someone to interpret the situation and tell me what to do next.

Once, when I missed a shipping deadline, he asked me what I thought the customer was feeling and what was going on at their end. When I did not have a ready answer, he suggested I call the customer and ask.

Scott believed that valuable feedback flows at us from all directions and gives us strong cues on what to do. Sometimes we need to ask people to help us see what they see.

The blinding glare of the obvious

It is also necessary to get people's brains in gear. Consider that our society has dumbed us down and often plays to the lowest common denominator. So we learn to sit back and expect to be told the simplest things.

David Sullivan, in his poem "Warning:,"[1] writes in a tongue-in-cheek fashion about how we often treat people as if they are unable to understand the simplest things for themselves. So we give warnings:

A can of pepper has a written warning that it may irritate the eyes.

A 13-inch wheel on the wheelbarrow is marked, "not intended for highway use."

The warning on the polyester Halloween outfit: Superman costume will not enable you to fly.

Sullivan calls this the "blinding glare of the obvious."

---

1 David Sullivan. "Warning:" in *Strong-Armed Angels* (Chicago: Hummingbird Press, 2008).

The restrooms at the Seattle airport have a small sign above every sink that says "Soap Dispenser." Hmm, thank you for sharing that.

We don't need everything spelled out and people should be able to figure things out for themselves.

This is a change from the usual dumbing-down of the team culture, where we allow people to hang back and say, "I did not know that was important," or "That's the first time I heard about that."

It is Managing Genius to create a team culture where everyone makes the effort to stay tuned to the "blinding glare" of ringing phones, unhappy customers, missed deadlines or scraped product. If sales are down 10 percent, that is clear feedback without stating the obvious.

Establish that it is in everyone's job description to act like the owner and pursue relevant and timely feedback as an everyday part of doing business. Here is what you can do.

You set the tone

In one HR manager role, I made a huge mistake. I received memorable feedback from Rob, one of the Managing Geniuses in this study.

A few people had complained about how accounting was processing employee reimbursements. It was easy to blame those turkeys in finance and I made known my negative feedback without restraint.

Eventually, my words reached Rob and it was interesting how he responded. When he first heard about my feedback, Rob had a momentary choice—he could launch out defensively, harbor ill-will or even sabotage me from a blind side or he could take a different approach. He certainly had the power to make my life miserable and this incident could have hung in the air like a gray Seattle fog.

Rob's response was pure Managing Genius. He acted like my feedback was a positive thing. As a learning step for his team, he had two of his employees collect feedback on the problem. As they interviewed me, the HR director, I realized that I had it all wrong. To my chagrin, I discovered that it was not an accounting problem after all.

Apparently Rob had trained them well and they treated me with far more respect than I deserved. This situation was a learning experience for everyone involved—stay open to new information and ask your customers for feedback to get all sides of the situation.

Moreover, an environment of feedback comes from the strong leadership of a Managing Genius who challenges the status quo and guides his or her people to be anxious to learn at every opportunity.

Point to what is important

On a sailboat, the *telltales* are nylon strips or woolen yarn attached to the sail in ways that indicate to the crew how the wind is crossing the sails. They look up at the telltales to get feedback on the nature of the wind, then adjust the sails accordingly.

It is Managing Genius to teach your employees about the telltales in the business. What information should we look at; what is critical to the success of the business? These are commonly called *Key Performance Indicators* (KPI). For example, in a manufacturing operation, KPIs would likely be safety, quality and production.

> Make sure your employees have all the feedback that they need to be successful.

Numbers assigned to these key areas give you an up-to-date status of how we are doing in the most important areas of our business. Teaching your people how to read the company reports and knowing which numbers are important will make them feel like an insider. Keep this as simple as the piece of string telling you the nature of the wind on the sail.

You may not give all the feedback but you manage and make sure they get all the feedback they need. Make sure they pay attention to what is important. It's like the parent monitoring the healthy diet of the family.

Team leadership should come from you. Do not just pass down exactly what you hear and see from your boss, the company or HR. Translate and explain things in your own words and make them relevant for your team. Let your employees know that these things are personally important to you and what you think about the issues.

Let people work on problems

People love to help solve problems. Don't you? We want to make things better and feel like we've made a tangible impact. We want to make real contributions with our personal skills, experiences and brains.

It's a double bonus when you thoroughly mine the talent that resides with your work force. Not only are they the best equipped to really know what will solve the problem but the process of getting them involved in finding a joint solution can create trust and community on your team.

Recognizing that someone understands and has mastery over a particular subject energizes and encourages. Take advantage of problems on the floor to enhance your culture.

Share the problem without sharing your solution. Good managers give people clear assignments. However, often these are in the form of a solution. "Customer feedback says our website is not user-friendly, so here are three changes I would like you to make." Look back through your recent to-do lists and assignments. Check to see if you are giving only bite-sized tasks. Do you give appropriate assignments that your employees can fully own?

The Managing Geniuses I've worked with have ways of drawing people in to get them mentally engaged with problems. "Take a look at the downward sales trends in this report. What can you do to turn this around?"

In doing this, you get your employees enmeshed with feedback where they can face real work and take ownership.

It is a good question to ask people: What responsibility do they think they own? What decisions have they figured out for themselves? What problems have they solved?

Watch yourself when people come to talk with you about their jobs. It's easy to jump in to help and then take over the problem. Leave room for people to figure things out for themselves. Make sure ownership is in their hands when they leave.

Even when you need to pass on a specific expectation, you can take a minute to share the background story and pressing business need. The bottom line is you need to trust your employees with responsibilities and decisions. Get them in the game; don't just give them solutions to work on.

You increase team morale by giving everyone the opportunity to study issues and solve problems.

Questions are a form of feedback

Feedback gets a bad rep because we think someone is looking for muck-ups. Instead, most effective feedback is when people *discover* and *uncover* the truth for themselves. It is like turning over ground to find the rocks in your garden that need to be removed. You ask insightful questions that turn the ground over, while not taking responsibilities for the rocks.

Gather facts and data, quantify and measure and understand the background history. Ask others who have relevant knowledge or experience. Discuss things from all angles.

> **Four key questions for problem solving**
> - What is the problem?
> - Why is it a problem?
> - Why is it important?
> - Who asked for this?

The trick is to not turn your questions into an exposé on mistakes, like an edgy TV show trying to uncover screw-ups. Instead, learn the art of asking questions that get to the heart of the matter and make people think.

Get a game face for receiving feedback

Steve Martin, playing the father, George Banks, in the movie *Father of the Bride*, has a great moment of self-reflection when he tells his daughter, "I come from a long line of over-reactors." I repeat that line frequently—I confess that I am an over-reactor.

People react to feedback in different ways. Richard, a senior vice president I worked for, would start tapping his glasses against his hand when receiving unfavorable news. The others in the meeting room knew what was happening. Gabriela would get stone-faced, staring straight ahead. Molly would cast her eyes out the window as if she was deep in thought. Charles would appear to be taking notes but I could tell he was doodling to avert the pressure of the moment.

How do you personally respond to feedback? Do you jump in with explanations? Do you ask questions to throw people off-guard?

Here is the trick: when someone wants to give you feedback, develop a simple physical pose that you use every time. *This is your feedback position— your game face.* It is a freeze frame where you gather yourself so you will not react in the moment.

> What would you tell me if you knew I would not get angry or defensive?

I learned this from Dennis, senior vice president and a Managing Genius. Dennis had a practice where he put his hand on his mouth to make sure he didn't speak while receiving feedback. This was his listening pose and I saw it a hundred times in meetings.

You could pull out a leather journal and take notes. You could capture feedback on the white board. You could make a show of turning off your phone.

But the two most important things to remember: 1. You listen with your eyes. 2. Wait for the period at the end of their sentence before you speak.

Take corrective action with a sense of urgency

To build respect for corrective feedback, you need to show people that the most important aspect of feedback is that it compels you to *do something*. Feedback is merely words until we turn it into action.

If you ask for feedback on your managing style, you will lose respect if you do nothing. You earn respect when you communicate to the person that you heard their comment. "Let me think about this."

You may see that people have feedback to share but they do not know how to share what they are thinking. Kate is sitting in your office sharing a complaint. She is so close to it that she may not be able to disengage enough to think straight. As she continues to talk, you ask: "What do you want me to do?" If you don't get an answer, ask again by saying, "So, Kate, what do you want me to do *right now*?"

It is a game-changer when people see you taking action on feedback.

2 GIVE MORE FEEDBACK TO THE WHOLE GROUP

The usual practice for most managers is to give individual feedback as they think about it or as the opportunity presents itself. They often react to problems by having individual discussions.

It is Managing Genius to discuss more feedback at the team table. This gives one common message and people will benefit from the shared discussion.

You can even share feedback aimed at individuals within the group if you have a supportive, socially mature team culture. You create an open culture when you bring discussion and confrontation to the team table. Your group facilitation skills will make a significant difference.

Take a new look at how you do business and spend more managing time leading group business. The following are some ways I have observed Managing Geniuses build a team culture that supports an open feedback stance.

Create a "safe zone" for feedback

This will not *just happen by itself.*

You need to set group norms and teach people how it works. You may need to step in to reinforce the group norms.

Suppose you agree, as a group, that members will not over-respond to feedback. You will need to step in at the appropriate moment to be sure that people do not shoot the messenger when there is bad news. "OK, everyone, remember how we do not shoot the messenger, so please chill as Xingeo shares the usage data on the website."

When people positively address mistakes and bring problems to the table, welcome it. Speak up to recognize and affirm when someone shares straight, unmitigated talk or shares facts and data to make their case. "Thanks, Amelia. Seeing numbers like this really clarifies the situation."

And watch your own response if you come from a long line of over-reactors (like me):

"OMG, tell me you did not do that!"

Shared results

It is a universal trait of every Managing Genius I have worked with to get their employees totally immersed into the everyday numbers of the business. They teach what data is important to follow and what matters most. This information serves to totally empower your people.

Everyone should have access to important information and participate in reporting and tracking results. Develop ways to measure and track results and make it a regular agenda item. Everyone sees and tracks the same information. (This is all feedback.)

The more people know about the group results, the more they can take initiative and self-manage. People see their own individual goals as promises to teammates and colleagues. Both group results and individual results should be discussed at the group table.

We do not like our mistakes pointed out. And no surprises, please.

Avoid hallway discussions where individuals attempt to explain their cases when, in fact, they owe the explanation to the group. "Hold on, Kevin. You need to share with the whole group why the schedule is going to slip."

As you get your team accustomed to discussing feedback as a group, it will seem more natural and you will see people bringing up weighty, relevant discussions at the group level.

Do not monologue

Christopher manages a group of 25 inside sales representatives. He is a nice guy who is full of himself. He talks way too much and loves to share his wisdom with his employees. He is the manager, right?

He will give Heather advice on her project and then move into advice on parenting. He has advice for Chip on speeding up customer calls but then the talk drifts over to a discourse on bottled water.

Christopher loves to "principalize" things. Last week a computer hard drive crashed, so today he preaches the importance of regular backups.

We may dislike the verbal barrage but Christopher is their manager and he holds the keys for anything good that comes your way from the company. So you need to listen to him.

Managing Genius
QUICK GUIDE

Effective Feedback

1
Preparation

Why are we here? Thoughtful and intentional, you understand the work. Look for the positive. Plan your words.

2
Current

Timely and relevant. Obviously applies to current situation.

3
Clear

Simple and specific. Cuts through obscurity and jargon. Avoid generalizations (never, always.)

4
Factual

Quantify and measure. Look back through what happened and share specifics. Your observations count.

5
Impartial

Focus on behavior, not the person. This is business, not personal.

6
Closure

Responsibility is the end goal. Everyone leaves the room knowing what happens next. Create a sense of urgency.

The key question is to ask, "Why are we here?" Feedback meetings should be focused on the pertinent issue and then stay on message.

Carry in a one-page sheet of talking points. Afterwards, follow up with an email that summarizes the message to provide closure for everyone in the meeting.

Some managers come into the meeting without a plan for what they want to convey. So they start talking and give lengthy explanations that include moral character and obligation to the company. It all seems like sales mode, thinking they can bring people around to their way of thinking through argument and logic.

The key question to ask after any employee meeting is, "Who talked most?" Do not play the expert and "fill the room." If people tune you out for some things, they can tune you out for the important things as well.

3 A SIMPLE FEEDBACK GUIDE

Forgive me for my love of the Green Bay Packers. Another story about our quarterback Brett Favre.

The fans loved his "gunslinger" playing style but the coaches sometimes had a difficult time giving feedback to Brett during a game.

A Simple Feedback Guide

1. Preparation
2. Make it current
3. Make it clear
4. Make it factual
5. Make it impartial
6. Closure

Coach Mike Holmgren and Favre had a deal. After a botched play, they would never stand next to one another on the sidelines. They had learned that in the heat of the moment, the communication often turned sour and testy.

Instead, they had a system: Coach Andy Green would step in between them on the sideline and he would relay communication back and forth between the two. This buffer worked for them when they needed to make adjustments during the game.

That is an example of how a Managing Genius might think ahead to choose the best way to pass on feedback. The alternative is to blurt it out when tensions are high.

This section will give you a simple, condensed flyover of how to give feedback to any person.

1. Preparation

Effective feedback requires thinking ahead before speaking. If you do not come in prepared, there is a good chance you will fall into mitigated communication and say things you will regret later.

How you start a feedback conversation—*your first few words*—is 90 percent of Managing Genius. Drift into the conversation and you lose your audience. Do this several times and people will avoid you when they see you coming.

Feedback is not reactionary. Don't yell or respond to some current crisis. Feedback is *never* communicated electronically.

> Good questions that make people think are the best feedback.

It is not that people do not want feedback; we want *well-planned* feedback. Connect today's words to previous discussions to show the big picture. This is all part of a plan, not today's special problem.

The trick is to prepare your best possible opening line to ensure that you get started on the right foot. Again, have a one-page set of talking points. This may sound simplistic, but here is an example:

- We are here to focus on your sales quota.
- Sales quota: $1M annually.
- Sales YTD (6 months into fiscal year): $222K.
- You are not filling out the sales pipeline reports, so we have no way to forecast.
- What will you do to ensure that you will meet your quota?
- Agree on your next steps.

Consider the agenda and participants when picking the right time and place—whether a formal meeting or quick team chats at your desk. Most feedback needs to be communicated face-to-face.

2. Make it current

For a team-building day, I took my employees on a whitewater rafting experience on the Wenatchee River. Whitewater rafting in Washington State is a nice, relaxing day floating down the river that is punctuated by moments of terror as you are forced to navigate through the rapids and avoid rocks, underwater trees and swirling eddies.

The group was talking and having fun and then suddenly the guide, with a stern voice, gave a heads-up that everyone needed to row to the left. Apparently he had spotted a tree trunk under the surface and we needed everyone to immediately paddle to avoid the danger.

> Sometimes feedback cannot wait. You need to catch the moment.

However, I was intent on finishing my conversation and was a bit too slow to transition. Finally, the guide cut in, "Shut up, Denny."

This was timely feedback that I needed that way, at that moment.

Later we laughed about the moment and I definitely learned from it. This feedback was obviously and literally part of current events. It was pertinent and appropriate in that moment.

Relevant feedback is all about current events.

There are other times where you can save your words for later. For example, you could affect someone's confidence if you try to give feedback in the midst of a presentation or you might choose not to have a "heavy talk" the night before a major deliverable is due.

Usually if you get the time and place right, people will forgive if you are not so good with your words. Just ask if this is a good time and place.

The key is to address issues when they are small, current and still under your control. Often we are too slow to speak up and we miss the opportunity to give people fair warning so they can make corrections.

3. Make it clear

On the TV show *America's Got Talent*, the judges know a good performance when they see it. They look right at the person and give him or her direct and honest feedback. Sometimes they give a standing applause for an exceptional performance. They also have a button to light up a big red X if they do not like the performance, and they use it regularly. I see Managing Genius in the *America's Got Talent* judges when it comes to giving effective feedback to the performers.

Next time you watch AGT, watch the judges:

They know a great performance when they see it. You can see it on their faces. They are leaning in and excited to share. That is how it looks when you see something you like.

They use "I" statements. The judges take owner-ship of what they have to say by using the first-person pronoun. This earns respect and gets people's atten-tion. "I noticed that you were late for the last three meetings," is far better than the all-too-common alter-native, "People have been complaining to me that you're always late."

> Make your feedback compelling by knowing in advance what you want to communicate.

They focus on what happened on the stage. The judges talk about the action or behavior they see on the stage. They are descriptive and factual. For example, you could say, "The budget was due August first. You were ten days late and this caused others to wait." This is much more helpful than saying "You were late again" or "Senior management is really upset".

They do not sound muddled. The judges offer concrete suggestions and they express importance and urgency in their voice. They do not hide behind obscure words and jargon like, "You have an opportunity to improve." Be direct and to the point with your feedback. Avoid being boring; people want to be inspired.

They are not asking scattered questions. When the judges do ask questions, it is not a causal conversation; it is not exploratory surgery. You hear short, pointed and pithy questions to get a complete and accu-rate picture of the situation.

There is a snappy next step. The judges share feedback that will make a difference. The judges are always clear on what to do to raise the performance to the next notch. Feedback should always point to what happens next. "If you had come in below budget and under schedule, you'd receive a superior rating."

The performer is on the hot seat. The judges are not jumping up on the stage to coach or help the competitor. The individual is standing there in the spotlight carrying the full weight of responsibility for their performance.

4. Make it factual

Charles Dickens wrote in *Great Expectations,* "Take nothing on its looks; take everything on evidence. There's no better rule."

Much of the reporting in American business measures activities and good effort. If we pack the schedule and send out status update emails, we just create a narrative around activity and enthusiasm.

"Just the facts, ma'am." Prepare for the meeting in advance with facts and data. Basically you are "preparing your case" and a few talking points will keep you on track. Your own personal observations and judgment are indeed objective feedback—that is what managers do.

Focus on the business needs and goals so you can correct the behavior, not the person. However, avoid personal annoyances, work style differences or sidebar excuses. Don't say, "You missed yet another deadline" or "I can't count on you." Instead, talk about promises and outcomes.

5. Make it impartial

Jay Leno says, "If you're a car salesman, and someone says, 'This is a terrible car; I'm not buying it,' that doesn't mean they hate you. They just do not like your product. I think that's a mistake a lot of people in show business make. They're so tied to their act they take everything personally." We need to advocate for the customer, the business and the team. This is business; it's not personal. You should be impartial and emotionally detached when you address performance.

6. Give closure

When sharing an uncomfortable message or presenting "bad news", it is a common tendency to talk too much and too long. We may be hesitant to share or feel apprehensive about a negative response. We can get into defensive mode where we feel the need to explain and reexplain our position.

Bottom line, it is more about how we leave the room. Make definitive statements that summarize the message. "That is all. Is it clear?" Make the transition to where words of feedback turn into action. End the feedback session with a clear understanding of next steps.

4 HOLDING DIFFICULT CONVERSATIONS

There will be people who challenge you and your judgment. Some will openly push back, while others may show their resistance behind the scenes or with a third-party. Remember, you are here to find resolution on a gap or behavior that needs to be changed. It is Managing Genius to rise above an emotional response and argument, *letting nothing get in the way of closure.*

Here are four best practices for when you need to hold a difficult conversation:

1. Act like you own the place

Managing Geniuses always find ways to reach closure under stress and conflict. They act like they are captain of the ship. People need to respect you and the business. You are never powerless. Pick the right time and place that puts you into the driver's seat. Act like you own this company. Remember that you sign the payroll checks. You speak on behalf of the company.

> **Best practices for difficult conversations**
> 1. Act like you own the place
> 2. Have a meeting agenda
> 3. End with closure
> 4. Understand how difficult conversations can unravel

2. Have a meeting agenda

Use the six simple steps in the Quick Guide on Effective Feedback chart (page 125) as a consistent way to develop your talking points and agenda for any feedback meeting. Confidence and poise comes from knowing in advance what you will say and do. Your goal is to hold an efficient, expeditious and effective meeting. I want you to look like you are confident and in control.

3. Make sure this meeting ends in closure

Make sure you close with a clear understanding (both you and the employee) about what happens next. Verbally check for understanding versus taking a head nod as an indication that the next steps are indeed clear.

It is a fact that each participant in an engagement remembers events in different ways. You can avoid repeat business by capturing what happened. Ask the employee to email you a summary of what was discussed, what was agreed to and what happens next.

If this has become a one-way conversation, you can also email *yourself* a quick update: "I met with Ben today and we discussed..."

Email allows you to search to retrieve previous history.

4. How difficult conversation can unravel

There are common ways people may try to derail a difficult conversation. These actions are often subtle and may slip in without you realizing it. Watch for these as they may pop up during the conversation:

Personal Criticism. One of the toughest sidebars to deal with is when a team member attacks you personally, trying to undermine your credibility and character. Remember to not take that bait and begin to defend your character or intentions to the individual or to your team.

Go to the individual and share what you have heard and bring everything to the light. Before talking about the issues, speak to the inappropriate behavior and explain the right way to address conflict. "On this team, we do not attack people's personal qualities."

In the long term, a critical spirit cannot stay on your team. If the person continues to "dis you", trust me that it will not work for long.

Emotionally disconnect. You sense the tension and see that your employee is showing signs that they do not like where this conversation is going. You imagine that they are thinking, "Why can't you be more affirming and positive?"

Yesterday you had a warm and convivial work relationship. Now you feel the emotional withdrawal. Can you live with that?

Whining. We all learn ways to get what we want in this life. Most of us have learned to take personal responsibility, talk directly to people and work towards mutually acceptable next steps.

However, some people will use whining as a form of manipulation to get what they want. This will increase in stressful situations.

They have learned that if they complain long enough, someone will give in and give them the attention they think they deserve. Whining allows people to play the victim role. Whining is usually not a specific complaint or issue that needs to be addressed. It is well-practiced behavior that has worked in the past and gets reused as needed. It is a tactic to avoid a difficult conversation. So when they whine they are actually saying, "Make *my* issue today's priority." Unfortunately, the cycle continues when whining works.

Consider that this world is never going to be right for some people. When you encounter whining, simply bring it to your employee's attention that the subject at hand is very important and focus on the original issue.

Triangles. An individual may pull a third party into the conversation for sympathy or support. They may go over your head or to HR to find a sympathetic ear.

Getting more people involved creates workplace drama as additional people weigh-in to share their opinion. Team members may see this as entertainment and play along with the fun. Whatever happens, it does not make you look like you are in control as the manager.

Here is how to get yourself back in the driver's seat.

1. Identify the triangles. Talk to all the participants face-to-face to shut down the drama. This will put you in control.
2. Ask people to stop discussing the matter.
3. Do not have conversations with others about the issues or participate in the drama.
4. Proactively go to your boss and HR and let them know them know that you have this matter under control.
5. Make this an agenda item for a team meeting. Succinctly close the issue and reiterate how issues like this should be handled.

Managing Genius
QUICK GUIDE

Holding a Difficult Discussion

1
**Why are
we here?**

You own this meeting.
- This is a necessary conversation.
- You feel a sense of urgency to close this issue.
- Say what you plan to say: With talking points in hand, announce agenda.

2
**Why is it
important?**

You own this meeting.
- Take charge of the meeting.
- Believe this: What you think matters. Exercise your judgment and discretion.
- Explain the business implications: You have customers, costs and consequences.

3
**What happens
next?**

Clear next steps: who, what, when.
- Adult-minded employees will accept responsibility and engage in next steps.
- Other employees may need detailed directions or "micromanaging."
- Only share consequences that you are willing to follow up on.

Participant shutdown. I was meeting with one of my employees for her first performance evaluation meeting. I had received feedback that she tended to act unprofessionally when she was around senior management, which was likely a result of her lack of experience. The senior team thought it was important for me to coach her.

As I began to give her this feedback, she suddenly got agitated, raised her voice and blurted out emphatically, "I'm not going to take this. You can't talk to me like this."

> An outburst of emotion can easily overpower present realities.

She then put her head down in a sullen posture. Of course, this shut down the communication and the meeting stumbled to a quick halt.

A magician calls this *misdirection*, which is defined as "a form of deception in which the attention of an audience is focused on one thing in order to distract its attention from another."

Lack of immediate response. You may think you are losing control when you do not get instant acquiescence. We focus on how people *initially* react to us. It is like we expect people to immediately say, "I am so glad you brought this matter to my attention!"

Even if they quickly respond positively, it may just be a superficial smile and a head nod. Give people sufficient time for processing so they can get their heart and mind into the new information or direction. Regardless of people's initial responses, focus on the final result.

Fixing people. You see an employee struggling and you feel a pang of compassion and empathy. They ask for help or advice and you find yourself jumping in to try to solve their problems. Before going too far, you need to ask yourself the basic question— should I try to "fix them"?

When you try to help an employee, be careful that you do not end up owning their problems. People need to leave the room owning their responsibility. There is also a danger in turning your employees into "projects" where you need to add them to your to-do list.

Giving your employee a "Get Out Of Jail Free" card to get themselves together may mean that you or your team will need to cover for them. *The show must go on.*

Face it, fixing people is probably not your strong suite anyway.

Backchat. After a difficult interaction, people may need someone to whom they can blow off steam or share personal feelings. That is backchat.

If people feel like they have to vent, you want people to vent to *you*. You do not want them to stuff their feelings or share this matter with just anyone willing to listen.

And you want people to share their backchat at the right time and in the right venue. If it is given at the wrong time and place (such as in front of the team or via a group email), you need to step up and explain your group norms.

Backchat can devolve into pointing out what is wrong with leadership to express disrespect and minimize authority.

Just remember to take the high ground and guide the conversation back to the issue at hand. When your employee leaves, what you are looking for is, "Thanks for listening. I feel better after this conversation. I am ready to get back to work."

Bunny trails. You have a scheduled meeting with Todd to discuss a cost overrun. As you get started, Todd interjects with a couple of new fires to put out. He asks for your help. Now you are working on his important items and your urgent matter got pushed out of sight.

One CEO I worked for was a master at keeping a conversation on track. He could easily navigate back to his message because he had a small, handwritten index card in his pocket with his list of what he wanted to talk about. He knew why he was there. I would leave our meetings with a sense of closure. Eventually, I started asking him, "So what's on your card?"

> A common power play is to change the subject to talk about what you want.

When an employee tries to change the subject from what you have on your agenda, simply write it down for later. Then emphasize that at this time you want to focus on the stated agenda item.

It's not a big deal or personal affront. Just press on with the reasons we are here.

"Todd, today we are here to discuss the cost overrun . . ."

5 FORMAL PERFORMANCE APPRAISALS

Most companies have a formal performance appraisal system that guides managers through an annual review process.

Actually, the year-end PA process is not the shining star of management practices in American business. It often feels like a time-consuming company administrative process where you fill out the form and check the boxes. Most important, I do not believe that the performance appraisal process makes the manager look like a leader who is in charge; it does not give you power.

First, understand the inherent flaws in the PA process as we know it at most companies. You will need to work around these issues:

Act like you own the annual company appraisal process.

- PA forms are meant to present a broad, comprehensive review. It is like your auto mechanic reviewing your car using a detailed inspection checklist instead of just saying, "Your water pump is leaking."
- It focuses on past performance, not current events. So it feels like reading a annual magazine highlighting the top news from last year.
- It puts a time lag into your feedback—it is like waiting for a future birthday to give your kids the new shoes they need today.
- By tying the PA to the annual pay review, you create edgy conversations that may cause people to withhold information or act defensive. No matter what work-related feedback you discuss, the meeting can become a negotiating session for a better rating and pay increase.

With that said, you are meeting with your favorite employees, so act like you want to be there. The PA is a great opportunity to:

1. Wrap things up and close out the year. What went well and what could we do differently in the future? Key learnings?
2. Catch up on personal goals and aspirations. Talk about upcoming jobs, assignments or experiences. Do they want new opportunities?
3. Use it to build a better working relationship. What frustrates you? How can I be a better boss?
4. Consider it "quality time"—two-way sharing with extra listening.

Discover Your Managing Genius

- Giving and receiving feedback is a business essential for any successful organization.

- Master the art of sharing feedback through your intentional words, delivery and timing.

- Ensure that your people know how they are doing so they can stay connected to you, the team and the business. Feedback calibrates us so we know where we stand in the company.

- Expect your employees to listen and heed your words. Feedback is not a suggestion tossed out with the hope that something happens.

- You are the number one source of feedback for your employees. You may not give all the feedback but you make sure they get all the feedback they need.

- Create an environment where everyone welcomes feedback. You set the tone through openness to receiving personal feedback from your boss, your employees and colleagues.

Guideback

Master the art of coaching,
correcting and discipline

Big Idea

You can confidently step in to resolve performance or behavior issues without the usual fanfare and drama. You take the lead and get to the heart of the matter to ensure that issues are effectively resolved. You make sure everyone concerned reaches closure. If needed, you can move the issue forward through progressive actions, including taking ownership for the firing process. People trust that you have things in control; you are not ignoring the elephant in the room.

I just think that sometimes we hang onto people or relationships long after they've ceased to be of any use to either of you.

—John Cleese, comedian

You can't be that kid standing at the top of the water slide, over thinking it. You have to go down the chute.

—Tina Fey, in her book "Bossy Pants"

Watch your mouth kid, or you'll find yourself floating home.

—Han Solo speaking to Luke Skywalker in *Star Wars*

I want you to do something for me, Pete. I want you to get a cardboard box and put all your stuff in it.

—Don Draper in *Mad Men*

I'm going to make him an offer he can't refuse.

—Michael Corleone in the movie *The Godfather*

Think of all that we've been through, and breaking up is hard to do.

—Neil Sedaka in classic oldie, "Breaking Up Is Hard to Do"

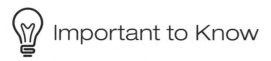

Important to Know

The "doldrums" is a colloquial sailing expression from historical maritime usage. This describes the area around the equator where sailing ships lose their trade winds due to a belt of calm and baffling winds. The doldrums can leave the sailing ship stuck for days of inactivity and drifting.

From my experiences, people problems are the *management doldrums* where most managers lose the wind to steer their own ship.

We lose power, over-analyze or just hope the problem blows away. We depend on third-party intervention, which tends to complicate the issues. As the HR leader, I frequently got called in to guide managers out of the management doldrums.

If you manage people, eventually you will face an individual with performance or behavior issues that, in your judgment, must be addressed and closed.

The Management Doldrums

1 Can you make tough decisions?

2 Would you stop the show for just one person?

3 Will you follow through on your words?

4 Is it OK if people leave?

5 Can you fire someone?

The conventional term, feedback, is all about communicating with employees so they recognize how they're doing in terms of job-related performance and behavior.

I conceived the word "Guideback" to describe the process whereby we address a specific problem that has breached the employment relationship. In your judgment, there are specific things that must be done to restore good standing with the business, the team and you.

So what do you need to know to stay out of the management doldrums where you look helpless and powerless?

Your employees need to see you in the lead role for employee relations. So you need to master the necessary skills to press forward confidently and without hesitation. This chapter will give you everything you need to know.

But first, there are five mental hurdles that will put you in the management doldrums. You will not be able to take personal ownership for this aspect of your work group without resolving these five questions.

1 CAN YOU MAKE TOUGH DECISIONS?

Most good managers can make snappy decisions concerning budget or business strategy. But add a real person into the mix and they tend to freeze up and analyze the situation from all angles or they simple ignore the issue and find a workaround.

This is not an *impersonal* decision—the person is front and center. How about an example of this hurdle?

Historian Doris Kearns Goodwin writes in a biography of President Franklin D. Roosevelt[1] that Roosevelt's "inability to get rid of anybody, even the hopelessly incompetent, was a chief source of the disorderliness of his administration."

Goodwin writes, "President Franklin Roosevelt's strength to be sympathetic and understanding to someone he liked became a weakness, as he could not find it in his heart to fire anybody."

One interesting anecdote in the book concerns Mrs. Nesbitt, the White House cook, who had a mind of her own and cooked food she thought people *should* eat, not what they requested.

Mrs. Nesbitt believed in cooking "plain food, plainly prepared." She insisted that Roosevelt eat oatmeal every day for breakfast. The leader of the Allied war effort during World War II, and the greatest industrial nation on earth, would surreptitiously ask his staff to lobby Mrs. Nesbitt for corn flakes.

Once when royal guests were dining at the White House, the call came to the kitchen for hot coffee for the guests. Mrs. Nesbitt sent iced tea instead, telling the president it was "better for them."

Roosevelt could not bring himself to fire Mrs. Nesbitt. After dinner on many evenings, he and his staff would assemble surreptitiously in a little kitchen off the president's study to cook egg sandwiches.

Sound familiar?

---

1   Doris Kearns Goodwin, *No Ordinary Time, Franklin and Eleanor Roosevelt: The Home Front in World War II* (New York: Simon & Shuster, 1994).

When we dance around the elephant in the room, it serves to lower people's respect for your ability to make decisions. It becomes easier to just "work around" this person rather than just talk to the individual. The key is to identify where such conflict and separation exists. You own it.

2 WOULD YOU STOP THE SHOW FOR JUST ONE PERSON?

Another mental hurdle is when we find it uncomfortable to ignore an individual need.

An individual employee comes to our door for help. How can we turn that person away? In that moment you see his or her face, not the faces of your stakeholders who are depending on your team.

You know it will make you feel good when you come to their personal rescue. The more you think about it, the more you cannot get this individual out of your mind. You lose perspective of what is most important to the mission. You may feel compelled to save this one individual.

In the book *Flags of our Fathers*,[2] James Bradley writes about the Battle of Iwo Jima, fought in February and March of 1945 during the Pacific Campaign of World War II. The US invasion, known as Operation Detachment, consisted of a plan to land waves of marines and equipment in order to capture the airfields on Iwo Jima.

The operation involved 800 ships coming together into one vast naval armada. There were 70,000 assault-troop marines on board the convoy. The planning and orchestration to make this work was an immensely complex management exercise.

As this armada was steaming toward a rendezvous at Iwo Jima, a lone, unnamed naval shipman became a small footnote in the history books by falling overboard at sea. By order, the armada did not stop for the one man adrift in the ocean. This was a weighty decision to be sure and one that could draw debate—especially if you happened to be the sailor who was left alone in the Pacific Ocean.

---

2 James Bradley with Ron Powers, *Flags of Our Fathers* (New York: Bantam Books, 2000).

In that moment on the sea, the senior admiral was responsible for coordination of the largest naval armada ever assembled. It was moving together in careful synchronization, with layers of antiaircraft and anti-submarine protection. He made the decision to ignore individual needs.

3 WILL YOU FOLLOW THROUGH ON YOUR WORDS?

This mental hurdle tests our resolve to follow through with our words. It is easy enough to proclaim some required action or behavior. It can be quite another thing to follow through *exactly as promised.*

Patricia is director of nursing at a multi-specialty medical clinic. Last year the clinic enacted new mandates regarding record management and privacy. It was clearly communicated that breaking the rules was a serious offense that would result in termination.

When you establish such a sweeping directive you should expect that someone will cross the line. Rebecca, a skilled and well-loved nurse with fifteen years of service had accessed the medical records of her elderly father, a clear breach of the new mandates. This resulted in a speedy and tearful termination.

Situations like this always draw fire from all sides. "She knew better." "Why can't they forgive her just this one indiscretion?" "This is a stupid policy."

Show empathy for individuals while advocating for your team, business and customers.

The important point is that if you are considering a new rule or policy, you must think through how it will be enforced and be willing to follow through, even if it is difficult.

Managers need to ensure that policies and directives are universally followed. When they are not, a predictable response from the manager should be expected. Never draw lines in the sand that you are unwilling to stand by.

This is more than just having the courage to make decisions. This is where you shouldn't even be thinking—this is an *automatic decision* that proceeds *as promised.*

This mental hurdle gives us the misguided notion that any decisions involving an employee always call for special analysis. This includes multi-step review processes that pulls in third-party involvement. This sends the message that employee issues are always complicated.

Patricia's decision to terminate Rebecca was simple and straightforward. This decision was made the day the new rule was implemented.

4 IS IT OK IF PEOPLE LEAVE?

We are in a Starbucks and Danica is sharing with me her latest reason for management anxiety.

One of her employees has resigned and she is taking it personally. She admits that this employee is not her favorite and she is not even unhappy that he quit. But last night, Danica had a panic attack so she asks me, "Is there something wrong with my management style?"

Danica is thinking that my HR role will allow me to get the inside scoop. "Can you find out if it was something I did wrong? Is anyone else planning to quit? What are my employees thinking?"

I did not need to investigate—I knew the answer. I responded to Danica with the plain truth: "Employees just move on from time to time."

Our employees are more like "house guests", not permanent family members. You are not adopting them. You don't expect house guests to move in and stay forever; they are just visiting for a period of time that makes sense and is beneficial to both of you. While they are in your house they should try their best to fit in and make themselves useful.

> Success may hinge on someone leaving so an amazing new person can fill that spot.

Then, just when you start to get comfortable with them in your house, they'll burst out the door and go on their own way. Now you have that empty bedroom waiting for another house guest.

Managers, like Danica, have a mental hurdle where they imagine that every employee is fixed frame on the org chart. Are you personally tied to your job for life?

People have highly personalized aspirations that drive them in different directions. Eventually we'll all part ways.

When a college draft choice is joining your favorite professional team, the fact is that the new player is *replacing someone* who is currently on the team. There are limited spots on the team. To manage this, you need to get your mind wrapped around the fact that someone coming means someone else is leaving.

This is the fourth mental hurdle. We think leaving is a bad thing. We have to accept that some turnover is typical. Of course, you want to retain the *right people* but even they will leave.

Danica should focus on becoming that Great Manager everyone wants to work for.

5 CAN YOU FIRE SOMEONE?

We often have a mental hurdle concerning firing people.

First, we believe that it is impossible to get the wrong people off the bus. That false belief may be joined by the equally false belief that if we hire the wrong person, we are stuck. All of a sudden, the idea of firing people seems like a huge negative.

Let me share an true story of a termination that was a quality decision at just the right time. This termination enabled the enterprise to move into a new space of creativity, innovation, and success.

The group was poised for big things. They had been working to bring creative new products to the market and there was a window for success that depended on everyone pulling together in just the right way. They had to get it just right.

But it was clear to the team that one member was not the right person going forward. The team felt certain that they would not succeed with Pete.

On August 16, 1962, three members of a rock and roll group in Liverpool, England made the decision to fire their drummer, Pete Best.

The Beatles replaced him with a drummer named Ringo Starr and the rest is history.

This termination may just be the all-time winner for a timely personnel decision that enabled the team to move into a new space of creativity, innovation and business success.

This last mental hurdle to overcome is when you are able to make the right decision at the right time for the band.

Is Pete a problem?
- He is playing to his own drum beat
- His skills are not at the level of the group
- We value collaboration and he is a lone wolf
- He resists changes agreed upon by the team
- He is holding us back creatively

Often when we are mulling over a termination, we can get consumed with the affected individual. We start thinking how this decision affected Pete Best. "It is a shame that Pete missed out on all that followed." We stop to ask, would you be mentally prepared to fire Pete?

We miss the fact that all that followed would not have happened if Pete had stayed. This was an open door that created rock and roll history. Was this a quality decision made at the right time?

Ask the customer: Our kids are still listening to fifty-year-old Beatles songs.

Inherent in your managing role is to make judgment calls when selecting people. When you pick one person you decide to not pick others. When you decide to hang on to someone you lose the opportunity that a new person brings. Sitting on the decision just weakens your respect.

Step back and consider that people come and go in the business world all the time. People come together and then part ways. Jobs change and business needs evolve. Moreover, individuals change in ways that can alter the match that once brought energy and synergy. The goal is to bring about this breaking off with grace and mutual respect.

What follows is everything you need to manage this. It is Managing Genius to take ownership for the door.

This Is Managing Genius

Imagine that you are standing on the fairway of a golf course, dithering over how to play your ball to get around a huge oak tree with branches outstretched in every direction.

There has to be a way. You study the lay of the ball and ask your golfing buddies for advice. You walk back and forth, thinking you might get a new perspective or find an easy solution. People are looking at you and wondering when you are ever going to play your ball.

Game Plan:

People Problems

1 What is the problem?

2 Turn around

3 Directed feedback

4 Corrective feedback

5 How to fire

If you continue to over-analyze the tough strategy decisions you face on the golf course, soon you will not have anyone who wants to spend an afternoon playing golf with you.

It is a far tougher dilemma to make decisions that affect real people in your work group. You know them personally and have work history. They are embedded in the layers of work relationships and anything you do has ripple effects.

Over-analysis can cause us to freeze at the very moment we need to make tough judgment decisions that affect people personally. In fact, you could keep staring at the situation and never find a perfect solution where someone's feelings will not get ruffled.

This chapter is critical. The Managing Geniuses I have known always take ownership for their own employee problems. There is never a sense of helplessness or passivity. They have a systematic way of bringing attention to what must be changed. They press ahead to resolve the matter as soon as possible, showing themselves to be a thoughtful and decisive leader.

Confidence and poise comes from knowing in advance how you will respond to people issues and reach closure for everyone. Even if you rarely use it, having a game plan for dealing with employee problems will give you a sense of authority and power.

Game Plan: People Problems

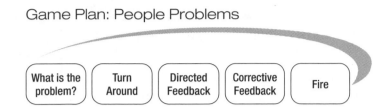

| What is the problem? | Turn Around | Directed Feedback | Corrective Feedback | Fire |

What is the problem?

John Swigert, Jr., on the crew of the Apollo 13 moon flight, reported a problem back to the base in Houston on April 14, 1970. He delivered the now famous line, "Houston, we have a problem here."

This phrase is a common metaphor to report any kind of problem. When it comes to defining the problem, take a leadership position:

- Identify that you do have a problem.
- Get to the heart of the matter—here is the problem.
- Attribute importance—per your judgment, this individual performance issue needs to be resolved.

When you narrow the agenda, you focus attention on a specific problem. When you get to the heart of the matter, you can *set* and *control* the agenda. You gain power when you simplify the discussion and focus on the problem at hand.

The smart strategy is to keep employee problems small, current and more readily solved within your team. When you quickly get to the heart of the matter, you can address a problem while it is still within your control.

> A Managing Genius has a knack for getting to the heart of the matter.

Just as important as focusing on a single problem, you can make decisions what *not* to talk about and what are topics for a different day. We are back to the core principle that you decide "why are we here" and you simplify this so everyone understands. You make sure sidebar discussions and distractions are off the table.

Imagine you are editing a document and you "bring forward" one item in the picture that you want to work on.

Here are five simple ways for setting up and focusing on a single employee problem so it has the highest potential to be solved.

1. Hold a narrow conversation

The key for successful resolution of an employee problem is to focus the conversation on a single issue.

This chapter is about specific problems that have run the course through Chapters 1 through 4. You've laid the right foundation and provided planning, expectations and affirmation. You now need to develop talking points that highlight the issue and elevate its importance.

If someone wants to avoid your message, they may try to diffuse or dissemble your words. (See page 132 in Chapter 4, Feedback.) Preparing in advance will prevent the issue from getting complicated during the meeting.

2. Focus on well-defined outcomes and responsibility

This is the time to focus on specific gaps, missed goals or unacceptable behavior.

Stick to your objective and lay out what needs to happen and who needs to do what by when. Avoid analyzing motives, taking personal feelings into account or trying to "fix people."

During times of stress and emotion, you will benefit from having a one-page list of talking points of what you want to say. That is a best practice for speaking in stressful situations.

When you think in advance and have preplanned words, you will be able to stay calm and stay on point in the heat of the moment.

This is not a secret script that you keep referring to covertly during the conversation. Tell your employee the agenda and let him or her see your talking points if requested. Why not, if it makes for clear communication? I would not give them a copy as it is a informal discussion guide, not a legal document.

"I have written down a few items so we can stay focused on the matter at hand. So let's get started." This sends the message that you have planned this meeting and know what you want to say.

3. Get the right time and place

Think about the timing implications to the action you might be contemplating. What about the ripple effects of the action you are taking given the current business environment?

In my HR role, I have observed that some managers just want to get the issue off their shoulders. They may feel irritated or annoyed, so they want to press ahead for an immediate change to clear the slate.

There may be good reason to finesse the timing. For example, there may be a hiring freeze, which means you cannot replace someone for several months. On the other hand, maybe team morale would benefit from a quick exit of the individual dragging people down. The key is to do what is best for the business, your team and you.

4. This is not about you

As he sits in my office, I can see the steam coming out of Richard's ears. He shares about today's presentation with corporate on the manufacturing plans for next quarter.

"Martha came to the meeting late holding a Starbucks cup. When we reached her agenda item, she was not prepared and I had to step in to help. She let down her team in front of senior management."

Richard pauses to catch his breath. Then he adds, "I have hit the wall. I want to write Martha up."

I know that Martha has bounced around the company and she seems to know how to skate right at the threshold of "good enough." She seemed to have a problem with *any* authority.

Richard is sharing a handful of problems that certainly merit attention and require change. I expect it will be a sticky conversation. However, Richard needs to avoid venting frustrations and personal feelings. This will just raise her defensiveness and give her an opening to share her feelings back.

Richard is doing the right thing to blow off steam before meeting with the employee. Now he can plan ahead for a feedback session with Martha with clear words that are objective. *In his assigned role, he speaks to Martha on behalf of the company. Speak less and say more.*

5. Manage the drama

In the classic movie, *Cool Hand Luke*, the Prison Captain explains how he views a prison behavior problem, saying "What we've got here is failure to communicate." (This is a classic line to add to your repertoire.)

In his own way he is simplifying things by saying, "Pay attention, this is a core prison rule." It is not a personal issue or social problem.

Rise above the heat of the moment and stay emotionally detached.

You are chief spokesperson for what happens on your team. Speak up or someone else will do it for you.

When you take control it will minimize spectators and third-party interlopers. Your team is watching and everything you do speaks loudly. Show that you are not ignoring the elephant in the room.

Without gossiping or sounding petty, you want to assure people that "you've got it." There is a strong leader steering the ship. "OK everyone, what we have here is a failure to communicate, so let me explain what is going on."

Turn Around

Managers often see and feel there is a problem with an employee but do not always see the way out. They hesitate to ask, does this warrant moving ahead?

Turn Around is a new step I am adding to your management tool kit. You are at a point where change is required. I want to empower you to know that there is always something you can do to get their attention.

House M.D. was an American television medical drama that ran for eight seasons. The main character is Dr. Gregory House. He is an unconventional medical genius who often clashes with his fellow physicians. His flouting of hospital rules and procedures frequently leads him into conflict with Dr. Lisa Cuddy, who is the Hospital Administrator and Dean of Medicine. In the pilot episode we see Dr. Cuddy (the boss) attempting to get Dr. House (her employee) to listen to her feedback concerning job-related performance that has been too-long ignored.

I have taken liberty to condense the script here. You should go to YouTube and find the pilot episode. This clip will help you understand this section on Turn Around and Guideback.

Dr. Cuddy: *I was expecting you in my office 20 minutes ago.*
House: *Really? Well, that's odd because I had no intention of being in your office 20 minutes ago.*
Cuddy: *I sign your paychecks.*
House: *I have tenure.*
Cuddy: *You're six years behind on your obligations to the clinic. I can still fire you if you're not doing your job.*
House: *I'm going home.*
Cuddy: *House, the only reason why I don't fire you is because your reputation is still worth something to this hospital.*
House: *We have a point of agreement—you're not gonna fire me.*
Cuddy: (as House walks away) *Your reputation won't last if you don't do your job. I want you to do your job.*
House, turning back: *But, as the philosopher Jagger once said, "You can't always get what you want."*

Dr. Cuddy is facing a talented employee whom she would prefer to *guideback* to the right standing in the organization. She cannot continue to allow him to disrespect the rules, procedure and herself as his boss.

You want to avoid the high conflict that comes when you start a formal disciplinary process. It is tough to restore an amicable working relationship amidst the broken glass that results once you start a formal process that draws attention and invites third-party intervention.

Are there intermediate steps you could take to give the employee an opportunity to turn around? Your goal is get people's attention and inspire them to make the needed changes without moving ahead and taking the formal, prescriptive steps with directed feedback.

Let me walk you through some intermediate steps that Dr. Cuddy could use to turn Dr. House back from the edge of the cliff.

Make it abundantly clear

I have sat with hundreds of employees who were totally surprised that their manager was having a problem with their performance. They may act incredulous to the specific problem or that it is in fact important. They were not aware that this behavior was such a serious matter.

Beware, this may be a tactic to minimize things and make them go away. Nonetheless, there are a lot of employees who really are oblivious to their current state of performance (or lack of it). So to be abundantly clear, you are clarifying "Why are we here?"

> You are giving feedback "with an edge." A specific response is required.

There is one thing you are adding: this is *feedback with an edge*. Something has to change to return to everyday normal. In my experience, guideback communication hinges on whether you are able to set the edge on your feedback.

Try this to effectively communicate your message:

- First, clearly communicate the problem statement. This is not exploratory surgery for Dr. Cuddy. She is prepared with specifics: Your billings are practically nonexistent; you ignore requests for consults; you're six years behind on your obligations to the clinic.

- Use the Game Plan illustration (page 149) to show "where we are in the process." This shows how you intend to manage and where this will lead. This sets an "edge" that we cannot ignore this problem.

How to show that "this is important"

Unfortunately, Dr. Cuddy physically puts herself into a position where Dr. House can ignore her. She resorts to speaking to his back as she chases him down the hall. Clearly, this puts Dr. House in a position of control.

You need to have a "this is important" voice and way of holding a meeting that *sets this subject matter apart* from everyday communication. You need to find ways within your own personality to ratchet up the communication and apply tension.

Here is a personal story. In one job, I was senior HR director for a high-tech business that grew from scratch to twelve hundred employees in ten states. In one memorable and painful learning experience, I had responsibility for planning and running an off-site senior management retreat.

To my chagrin, I botched the planning of this event. I had delegated administrative details with half-formed thoughts and had casually passed on requirements and details for the agenda and logistics to folks without clear specifics. I realized after the event that I had not paid close enough attention to the details and logistics.

The next day, Larry, my boss and the senior vice president of the business unit, did not swing by my office to chat about the event. (His office was twenty steps away from my office.) Instead, his executive assistant called me to set up a meeting at his desk at 4:40 p.m.

Hmm. First, his assistant worked out of her home in New Jersey, so Larry called her—three thousand miles away—to schedule a meeting with me—twenty steps away.

The meeting was scheduled for 4:40. Not "around 4:00 or see me sometime before you go home." It was at his desk. There was no agenda stated.

You need a way to say, "This is important."

When I arrived at his office he had his desk cleared. There was obviously something important on his mind that he wanted to discuss. I swallowed hard.

I quickly jumped in to apologize for the glitches and take full responsibility for the management retreat. I made promises for how I would change. "My bad, I am so sorry."

Interestingly, Larry was not interested in my apologies. I understand now that I was trying to identify the problem for him. He wanted me to understand *what he perceived as the problem.*

Our technology organization had grown so fast that the senior management team had gotten used to operating in a slapdash, jury-rigged mode of operations. We were doing whatever we had to do to get the plane off the ground. It was the wild and woolly technology frontier.

He wanted to communicate to me that I could not continue to operate in this manner as a leader in his organization. He wanted me to make a major shift to act like a senior leader who uses planning and forward-thinking to insure excellent execution.

I left understanding his view of the problem and what he expected of a senior leader in his organization. I understood the importance of the desired change and this was not optional. In the end, I believed that he continued to hold confidence in me.

The way he delivered the message was Managing Genius.

Do something

You are never completely powerless. Guideback is not always a huge show of force. We always have options to take some kind of action. Take note: *The alternative is to do nothing.*

Back to the *House Pilot*, Dr. Cuddy decides to do something, so she pulls the hospital privileges of Dr. House:

> House *(angrily): You pulled my authorization!*
> Cuddy: *Yes. No MRI, no imaging studies, no labs. You also can't make long distance phone calls…or photocopies.*
> House: *So, you're not letting me treat patients?*
> Cuddy: *I need you to do your job. And…I looked into that philosopher you quoted—Jagger. You're right; you can't always get what you want. But as it turns out, "If you try sometimes, you get what you need."*

See that you do have power. It should not be a heavy-handed power play or official proclamation with fanfare and lights. This is just everyday management that you can use to step up and make discretionary decisions.

Change jobs and assignments. No job is an entitlement. If a basketball player is having a bad streak on the court, the coach sends in a substitute. If a lineup is not playing well together, the coach may mix it up with a different lineup.

You can shift many things within someone's job. You can alter responsibilities. You can pull back things like training, travel or committee participation. You can easily change the meetings that they attend.

Micromanage. If you are concerned about an individual on your team, it might be time to pay closer attention to his or her work. Give well-defined short-term assignments and expect timely updates and results.

Maryanne has been concerned over a lack of team skills in her employee, Katie. She hears reports of Katie's noncooperation in shared group projects and that Katie sits on information that ought to be dispersed to her teammates. Katie has apparently been keeping a few participants in the dark and not inviting them to meetings.

> People earn the right to enjoy autonomy and trust.

Maryanne decides to temporarily get more involved in Katie's projects. She asks to be copied on all emails for Katie's group involvement and she arranges a weekly meeting with her to review group activities.

This close managing is something Maryanne would not do for a long period. It would spur most employees to make immediate changes.

Deep dive. Larry had a practice of doing what he called a "deep dive" with direct reports whom he felt needed the "extra attention." If he asked you to hang around at the end of the meeting for a "deep dive," it was clear to you—and to everyone else—that you had missed something. It was as if Larry wanted to check your math homework.

Larry was giving you extra attention to get your attention.

This was not a public defrocking; it was just a way to show it was time to stop sleepwalking and step up to change.

In the deep dive, Larry would pepper you with detailed questions to discuss your work and expose the gaps. You definitely felt like you were under scrutiny and you knew you did not want to go through this process again.

The deep dive became part of our team culture and it became a source of friendly banter when others knew you were on the hot seat.

Mixed signals. It's important that you don't send mixed messages to an employee with a performance problem. People receive confusing messages when they receive a three percent merit increase at the same time when you share concerns over their last-minute work habits.

The key is to make sure you take control of anything coming to your employee who is on the hot seat. Make sure there are not conflicting messages through awards, bonuses or pay increases.

An employee discipline process becomes much more difficult when the employee has received mixed or contradicting feedback or other signals. Make sure your performance documentation is consistent.

Move people away. Early in my engineering career, I worked for a Research Director who was a maverick. He was once a rising star in previous administrations but a new senior leader had plans for a more collaborative management style.

The entire research organization went through realignment and our group was moved to a separate building away from the main seat of power. It was a subtle shift that put my boss a short walk from center of things. I remember my manager looking flustered when he announced this, as if he had lost a position of favor.

> Managers always have something they can do to get people into listening mode.

Not surprisingly, he became a model director and stellar program manager. A year later, our group was back into the main research building while another group replaced us in the outbuilding with their own story.

Coaching people. In this turn-around phase you may consider trying to coach people back. Coaching is a popular leadership topic with plenty of consultants wanting to help you.

Let me share a fly-over of the coaching concept that is more practical and pragmatic. I am hoping that this will enable you to make an objective decision whether to coach someone as a turn-around strategy:

- First and foremost, understand that you cannot personally fix people nor can you infuse them with motivation to make changes.
- If you do coach, address issues that have immediacy. You should see a short term goal in sight; this is not an extreme makeover.
- Be realistic and pragmatic: What is on your plate? This is a business and the show must go on. Can you wait for the individual to achieve a hoped-for outcome? Can you or your team carry the extra work?

- Coaching is not a reward or a way to achieve advancement. Some people want to be coached by senior management because they think it will earn them special attention or access.
- Just because someone asks for help does not automatically mean you should invest your time and attention. Does this individual merit more of your time than others in your organization? Is it in the best interest of the business?
- Coaching to help people should not become an excuse or a delaying tactic. Why do they want your help three weeks before the deadline?
- People work within their gifts and abilities. Sometimes we try too hard to encourage people to make changes that may be outside their natural desires and abilities.
- Expect people to have thoughtful and specific requests for what they are hoping to achieve. Avoid telling people what they need or giving unsolicited advice.
- Here is the kicker: Coaching people calls for special skills that most managers do not have in their leadership tool kit. You have to ask yourself if this is what you do best.

> **Invest in the people who:**
> - Take ownership
> - Contribute job ability and desire
> - Show respect for the company, the team and for you as their boss
> - Are in "listening mode"

Directed Feedback

This next step is called directed feedback, which is meant to imply that this is a one-way discussion. You are sharing a message that must be delivered and must be heeded. This ratchets the communication up and moves the issue forward. We are now on a narrow road leading to a destination.

You can and should insist that: 1. This employee is in listening mode, 2. This person accepts responsibility for this problem, 3. You believe a change is required. You are now in micro-managing mode concerning the agenda and required next steps. Express your desire to see this issue reach closure in a reasonable time frame (define a specific time). You are not seeking a win-win or middle ground and *you are not bargaining*.

Your judgment, observations and conclusions are not in question at this time. Use facts and data whenever possible. Remember that your objective and unbiased opinions are also important facts and data.

Avoid broad statements and general requirements like you have to get along with others better or your attitude needs to improve. Stand by your own words and do not say "everyone thinks this about you" to bolster your opinions.

The warning should communicate next steps and specific follow-up actions. Most people will take this special attention to heart. Document this conversation via email (you can search your email box later).

Do not banter further by email or through third parties. Do not allow new agenda items or side skirmishes. Hold additional face-to-face meetings if more clarification is needed.

Finally, maintain a level of professionalism and emotional detachment. No need to respond to every emotion or reaction. What is key is to make a quality decision up-front, then stay your course.

Corrective Feedback

The business world is in continuous flow—we come together and then part ways. A Managing Genius manages the breaking off with grace and respect.

In your judgment, the problem presented is unresolved and this issue is in jeopardy of affecting the employee's continued job status. You may have serious doubts as to whether this person is even right for the organization. You have reached a point of no turning back, unless of course the employee quickly shows a genuine willingness to comply.

Craft a written warning that includes a specific performance improvement plan. Include sufficient details about what will happen next if the person fails to fulfill this directive.

A written warning should clearly communicate the unacceptable behavior and the fact that the employee has been previously instructed that the behavior requires improvement. The warning must be very specific as to what needs to happen in regards to mandatory improvement and what happens next should the performance not improve as directed.

The warning needs to be signed and dated; give a copy to the employee. This does not need to be a legal letter or contract. Just carefully lay out the details using as few words as you can and be specific about next steps.

You could label this a "written warning." You should give a deadline with specific required behavior and present a clear choice for your employee to either comply or face serious consequences, up to and including termination.

Fire

Donald Trump says, "I mean, there's no arguing. There is no anything. There is no beating around the bush. 'You're fired' is a very strong term."

It is Managing Genius to have the *ability* to fire people when it is time for them to leave your team. It is important for you to take ownership for this process.

The ability to fire people is an important skill that you may not use much in your career. However, when you need to, it becomes extremely important. You should have knowledge of how to fire people or you should at least know where you would go to get that information.

If you hesitate or act helpless, people will pick up on this and may begin to doubt your resolve. I want you to feel powerful and decisive. You own this decision and you make it happen.

You will feel greater ownership and confidence if you see a way to carry out the process.

> You can only learn how to fire someone by doing it few times.

Follow the simple, prescriptive process as shown in the Quick Guide on the next page. In fact, when you fall into a mechanical mode you will stay objective and unbiased.

Firing is one of the most difficult things you will have to do as a manager. Having a game plan will make you feel confident and in control.

Managing Genius
QUICK GUIDE

Firing Process

1 **Quality Decision:** Pull together facts, data and direct observation. Check history and previous disciplinary actions. Seek objective advice, then make your decision.

2 **Align:** Get approval from your boss. Communicate your plan with key stakeholders. Arrange with Human Resources and IT for needed support.

3 **Plan the Delivery:** Set up a short and professional 10-minute meeting. Prepare a one-page termination letter and give the employee a copy. Plan how you will exit the room.

4 **Run the Meeting:** Everything needed to physically leave is ready on the last day: final paycheck, benefits info, FAQs. An efficient exit gives closure.

5 **Reset Team:** Walk the floor for a series of quick updates with individuals and small groups. If you don't, others will speak for you. Quickly reset the work space. Restart your team.

Zero tolerance

A senior staff engineer had submitted an expense statement. She had added the cost of a hotel room to her expense statement, when in fact the hotel had been paid for by a customer.

She had worked for the company a decade. She was a top performer and a great team contributor. She often spoke at new employee orientation.

As I entered the room she was tearfully explaining her story to her boss, the Senior Director of Engineering. She explained that it was just a stupid mistake, an oversight that she would be happy to fix.

When her boss asked my input, with a sad heart, I opened a file of past expense statements. I asked if we could ask her some questions about some other expense submissions.

She immediately burst into tears and the real story unfolded. She had recently experienced a painful divorce. She was a single mother of three with private school tuition.

The Senior Director cut off the discussion with a wave of his hand. "Sorry. You lied. Frankly, we do not care why. We never lie here and what you did calls for immediate dismissal."

As he got up to leave the room, he said to the now-fired employee, "I wish you would have come to us for help." That was it.

At this company, lying was a *zero tolerance issue* and an immediate ticket out the door, no matter who you were.

Zero tolerance means not every inappropriate employee action deserves review, further discussion or a corrective process. Some actions fall into "automatic" decisions concerning behaviors that are never acceptable. Your decision to fire someone for a zero tolerance situation is not based on the person. It's automatic, impersonal and it applies in every case.

Some employee actions deserve immediate action. You need to send a clear message to everyone that the company considers this matter gravely serious. Your immediate action communicates that the company has no leeway for zero tolerance issues.

Discover Your Managing Genius

- Step up and take the lead to resolve people issues in your group.

- You can confidently resolve performance or behavior issues without the usual fanfare and drama. This comes from knowing in advance how you will respond to people issues and taking ownership for your own employee relations.

- Learn the five-step Game Plan for People Problems (page 149). If necessary, you can move the issue forward through progressive steps and reach closure for everyone concerned.

- Be prepared with a simple, straight-forward process (page 162) when it is time to fire someone—a necessary skill to have in your back pocket.

- Act as the chief spokesperson for what happens on your team. Speak up to show that you are not ignoring the elephant in the room. Build trust that you have things in control.

Captain of
the Ship

This is your team—
establish respect for you
and for the business

Big Idea

This is your team and you have responsibility for the work. You will need to establish respect for your managing role and find effective ways to ensure that people are listening. Learn the art of combining authority, power and influence to delegate and direct people.

I think there should be a Captain in there somewhere.

Jack Sparrow, *Pirates of the Caribbean*

People just don't realize their dog must respect them as leader of the pack. You can't change unstable ways with affection. The most important thing that we have to provide every day is that we are the pack leader, that we set the rules, the boundaries and the limitations, and then we love.

—Cesar Millan, the Dog Whisperer

If aliens are watching this through telescopes, they're going to think the dogs are the leaders of the planet. If you see two life forms, one of them is making a poop, the other one's carrying it for him. Who would you assume is in charge?

—Jerry Seinfeld

It is a curious thing, Harry, but perhaps those who are best suited to power are those who have never sought it. Those who, like you, have leadership thrust upon them, and take up the mantle because they must, and find to their own surprise that they wear it well.

—J.K. Rowling, *Harry Potter and the Deathly Hallows*

Any peanut stand needs a manager.

—Rudy Giuliani, former mayor of New York

💡 Important to Know

Mark reflects back on an early experience after his promotion to Managing Director of this large senior care facility. He saw this as an amazing opportunity to lead the whole business unit.

In his quest to start well, he held a series of all-team meetings to share team goals, policy and practices. Unknowingly, Mark had begun to put into place the makings of a *Managing Genius* work culture.

Captain of the Ship
1 Why bother?
2 Your management prerogative.
3 Third party intervention.
4 Who is the boss?

Diving down into the organization, Mark learned he had inherited an employee with a long history of below average performance and poor attendance.

Wendy, a nursing assistant, was one of those employees who knew how to do just enough to get by. The staff had grown accustomed to covering for her tardiness and absences.

Mark met with Wendy to discuss expectations and policy. Wendy always had personal excuses and tearful promises. But her performance didn't change and in due time Mark methodically followed the company process to fire here. The staff expressed a collective sigh of relief.

However, a few days later, Mark got a meeting request to meet with the President and HR. When he arrived, he learned that Wendy had already met with them to share her story and plead her case.

The President quickly got through the pleasantries. Then he proceeded to chide Mark, "What were you thinking? Wendy has been here eight years and deserves better. Did you take the time to learn that she is a single parent with two small kids?"

His phone beeped and as he turned to take the call, he added, "Can't you find a way to solve these issues amicably without causing problems? Next time, don't let your personal feelings interfere with common sense."

HR told him next steps. Mark drove back to his office feeling stunned, wondering how to face his team and how he would manage Wendy.

As I listened to Mark's story, I could see that this was a pivotal experience that many managers face, where they ask, *"Why bother?"*

1 WHY BOTHER?

If you are visiting Seattle, you may want to learn the unique names for various coffee drinks so you can feel like a local.

For example, if you want a decaf latte with nonfat milk, you order a "Why Bother." Ordering a Why Bother is a way to go through the motions of drinking a hot beverage that looks like coffee...while the coffee fanatics in line behind you are thinking, *Why bother?*

Many managers can relate to Mark's experience. They run into a tough situation and step up to the plate, only to get their legs cut out from under them. They begin to doubt themselves. This can cause them to shrink back and act passive or helpless. It can affect their ability to think objectively. They may punt issues over to HR or just do nothing and wait for the tension to pass.

So they begin the long dance where they are constantly looking over their shoulders to see what others want them to do. They may come to the same conclusion Mark came to—*Why bother?* Team members can pick up on your plight and they may start asking, W*hy bother listening?*

2 YOUR MANAGEMENT PREROGATIVE

I spent four years as a labor relations manager at a unionized pulp and paper mill. In this role, I would often mix it up with the union president over various personnel problems and contract issues. Sometimes the discussion became more sport than necessity.

Once I was working a little too hard to win an argument with the union president. He let down his guard to give me some friendly advice, "You don't need to win every argument...you do realize that you have management prerogative, right?"

This made me think, *I could decide.* Unions are there to challenge and watchdog our management practices. They are speaking and acting in a variety of ways for the profit and gain of their union members.

"You have no right to make that decision concerning our union member." But wait—in fact we do. It is called our "management prerogative."

I began to remind myself that union members are first of all our employees. Their paycheck comes from the company and we have the ability to exercise management prerogative.

Management Prerogative: Make decisions using judgment and discretion.

3 THIRD PARTY INTERVENTION

Here is an experience repeated a zillion times in my HR career. Employees come to me to complain about their manager. The concerns are usually the garden-variety stuff like personality conflict or differences of opinion. Once they have shared their concern about their manager, they pause to ask what I think.

I always ask this question first: *"Have you talked about this with your manager?"*

It is a phenomena in America business to depend on third-party intervention for employee relations issues. In many companies this is built in, just like when union employees bring along their shop steward.

This creates triangles where employees can avoid direct communication versus where they take responsibility for their words. Eventually this becomes the accepted system and we lose our skills at "just talking to the person."

Use staff support for the exceptional employee relations problem. That support can also be helpful for complex legal and policy issues. However, it has become standard operating procedure to bring in a third-party for *every* personnel issue.

Break up triangles and ask for direct face-to-face communication.

Managers complain to me about interference from HR and legal but often *the problem is you.* You may fear making tough employee decisions, so you too quickly walk down the hall to HR to ask for help.

This invites third-party staff into the problem. In turn, this diminishes respect for your authority when your employees see you asking for help.

You may even say out loud, "Let me first check with HR." This invites employees to just bypass you the next time and go straight to HR or over your head to your boss.

Instead, keep the ball. "Let me ponder this and get back to you."

One Managing Genius I worked with had a passion to eliminate triangles. If you came to him with a complaint about someone, he would escort you to that person's office and say, "You two need to talk. Let me know what you decide."

Talk with your team, your boss and HR so everyone identifies and avoids triangles. Become faster to address issues when they are small, current and more readily resolved within your team. A delayed decision often invites third-party intervention.

Become adept at everyday HR matters. *Speak for yourself.*

4 WHO IS THE BOSS?

When my daughters were in elementary school, I volunteered to chaperon a zoo outing. At one point during the day, the child of one of my fellow chaperons ran up to his mom and *told her* where he was going next.

The mother paused and said to her son with a patient but firm smile, "I'd like to see a question mark at the end of that sentence."

After her son scurried away, she shared from her experience raising three teenagers, "Never forget who is the parent and who is the kid."

Parenting 101: Never forget who is the parent and who is the kid.

As a father of two daughters, I have learned that this one key principle shapes everything we do as parents.

In the same way, we should ask, "Who is the manager and who is the employee?"

Managing Geniuses always act with confidence and assurance concerning their management prerogative. They are not questioning their role or their authority to proceed.

This chapter is a summary of the basis for that confidence.

This Is Managing Genius

It is Managing Genius to act and speak in ways that will cause your employees to respect your role and listen to you. Do not sit back and wait for others to define this for you. You need to step up and use effective ways to take leadership and control as Captain of the Ship.

Establish Your Managing Role

1 Responsibility

2 Authority

3 Power

4 Influence

The following four elements are key to defining and communicating your management role. See these as a single picture that shows people what they can expect from you.

Important to note, clearly establish your responsibility, authority and power early to give your team confidence in you.

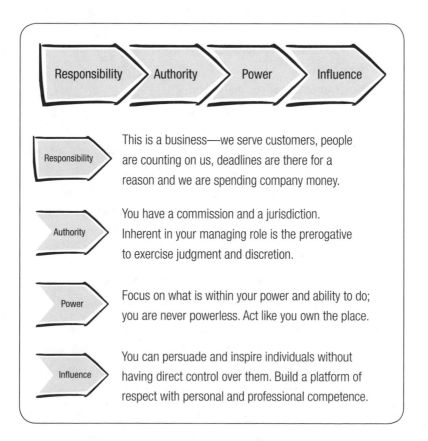

| Responsibility | Authority | Power | Influence |

Responsibility — This is a business—we serve customers, people are counting on us, deadlines are there for a reason and we are spending company money.

Authority — You have a commission and a jurisdiction. Inherent in your managing role is the prerogative to exercise judgment and discretion.

Power — Focus on what is within your power and ability to do; you are never powerless. Act like you own the place.

Influence — You can persuade and inspire individuals without having direct control over them. Build a platform of respect with personal and professional competence.

1 RESPONSIBILITY

Responsibility is the reason why we are here. Whatever is said or done between you and your employees, there is a business reason to be here. That reason is to provide products and services for customers. There is a business plan and money is being spent. Responsibility is why we bother to come to work.

Required duty.
Burden of obligation.
Accountability.

In the role of manager, you have responsibilities that you cannot accomplish without the contribution of other people. Your company asks you to get work done through your employees. You have authorization to spend budget dollars to hire employees. You delegate your responsibilities and free yourself for bigger things.

However, you manage people and when all the talking is done, someone must take responsibility for the work.

Talk about your own responsibility

It is important to communicate that you are responsible for getting certain work done. Your company requires you to manage people within the realm of your responsibility. It is your job to share responsibility linked to the particular work that was assigned to you.

Remember that you are an employee and you have a boss. Your work rolls up into a larger entity with overlapping umbrellas of responsibility.

We all have work we *must* do

> *Freedom is just another word for nothing else to lose.*
> —Janis Joplin lyrics, "Me & Bobby McGee"

Everyone would love to work in an environment where we had complete freedom to do what we want, in the way we want. It is human nature to prefer a "free range," do not tell me what to do. But then we would also own the company and be responsible for paying all the bills, right?

As manager, you are not free to pick and choose what you want to work on. Your boss asked you for something specific today and it was given to you with a sense of urgency. *The show must go on.*

Responsibility is always assigned. If not, people can sort through the pile and hand-pick what they want to work on. There are many parts that make up a person's job. Over time people may try to cherry pick and do only the "shiny parts."

So we ask: If riding the horse is the "shiny part," who cares for the horse? Who cleans out the barn? If your team leaves without claiming full responsibility, you will be left cleaning out the brown stuff.

Compromise

It is a great thing to seek input and reach mutual agreement when you pass on responsibility. No one likes work dropped into their lap without a chance to discuss. However, leaders may look for "middle ground" where everyone leaves happy with work decisions.

Important to note: How can there be compromise with the responsibility? There are always alternative ways to reach the same outcome and we can fine-tune strategy and tactics. However, when we leave the room, someone has to pick up and own the responsibility.

Anything else is bargaining.

2 AUTHORITY

It follows that if you have responsibility you must have the authority to perform those responsibilities. In the same way, when you delegate responsibility you also delegate individual or shared authority to do that work.

Authority

Professors and pundits talk as if authority is a bad thing. It's an outdated term bottled up with giving orders and expecting obedience. It sounds like we are taking advantage or manipulating people. People have learned to question or push back on authority.

The right to direct, judge or control the actions of others.

This is not a recent trending topic. In fact, Lord Acton was a mid-1800s English historian, politician and writer who gave us a famous quote: "*Power tends to corrupt and absolute power corrupts absolutely. Great men are almost always bad men.*"

This all-encompassing quote sounds like the "dark side of the Force" from *Star Wars*. Too often in the business world, we paint all managers with the "dark side of the force" brush. We do not trust managers to use authority and act with good intentions.

This brings us back to where we start questioning our ability to direct the activities and actions of our employees. So we find ourselves back in the pulp and paper mill, where we let the union push us around and challenge our management prerogative.

If you don't have authority, *why bother?*

Establish your own authority

You need to believe that you have the authority that is tied to your managing role. Without authority, there is no way to manage your responsibility. *So again, why bother?*

> Lt. Bailey: *We have phasers. I vote we blast 'em!*
> Capt. James T. Kirk: *Thank you, Mr. Bailey. I'll consider that when this becomes a democracy.*
>
> —Original *Star Trek* TV series

Your position comes with a commission and a jurisdiction. Authority is not all-encompassing or global. It is tied to your company goals, responsibility and budget. *You are a boss and you have a boss.*

Whether you are in the office, away from the office, deciding to take action or doing nothing at all, you still have that authority.

One hot summer day at the mining operation, I was on a ride-and-learn with Pete, an experienced shift operations manager. We drove up to a work site where one of his employees was not wearing the required hard hat. When he delivered a friendly reminder of the safety rules, the employee responded, "No frigging way, it's too hot!"

Pete winked at me and asked the employee to get into the pickup truck. (Later, he explained that the first step is to separate the person from his grinning peers.) Then he drove toward the main office, continuing his review of the operations with me.

The employee eventually asked where we were going and Pete informed him, "We're heading to the main office so we can clock you out. You know you can't work here without the required safety gear." The

> Only you can establish your authority.

employee softened and smiled broadly, putting on his hard hat. "You can take me back."

Pete drove the employee back to his work location but dropped him off fifty feet short so he could walk up to his peers with his hard hat on. It was a magic managing moment—something you do not learn in college.

Be aware of the importance of pivotal moments where you can send a clear reminder of how people need to respect your authority.

Establish authority early and you will not need to use it often.

Believe that authority is a good thing

Authority gives us prepackaged directions for items that do not need to be rehashed every day. For example, authority is the flashing light that tells us to stop at the crosswalk. Parking lots are painted so you don't have to decide where to park your car. Even boxing has rules of engagement.

Authority provides organization and predictability that allows a large group of individuals to cooperatively work together. It makes it possible for dissimilar people to share close spaces and common resources. It provides a way to solve problems and conflicts. It creates a system to exchange individual desires for the greater good.

> Taking a leadership position over other people has one huge advantage. You can do more good than anyone else can.

Everyone needs to have a healthy respect for authority, rules, procedures and process. Simply stated, people need respect for the game to play the game. This can be a problem in a society that so highly encourages and rewards individualism.

In business, we see the necessity of authority established in safety rules, spending approvals, handling of hazardous materials or guidelines for using company property. If you allow your people to push back or water down authority, people will sense your hesitancy and think everything is open for discussion. You will twist in the wind at the slightest hint of conflict.

Eventually people may begin to fend for themselves or look for another leader to follow. They may "play you" like the easygoing, bumbling Henry Blake in the classic TV series M*A*S*H.

Everyone needs to have a healthy, mature respect for the company, the customer and you as their manager.

> Can people go over your head? Only with your cooperation.

Think about this: it may not be that they disapprove of your personal authority. They could be resisting authority *in general, from anyone.*

Face the emotional disconnect.

Few of us, when upset, can take a balanced point of view. You need to step back to collect yourself. Find the emotional strength to take the heat and face disapproval. You should be unwavering and unflappable.

Exercising authority mean that you may have to live with some emotional disconnection and ambivalence from your employees. Believe that you hold a position independent of their favor and attitude.

Establish authority at the right time and place

When you've taken issue with the way that your boss exercises direct authority, it is often because he or she picked the wrong time and place to communicate the message.

People will show more personal resistance when you surprise them or talk to them in front of others. No one likes to be cornered or be the recipient of a surprise attack.

You build trust and reduce personal resistance *by picking the right time and place.*

Reflected authority

My first job after college was at an open pit mining operation. As a crew leader, I was uncomfortable assigning unpopular work, like telling the crew to go out into the frigid winter weather to redo a job.

I found myself name-dropping my boss's name to deflect the sullen stares. "Sorry, guys, but Joe wants this." "You can blame HR for this." However, name-dropping invites your employees to tune you out and go directly to those third-party people you mention. *Why bother with you?*

Getting the last word

Getting the last word has become a pejorative phrase that means you do whatever you have to do to win the argument. We mistakingly think that whoever gets the last word wins the argument.

We have all worked with at least one last word manager who had a psychological need to over-power people to get the last word. Later, the last word gets spoken down the hall where beleaguered meeting attendees get the last word and the last laugh.

However, the key question is always why we are here and everyone in your group will need closure on what happens next.

Managing the "last word"

1. Who got the last word?
2. Who should get the last word?
3. How did we reach the last word?
4. What was the last word?
5. Did we reach closure?

Here is how to manage the "last word":

1. **Who got the last word?** It is often the same people who speak up in the meetings who carry the group discussion. If you do not want to be the person who gets the last word, do you care who does? Make a chart of recent decisions and check whose opinion prevailed through persuasive sales skills or hallway arm twisting.

2. **Who *should* get the last word?** Decision making should be tied to responsibility. Make sure the right people are making decisions that affect the responsibilities they own. Once group input has

fine-tuned the options, turn to whoever is responsible and ask, "Is this what you want?"

3. **How did we reach the last word?** When you throw up a jump ball and allow anyone to grab the ball, you could be relegating the last word to the most persuasive extrovert. Do you see healthy discussion and mutual respect? Did the most knowledgeable and prepared person carry the discussion?

> Your boss will assume that you own the last word for every group decision.

4. **What *was* the last word?** When we talk about the work, do people then leave the room with closure? This is a paradigm shift—even if you do not exercise authority to get the last word, you provide oversight to know *what was the last word.*

5. **Did we reach closure?** No matter what is said or done, you have responsibility to make sure that everyone leaves the room with clarity on next steps. Always be sure that when work is discussed, everyone in the room knows what the plan is going forward.

What is your default style to seek people's respect?

When we need others to do work for us, we often fall into familiar patterns to seek cooperation and try to convince people to listen to us. We have seen different styles from the authority figures in our life. We all have different temperaments and tolerances for anxiety and ambiguity, so we each find a default managing style.

- Stephanie is a people person; she depends on relationships to win people over and get their cooperation. When pushed she will suggest, "Lets get coffee and talk this through."
- Jack gains authority by name-dropping senior management or using his insider knowledge to get people to listen to him.
- Sanjay believes people should look up to him because of his vice president title. He scans the meeting room to see who is senior. He may not attend if it is below his "senior status."
- Karen is the division CFO; she enjoys the power that comes with holding the purse strings and the company assets.

- Deepak has a PhD in electrical engineering. He carries himself like a distinguished scholar who deserves respect and special recognition for his academic achievements.

Are these methods effective? The styles mentioned above require repeated stroking by you, they wear out in time and they often will not work in the midst of stressful situations. Understand that we can over-depend on certain tactics to gain an edge of authority.

Note that all of these tactics are a form of superiority.

Interestingly, your employees and coworkers have already figured this out about you. They know your preferred management style and they may just play along. If they see that you enjoy status to get work done, they may just "suck up" to you to win favor.

Admit your mistakes

Michelle starts the meeting with an update on a recent group endeavor that completely went off the train tracks. "It was completely my fault, my bad," she shares in a upbeat fashion. "I made some assumptions that fell through. Let me walk you through how I made the decisions and what I have learned from this."

Making a mistake does not diminish your authority.

This approach builds respect from her team as she demonstrates humility and learning. Bring mistakes and miscues to the team table to discuss learning opportunities.

However, admitting a personal management mistake *does not diminish your responsibility or authority.*

You are not saying "I screwed up so I next time I should listen to my employees more."

Instead, explain that you made a judgment call based on the situation and the input you received. Remind people you will seek input if possible. "Now we need to reset and move forward."

You are still their manager, although chagrined and much wiser.

Build your personal authority

It has always been a basic tenet that managers had the authority to set the goals and direction for their employees. You *have* inherent authority within your management position in the company.

In the last two decades companies have invested too much time and money searching for the "magic key" to connect people with a higher purpose. Senior management, HR and hired experts have kept tweaking the company structure to find the perfect system. First, they make the organization flat to eliminate hierarchy. Then, they try a new "matrix management" strategy, "details to follow."

The company tries to solve management issues with the latest trendy system that promises to create a happy workforce. Compensation may be handled by a forced ranking appraisal system that even further reduces manager judgment and discretion.

> **Simple ways to guide**
>
> 1. Teach and explain
> 2. Use show and tell
> 3. Ask probing questions
> 4. Walk through recent events
> 5. Share from your experiences
> 6. Believe and encourage

When the dust settles, we still work within an org chart that is in continuous flux. People move into different positions, reporting relationships shift and responsibilities get shuffled. Multiple managers may carry parts of the work in their personal department budgets.

So what? Managing Genius is about you.

You cannot always depend on *formal* authority, rules, policy or management systems to give you the ability to lead your group. As you rise in the organization, you will increasingly need to lead people without having direct authority.

It is important to remember that your authority will not always be based on your position on the org chart. You must build personal authority based on your professional, competent ability to take charge and make decisions. Your employees, colleagues and senior management look to you as a person who has authority.

Here are a few simple ways you can enhance your platform of authority:

1. Become an authority.

You attain authority by walking into the meeting as the most knowledgeable and prepared person in the room. If you are in the mode of flying into meetings late and looking scattered, do not be surprised if people lose respect for your authority. Revisit Chapter 1 to "get your ducks in a row" so you can speak with authority.

2. Act like you are supposed to be here.

Before we respect your authority, we want to know if you have a reason to be here and you want to be here. You can get ignored if you act disinterested or distracted. You speak from authority when you walk into the room like you belong there. Act like what you have to say is important. It is a feeling you need to cultivate in yourself.

3. Watch how you personally react to conflict and stress.

Steven Ambrose wrote about the leadership of General Eisenhower during World War II. As Supreme Commander of the Allied Expeditionary Forces in Europe, Eisenhower had to work with, through and around leaders and generals from the Allied nations, all who had strong opinions that pushed and pulled against his overall plan.

Ambrose writes that Eisenhower never passed these problems down to his staff. They were often unaware of the political turmoil and second-guessing, because Ike wanted his staff to focus on their immediate goals.

Eisenhower wrote, "When pressure mounts and strain increases everyone begins to show the weakness of his makeup. It is up to the Commander to . . . conceal doubt, fear, and distrust."

Eisenhower wrote, " A Commander's optimism has a most extraordinary effect upon all with whom the he comes in contact. With this clear realization, I firmly determined that my mannerisms and speech in public would always reflect that cheerful certainty of victory." [1]

Avoid sharing your fears and apprehension with your employees.

---

1 Ambrose, Stephen. *D-Day: The Climatic Battle of World War II.* New York: Simon & Schuster, 1994, 61.

We often have an automatic first reaction to bad news or emotions. It is critical to spot your personal cues when you are feeling out of control or sense that you are overreacting to the stress. "Let me think about this and get back to you by the end of the day."

4. Professional demeanor and appearance.

Since the beginning of time, leaders of clans or military groups have used costumes or markings to distinguish themselves from their followers. Today, we tend to disparage these outward trappings of position.

Even Jack Donaghy on *30 Rock* was concerned about how he looked when he was demoted to the twelfth floor of the NBC building.[2]

It is not important that the manager looks different or superior. However, you strengthen your authority when you look organized, in control and professional. Make sure you come to meetings on time, prepared and ready.

Does your professional demeanor causes people to *take you seriously?*

5. Someone has to make the decision.

Too often we stop to ask for permission where it is not needed. What's worse is we stop midstream in the meeting to question whether or not we can proceed.

In that moment, you may notice that respect in the eyes of your employees is wavering or lost.

A Managing Genius gets the "last word" at the front end.

Try to anticipate problem situations and get advance support from your boss or HR. Do not get yourself stuck in situations where you "twist in the wind" in the eyes of your team and coworkers.

In most cases, you should step up and make the decision. We often doubt ourselves when in fact we have the answer and need to press on. It is important that your team sees you in a decisive, forward-moving mode.

Your team is watching. *Whatever you do speaks loudly.*

---

2 Watch *30-Rock*, Season 2, Episode 14, "Sandwich Day."

3 POWER

First, step back to understand the nature of power.

When you see a police officer in uniform directing traffic, you do not question whether that officer has the authority to stand out there and wave his or her hands to direct where you should drive. But—it's important to note—a police officer does not have the *power to physically control your car.*

Power

The ability to do or act. The capability to make things happen.

In the same way, you do not have power to control the actions and behaviors of your employees. People are not an avatar in a video game.

However, as a manager in your company, *you do have power.* Your company wants you to get work done through your employees. First understand the power that comes to you through your managing position in the company.

Clarify the power that you have

Managers *have* power that is inherent within their managing role. Power—your ability to do things in the company—needs to be in the background of any discussion concerning your managing role. For example, you approve payroll and allow people to be paid.

First, discuss with your boss how he or she sees the power that you possess within your managing role. Solidify this up-front so you are not left scrambling at every turn of the road. Ask for clarity concerning how you can exercise judgment and discretion.

For example, what layers of review are required for an employee relations decision? Can you make hiring decisions? Can you send people home or fire them? Clarify what decisions you can make without special approval.

It is not always a skills issue. Understand your ability to make decisions.

Put it on the table if you have to jump through hoops or seek approval. You look more powerful if you know the limits of your own power. You do not want to act surprised when someone pulls you back midstream.

You need to exercise your power

You have more power and ability than you think you do. If you have the responsibility, assume you have the power to do the work.

Your boss, HR or employees will not walk down the hall to formally grant you power and the ability to make decisions. Your boss will not always be there in the room to back you so people pay attention to you. HR does not hand out power in a training class.

"This station is now the ultimate power in the universe! I suggest we use it!"
Admiral Motti in the first *Star Wars* movie.

Hands-on experience is the catalyst for Managing Genius. You master the art of managing through ample opportunity to try things, see what works and make mistakes. *Press on.*

Power is not something that you *earn* based on successful outcomes or whether or not you are able to maintain "peace in the neighborhood."

Choose to step up and exercise your power.

In advance, discuss with your boss, senior management and HR how you and they will react to sticky situations and unintended consequences.

We know that employee issues often turn down unforeseen roads. "It's complicated." Have a strategy for dealing with whining and complaints.

You need to step in to exercise your power make things happen. Do not doubt yourself. This is your job; you are supposed to be there.

Power that is undefined

You will face situations where power is undefined or shared. It is common to have multiple bosses where lines of authority and budget overlap. This can result in mixed signals and conflicting priorities

Do not over-analyze personal power or who is in control. In any meeting you can take the lead by focusing people on *why we are here, what is important, and what happens next.*

Master the art of exercising power in any situation. Start with anything you see in Managing Genius—this is what great managers do.

There are always things you can do

It is essential that you believe you must have power as a manager in the company. More important, *you are never totally powerless.*

An example of where you may lack power is how difficult, if not impossible, it is to fire someone. You certainly cannot pursue that course without approval and advice from above and HR. Likewise, you rarely have the power to give pay increases linked to today's performance.

Nevertheless, if you focus on what you *cannot* do, you will communicate to your people that you feel helpless or lost. People may see you as just an administrative manager who processes forms and serves as

> You have power pre-loaded into your managing role. Focus on what you can-do.

the watchdog for policies, schedules and time and attendance. You will fall into indecision. You may begin to over-analyzing issues and second-guessing the decisions you have already made.

A Managing Genius sees himself or herself with the power and ability to exercise judgment and make decisions. In fact, everything in this book is within your power to do without approval or fanfare. Your management role gives you power.

How do you say, "This is important"?

One aspect of your managing power is to have acceptable ways to get people's attention to assert or declare, "Pay attention. This is important."

For example, I worked as a logger one summer during college. On a rainy day, we used the wet conditions to create an enormous brush pile to burn. I applied gasoline around the base and was about to light the pile.

My boss, the woods foreman, marched up to stop me and he proceeded to tell me I was a flipping stupid idiot. He ripped me to shreds with every swear word known to man. He was so angry, spit was hanging from his beard. Of course, I was incredibly embarrassed in front of my coworkers.

Later, the foreman pointed out that I was about to light the pile with the gas can at my feet. Whatever your style, people need to know when the message is important. (I will never forget this experience.)

You will get what you give

The early days of TV were filled with classic shows like *I Love Lucy*. The common story line was Lucy employing devious and shrewd tactics to get her husband, Ricky, to do something she wanted. These manipulative tactics have a way infiltrating every generation.

Power Plays

- My way or the highway
- Bargaining
- Use rules and policy
- Withhold information
- Carrot and stick rewards
- Leave ambiguity so they have to depend on you

Consider the tactics listed in the chart. It may remind you of managers you have worked for in the past. You could put names by the power play.

These tactics might help you get through today's stressful confrontation or crisis. However, they will not work for the long haul. In time they will diminish people's respect and confidence in you. This is not Managing Genius.

Important to note: When you use these power plays to get what you want, be aware that these same tactics may be used against you.

Give your employees processing time

Another way to fine tune your managing power is to not force people into instant compliance. You do not get to yank the leash and expect immediate obedience. Instead, give patience and space to think through your request.

It is understandable to want to quickly get things done. You have already thought about the problem and as you walk down the hall you may already have a solution in mind. You may have ten pressing items in your head, so in this moment you would love the instant gratification that comes from immediate compliance.

However, power does not give you freedom to be impatient. If people pause at your words, they are not always "dissing you." Maybe they just need time to process or space to catch up. Most of us prefer gradual versus hard turns, so show patience and focus on outcomes.

Sharing power through employee participation

Leadership pundits have taught us over the last few decades that the best ideas come from the "collective wisdom of the group." The experts tell us to disperse power and decision-making. From my experience, here are some observations for sharing power and making the most of employee participation:

Goals. At the front end, clearly state why we are here and what take-aways you hope to achieve.

Responsibility. If you share power, people should share in the responsibility. It is fun to participate in discussion to make decisions, but who owns the work?

Sense of urgency. Many business decisions require timely decisions. Make sure employee groups are operating with a required urgency.

Define power and scope. Define the power of the group, such as decision making or spending limits. Your team may feel frustrated if their shared ideas get too easily discarded or ignored. This includes follow-up work and future decisions—once asked, people may expect to be included in future decisions. Explain your "power sharing philosophy" in advance.

> Committees should feel that they are sharing in responsibility.

Understand group dynamics. It is naive to think that people will always work together in an inclusive and democratic way to reach a shared consensus. Private agendas can spring up that cause compromise and deal-making. Some find debate an interesting sport. When it is all said and done, the extroverts may carry the discussion and get the last word.

Who said everyone should speak? Instead of the word "everyone," how about making sure the right people get to speak? You should show value for the people who are prepared and ready to contribute.

Is this what your employees want? Not everyone wants to participate in leading the company. Sharing leadership may not be their cup of tea. Some people may just want to get off work on time to meet their carpool. They may be more concerned with picking up their kids on time from daycare. Understand what your people are thinking.

Capability. Managers often assume that their employees can do exactly what they can do. Your employees may lack the power and ability that you can have as a manager. You have a greater awareness of the business and organizational issues. You have access to available resources, senior management and information. You have budget and spending authority. All this allows you to get things done by managing through ambiguous and competing priorities.

Too often we throw together a group or let people volunteer, assuming they have the same ability to get things done as we do.

Best practices for employee participation:

- **Business reason to assemble the group**
  Communicate the agenda so everyone knows what to expect and how they can contribute. Are you assembling people to get input, announce changes or plan out a detailed implementation?

- **Define the scope of power for the group**
  Set limits, boundaries and budget limitations. Are we here to generate potential solutions that others will sort through? Clarify who reviews or approves the final decisions. This will make people feel more vested in the meetings.

- **Fully engaged facilitator**
  Any assembled group needs someone to guide and direct so they can stay on agenda and reach the finish line. This is a great opportunity for training future leaders.

- **Invest in more front-end coordination**
  Managing at the front end is more important with groups of people who may be unfamiliar with each other. Get the group started well and overcome "new-group" inertia. Be sure to coordinate the first meeting.

- **Invite the right people**
  Managing the meeting attendance is as important as defining the goals of the group. Invite people who have a vested interest, something to contribute or people whom you want to invest in for the future.

How to effectively communicate your power

1. Talk about the whole picture

Just after presidential candidate Barrack Obama defeated Hillary Clinton, CNN news commentator David Gergen was asked, "What was the one mistake that Clinton made in her 2008 presidential campaign?"

Gergen explained, "To win a political campaign, you need to do a dozen or more things well. Any one item can cause you to fall short of winning political office." What Gergen was saying was that politicians need to do a capable and competent job *across the whole board*.[3]

In anything you lead, take ownership for the whole job. You earn respect when you show that you understand the whole picture. People get jazzed when they see the big picture.

Managing Genius was written in this spirit. To be a successful manager of people, you must succeed at a decathlon of essential elements. For example, would you need to go through all this employee drama if you gave clear expectations and directions at the front end? Did you give effective feedback? Was the work planned?

Think about the whole picture when you are speaking to your people.

2. Focus on what you can change

Daniel A. Wren, in his seminal work, *The History of Management Thought,* takes the reader through the evolution of management practices from the advent of the Industrial Revolution to today. Wren shares that the role of any people manager has always involved four basic elements: "recruitment, training, motivation and discipline." [4]

What a paradox—today, all four are essentially outsourced to HR, with managers left to jump through hoops to get things done. So I propose that you make an important paradigm shift: *Focus a management strategy on what you can change and own yourself.*

---

3 I heard this on CNN while working out at the YMCA. I have done my best to reconstruct the gist of the interview.

4 Wren, Daniel A. *The History of Management Thought.* New Jersey: John Wiley & Sons, 2005, 44.

For example, notice that I do not discuss compensation in this book. This is not to say that pay is unimportant or irrelevant. In reality, any manager below CEO has little power to use pay as an incentive linked to *current* performance. You try to make sense of the compensation process but your explanations keep falling short. Your *lack of power* to directly manage compensation, as you would any other important team process, does not make you look powerful in the eyes of your employees.

The good news is that you do have power. For example, there is nothing stopping you from singing the praises of a star performer or you can assign plum projects to your most deserving employees. Actually, everything in *Managing Genius* is readily available to use and own.

You make yourself look powerful when you become a can-do leader.

3. Simplify everything

Americans spend millions every year on fancy cookbooks and expensive cooking gear that looks great in the kitchen. The experts whip up amazing recipes and cooking techniques that pave the way to healthy living and culinary excellence. But we stop to ask, are we eating better?

Powerful leaders are simplifiers. They choose simple techniques to cut through the clutter to get to the heart of the matter. Simplification reduces unnecessary frustrations and makes the work feel user-friendly, understandable and easy to own.

> The Internet has inundated us with information. You serve people by simplifying.

You earn respect by directing people to clean up the deck by tossing unnecessary things over the side of the ship. This demonstrates power when you can make tough choices to improve the workings of the ship.

An important form of simplification is knowing when to accept "good enough." Allow people to finish and feel successful instead of chasing the elusive goal of "unobtainable perfection".

Actually, I wish someone would write a book titled *Great to Good-Enough*—the chase for perfection often keeps us from finishing things.

Powerful leaders are great simplifiers.

4. Do-it-yourself philosophy

In the mid-1920s, the new age of aviation pioneers began flying variations of small, fragile and poorly equipped airplanes. The historian David McCullough writes, "What was so unique about the early aviators is that they flew with the land."

He explains, "The early fliers were never detached from the land in mind or spirit. It was a necessity to keep their bearings, so they flew with rivers and kept eye contact with landmarks and roads. That is how they navigated above the countryside.

With the wind in his face, he is close enough to the farmland to pick out details, he is in touch with the Earth, and in touch with his fellow man as he waves a hello." [5]

All this has changed today. Modern flying is a skill learned on flight simulators and captured on the computerized instrument board. The word *autopilot* has taken on a broader meaning in business. To describe someone as *flying at 20,000 feet* is a way to express a great visionary leader who is unburdened with the details of what is happening on the ground.

> Everyday team operations should feel like a locally run initiative, with you in the lead.

Like the evolution of the flying experience, technology and systems have created distance between us and the people who are working for us. We find ourselves flying on autopilot.

Remember the first time you managed people? People had names and you loved seeing their faces at your office door. They represented opportunity, not problems.

Somewhere it stopped being fun flying your "managing biplane." People became tiresome and annoying. You became hesitant and wary of how your words and actions might get construed. You realized that with the managing job comes tough decisions concerning real people working on the ground.

We have a few "close calls" and we stop flying the plane ourselves. We bounce the problem up the ladder or over to HR.

---

5 McCullough, David. *Brave Companions: Portraits in History.* New York: Simon & Schuster, 1992, pages 125-133.

Managing Genius
QUICK GUIDE

Do-it yourself team leadership

1 **Captain of the ship:** You carry responsibility for all things concerning your team and your corner of the business. Step up and act like the owner.

2 **Team HR director:** You should be the "first phone call" for your employees. Become adept at handling everyday people issues and HR matters. Speak for yourself.

3 **Team training manager:** You are in the best position to facilitate individual and team growth. Plan, budget and schedule team training as you would any business need.

4 **Team communications officer:** Your people trust you to keep them informed on what is important. People want to hear it from their boss. Speak early and often.

5 **Chief morale officer:** You manage the work environment and shape the employee experience. This will not happen by itself—build a vibrant, colleague-friendly work neighborhood.

6 **Manager of rewards/recognition:** You are in the best place to link effort to reward. Make sure good news comes from you. This gives you power in the eyes of your employees.

History lesson. The first recorded attempt to establish an office for "social welfare" was at the National Cash Register Company in 1897. Lena H. Tracy was hired as Welfare Director to "manage the changing relationships between managers and workers." [6]

This "Welfare Director" handled grievances, provided recreation and education, administered dining facilities and looked after the moral behavior of unmarried female factory workers. *This was the birthplace of HR.*

We stop to ask, will you take ownership for the "welfare of your workplace?" Is this your team? Will you speak for yourself?

It is Managing Genius to develop a do-it-yourself philosophy for your workplace. You gain power when you become a hands-on manager who is adept with the everyday matters listed in the Quick Guide on page 192. Recast your managing job to take ownership for what is important to your team.

Become a do-it-yourself people manager.

5. Sense of urgency

I was walking with Kaylia, a Director of Education Programs in Chicago. As we weaved through the crowded Chicago streets, she explained how to navigate through the traffic, "You have to walk with a purpose."

You gain power when you manage with a sense of urgency:

Focus on ownership. Giving ownership will wake people from their sleep-walking. Responsibility has a way of tugging at your sleeve. Bring goals to the team table—people are more likely to follow through with goals that they make explicitly to the whole group.

Demonstrate an incredible awareness of current events. Show that you are a master of the group schedule. You can identify and talk about key milestones and delivery dates. Your drive and enthusiasm makes everyone aware that the clock is running.

---

6 Wren, Daniel. *The History of Management Thought.* New Jersey: John Wiley & Sons, 2005, 186-87.

Develop a mainstream mentality. Be focused on the center of the business, not on the distracting side stuff and corporate noise. Everyone gives importance to what is really important.

Be forward-minded. A Managing Genius is always looking for what should happen next. It is easy to fall into side conversations or innuendo. Press on.

Show zeal for closure and completion. Urgency always presses for the finish line. Show this in your questions. If someone says that work will take a month, you ask, "A month is 22 work days. Can you walk me through your time line?" This makes people understand that every day counts.

You gain power when you manage with a sense of urgency.

4 INFLUENCE

The secret ingredient behind Managing Genius is the art of influencing people. Influence allows you to persuade and direct people without direct control. Influence builds cooperation and commitment.

Influence comes from *you personally*. People respect you so they choose to listen to you.

People hold the start of the meeting until you arrive. When you walk into the room heads turn and people want to know what you think. Your presence lowers resistance and "disarms people."

Influence

The capacity to sway or persuade other people's thinking or actions.

Influence is built on hundreds of data points collected from everyday interactions with your employees and across the workplace. Through your actions and behavior, people know what to expect from you.

You cannot market yourself at work like you would on social media. A business is like a small village. The word on the street, in regards to who you are in the village, is rarely far off. You are building your reputation in the company by everything you do and say.

The ultimate example of using influence

Just for fun, let me give you a visual image of influence from the first *Star Wars* movie. Don't you wish?

Ben Obi-Wan Kenobi: *These aren't the droids you're looking for.*
Stormtrooper: *These aren't the droids we're looking for.*
Ben Obi-Wan Kenobi: *He can go about his business.*
Stormtrooper: *You can go about your business.*
Luke Skywalker: *I can't understand how we got past those troops. I thought we were dead!*
Ben Obi-Wan Kenobi: *The Force can have a strong influence on the weak-minded.*

Think about this: If Han Solo was in this movie scene, he would have used his blaster weapon (power) to break through the road block. Ben Obi-Wan Kenobi chose to use influence—a well-developed skill that he could readily use to get through such conflict situations.

Working for two different leaders

I have had the opportunity to work for two different senior executives in the same Fortune 50 company. They were both highly competent and highly successful leaders. Both had accomplished careers with amazing business results.

Here is how I would sum up the difference in working for them:

If Rich asked me to do something, I would do it.
If Matthew asked me to do something, I would want to do it.

Rich was a top performing executive with years of results managing major businesses. In this role, he pulled together his senior team to perform excellent execution and implementation. His organizational execution was flawless. He demonstrated the superior interpersonal skills and social graces that you need to be able to advance to the highest ranks of a large corporation.

As his direct report, I felt as if I was working *for* Rich. I was on the line to please him and follow-through on his direction. Ultimately, I felt that I was there to serve Rich and help him look good to the company.

You did not want to disappoint a senior executive like Rich. One day you are playing a key role on the ship. At the next port you are left standing on the dock watching the ship leave. Been there?

In a different experience, Matthew made me feel like I was working *with* him. He explained the mission and what was important. He took that extra time to explain his thinking and share insights from his knowledge and experience. We worked together on how to best implement goals.

Matthew would ask probing questions to get my opinion or perspective and then he would actually pause to wait for my answer. He listened to my input.

Would you want to work for you?

Matthew was an excellent teacher, willing to share from his own experiences. He was free with wisdom on getting work done through others. He taught me strategies for navigating the company and gaining cooperation from people. On one memorable occasion he stepped in to cover my back.

Matthew's management style had a positive impact on our entire senior management team. This was the strongest team I have ever worked on.

Influence creates cooperation and commitment. You get work done through both the head and the heart to win people over without having direct control over them.

People want to work for you.

Master the art of influencing people

Rich and Matthew were both highly effective using authority and power.

Authority and power *without* influence defined Rich's management style.

Matthew saw authority, power *and influence* linked together as a package. He understood how they come together and built a platform of respect for himself and the business.

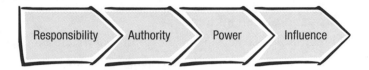

Responsibility is the reason we are here.

Authority gives you the right to direct, judge or control the actions of others. Authority can get you a seat at the table because of your position. You can also get authority because of where you are positioned on the org chart, your budget authority or "who you know."

But, authority *alone* may only give you a way to get work done through a compliant workforce. In time, people may find a way to work around you.

Power gives you the ability to delegate and direct the work of your direct reports. Your company has "pre-loaded" your managing role (hopefully) with power so you can have the ability to make judgment calls, exercise discretion and reset priorities.

> Be aware that you may be more comfortable relying on authority or power.

But, power *alone* may create a workforce dependent on your presence and your repeated application of power. In time, people may learn how to just pay you lip-service and do only what is minimally required or just enough to get by.

Influence gives you the ability to initiate and guide work without using direct authority or power. People *willingly listen to you* because they respect you for who you are and how you get work done.

Note that influence *alone* is just sales.

The influence of a Managing Genius is always visible and front and center in their management style. They know how to use responsibility, authority and power in the right way to enhance their influence.

Authority and power should be established early so you will not need to exercise them often.

What's next: Find simple ways to obtain attributes that build your influence in your team and throughout your organization.

Simple ways to obtain influence

In the movie *Avatar,* humans in the 22nd century are mining a highly valuable mineral named "Unobtanium." The mineral was so named because it was extremely difficult to obtain. I share this because, in my humble opinion, many leadership books sound interesting but the teaching seems "unobtainable" in our lifetime.

Obtainable influence

1. Become a Managing Genius
2. Professional competence
3. Amazing conversational skills
4. Circle of colleague
5. Character and values

I sought to uncover what gives a Managing Genius such high levels of influence. Then I narrowed the list to five ways that are *obtainable.*

1. Become a Managing Genius

Have you ever followed a boss to make a career move? In the long term, you will not stick with a leader just because of likability, friendship or charisma. Once the senior leader resigns, the power to help your career "just left the building."

The managers you choose to admire and follow will always show exceptionable skill in managing people. Would you like to work for a senior manager who masters all ten of the elements in this book?

In the end, you prefer to sail on a ship that operates smoothly, can weather storms well and makes it effortlessly to the right port. Everyone wants to work for a Managing Genius.

Everything you see in Managing Genius is obtainable.

2. Professional competence

We were growing fast in our new division and there were always special projects and high level decisions needing to be made to expand the business.

We had two financial analysts and they were both highly competent professionals. Brian came to me to complain that Michael got all the cool projects. It was not fair.

However, Michael anticipated potential questions and brought new ideas to the meeting. He seemed prepared and ready for anything. Without being asked, he developed a detailed spreadsheet that quickly became the tool for analyzing potential business deals.

Michael clearly outworked Brian. He became the senior management team's first choice for making financial decisions for the business.

Who would you invite to your meeting? Michael acquired influence because of his professional competence.

Professional competence is obtainable.

3. Amazing conversation skills

We have the best communication tools that have ever existed in the history of mankind. We can stay in touch real time and increase the speed of getting work done. However, smart phones and email have slowly replaced talking face-to-face with real people. Conversational skills is a lost art.

Trust me, anyone who aspires to advance in their careers must master their ability to talk face-to-face with real people. These simple items will build excellent conversation skills and make you an influential leader:

- Listen with your eyes. Body language is 90% of showing great conversational skills.
- Focus on the people in the room. Visibly turn off your smart phone.
- Use thoughtful, open-ended questions to unfold the topic. Questions are the key that unlocks employee engagement.
- Punctuation matters in verbal conversations. Look for the period at the end of their sentence.
- Let people answer your questions without interruption.
- Speak professionally and avoid everyday banter and low-talk.
- Make your conversations continuous. "The last time we talked you were worried about the sales presentation. How did it go?"
- After every meeting ask yourself: *Who talked most?* Listening is always increased when you speak less.

Developing conversational skills is obtainable.

4.   Circle of colleagues

I find it interesting that Managing Geniuses always have an inner circle of exceptional colleagues and business associates. They hang with smart and savvy people who make them better. They have the social graces to work well with just about anyone but they have the ability to develop insider relationships with influential leaders.

You will also see that Managing Geniuses hire top people. They can attract key people because the best people want to work for them.

Picking strong colleagues and top employees is obtainable.

5.   Character and values

There are some common personal values that are all *obtainable*:

- Humility: Confident leaders are not concerned with touting their capabilities or acting superior. They do not seek excessive control to maintain their status. Instead, they make others feel important. They are gracious, self-effacing and unpretentious.

- Transparent: "The sins of some are apparent today...While the sins of others follow closely after them." (1 Timothy 5:24) We have all worked with amazing leaders who make poor choices that eventually catch up with them. It is best to work openly in the light of day.

- Open communicator: Treat everyone in the org chart with the same courtesy and respect. Master the art of face-to-face conversation. Show you are approachable through your non-verbals.

- Giver: Some of us are givers and some are takers. The people around you already have you pegged. Do not only give to people who can serve you or pay you back. As you walk around at work, look for opportunities to be a giver.

- Learning attitude: As we gain career experience, we often lock in on ways of doing things, narrowing our interests and shrinking our willingness to try new things. Politics can lock us into positions or status quo. Special note: You will marginalize yourself if you do not embrace new software, IT systems and technology.

Developing character and values is obtainable.

Character and Values

These are all *obtainable*.

Humility

Make others feel more important than yourself. Gracious, self-effacing and unpretentious. Open to input.

Transparent

Stay in the light to avoid the appearance of inappropriate actions. Stay open and accountable to someone who can challenge your thinking.

Open Communicator

People will give you the benefit of the doubt when you show that you are an open-handed communicator without guile or game.

Giver

Make it your goal to be a giver to all, regardless of where they are on the org chart. Do not just give to people who can help you.

Learning attitude

Have a great deal of curiosity and willingness to explore. Ask great questions that unfold issues and show new ways to do things.

Discover Your Managing Genius

- This is your team. You will need to establish respect for your managing role and find effective ways to ensure that people are listening.

- Learn how responsibility, authority, power and influence work together to create the Managing Genius:

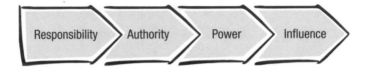

Responsibility › Authority › Power › Influence

  - You *have* responsibility for the work. This is the reason we are here.

  - You *have* authority. This gives you the right to direct, judge or control the actions of your employees. You establish authority early so you will not need to exercise it often.

  - You *have* power inherent in your managing role. This gives you the ability to delegate and direct the work of your employees. Everything in Managing Genius is within your power.

  - You *earn* influence. This is the ability to sway or persuade other people's thinking or actions. Influence builds cooperation and commitment.

- The secret ingredient behind Managing Genius is the art of influencing people. This multiplies your personal effectiveness across the organization.

Value
People

Show respect and value
for every team member

Big Idea

Show respect and value for people independent of their job title or performance. This builds long-lasting commitment beyond today's work. Consider how this one element serves as a catalyst for the other elements. Role model this group norm and pump it into the air at work.

Do you know why I hired you? I always hire the same girl—stylish, slender, of course ... But so often, they turn out to be disappointing and ... stupid. Anyway, you ended up disappointing me more than any of the other silly girls.
—Miranda Priestly in *The Devil Wears Prada*

Nobody ever asks "How's Waldo?"
— Waldo commiserating at a bar in a cartoon in *The New Yorker*

I care about the job, of course. But mostly, I just want to be inspired.
—Dorothy in *Jerry Maguire*

I was influenced a lot by those around me—there was a lot of singing that went on in the cotton fields.
—Willie Nelson

What's important is that you have faith in people, that they're basically good and smart, and if you give them tools, they'll do wonderful things with them.
—Steve Jobs

Reserving judgments is a matter of infinite hope.
—F. Scott Fitzgerald in *The Great Gatsby*

Important to Know

I am meeting with Alex, a senior vice president, in his private conference room. We're going over a to-do list concerning the staff and organization and this meeting is a chance to catch up on loose ends.

As we start talking, his admin, Stephanie, comes in with our boxed lunches. Without looking up at her, he looks at his box and chides her, "I wanted a sandwich, not a stupid salad." Stephanie holds her ground and cheerfully reminds him that last week he asked her to remind him to start eating more salads. There is a pause in the room and then he says without looking up, "Forget it, Stephanie. My bad. OK, come get me at one o'clock." She slips out of the room as quickly as she came in.

How You See People

1 If I only had a heart

2 The incredible worth of people

3 Take the high road

4 Showing respect and value

Alex tears into his lunch and starts freely sharing what's on his mind.

Chuck, one of Alex's direct reports, needs a fire lit under him. Alex proceeds to tell me a story that demonstrates that Chuck just does enough to get by. I am taken aback, as the story involves casually sharing personal information about Chuck that I would rather not know.

Next, Alex shares that although Michael is a good enough controller, he is so annoying to be around that he is considering getting rid of him. He shares another long-winded story that demonstrates how "stupid" Michael can be in meetings. "Michael is hopelessly stuck in the basement, sucking air out of the room," Alex declares.

Then his voice gets quiet and Alex confides that it's a slow, painful death to be with Susan when she is wearing her "bitchy face." He has learned to stay away from her when she's in one of her moods. Alex shares the story about how he had sponsored Susan through a company program and he thinks he should get double points for mentoring a black woman. "She is here because of me but of course now we're stuck with her, if you know what I mean."

Alex is mostly happy with Martin but he's too concerned with kissing the asses of corporate people in order to secure his next promotion, so

Alex has stopped including him in insider issues. "I cannot trust him if he is going to suck up to corporate." He instructs me to keep Martin in the dark on important stuff.

He goes on to fill me in about a feedback session with Gerry. He describes the meeting as tense and says that Gerry did not seem to get what Alex was telling him. So Alex believes Gerry is doomed to keep making stupid mistakes. Before Alex can say another word, Stephanie pops her head in to advise him that his one o'clock is here.

While we are still alone, Alex speaks quickly and asks what I can do to secure an intern job for the son of a recently hired senior executive at corporate. He confides, "We may need a favor down the road."

As I walk down the hall, I realize something: the only direct report Alex did not talk about in our meeting was me. It occurs to me that Alex is probably talking about me in his next meeting.

1   IF I ONLY HAD A HEART

I have to admit, Alex is a very good manager. I have never worked for anyone who has a better understanding of the business. He earns respect for his knowledge. He is a walking expert on the technology and the industry.

Alex is truly the captain of the ship. He is smooth and consistent in establishing goals and direction.

Do you believe that people are important to you and the business?

You always know where you stand and he gives clear feedback. He gets my grudging respect for his ability to lead and direct all aspects of the business.

So what is missing in his management approach? He treats people like things—human ATM machines. He asks for something, you give it to him and then he gives no acknowledgment of appreciation whatsoever. He chooses to mentor a manager like Susan in her career and then he makes her sound like a project.

He chooses to connect with people for "give and take relationships." He is always looking for an edge with his employees. He constantly assesses where he stands with people. Alex has a knack for using people he perceives as holding power and influence.

To quote the Tin Man in the *Wizard of Oz*,

> *When a man's an empty kettle he should be on his mettle,*
> *And yet I'm torn apart.*
> *Just because I'm presumin' that I could be kind-a-human,*
> *If I only had a heart.*

Managing Genius is built on showing respect and value for every member of your team. It is important to note that it is not important what you think of yourself. People are smart; they can usually figure you out. Our true selves will often pop out in moments of stress and conflict.

Some might say that managers like Alex have no values but actually they use their authority, power, and influence to deem who is valuable. It comes from their sense of superiority.

Unfortunately for the people he works with, the application of such external values can seem capricious and is merely based on Alex's exchange rate. The only way that you can continue to connect with Alex is by performing. You are on edge and you can never be sure of attaining his good favor.

It is difficult to feel comfortable around Alex when he is judging you and assessing your value based on his needs and wants. It is hard to trust someone who allows personal traits to bias his thinking. It is difficult to commit yourself to someone who has such a low regard for women. All of this affects how would you feel about working for Alex.

2 THE INCREDIBLE WORTH OF PEOPLE

We can get so busy with work that we forget we're dealing with people.

Arnie was a maintenance manager at the pulp and paper mill. He had worked his way up from the rank and file as a skilled journeyman, moving into the salaried ranks and becoming the department manager when his boss retired. He would drive to work in classic cars that he found in junkyards, and in his spare time, he would restore these junk-yard cars into works of beauty. He had a 1969 Mustang and a 1973 Dodge Challenger.

Arnie would often park outside my window, in a stall that was protected from car door dings. When the shift ended in the mill, I could sit in my office and watch Arnie showing off his car to his coworkers. Although I could not hear their words, I knew they were amazed at the incredible work Arnie had done to his automobile.

People do things not just because they are asked to but because they *want* to.

As I watched these scenes unfold, my mind went beyond the car with the incredible paint job and the painstaking eye for detail to admiration of the real work of art: Arnie.

It amazed me that a human being could use his hands to shape sheet metal in such a fashion and apply paint with such amazing artistry. He could transform a forty-year-old assembly of metal, chipped paint and rust into a street-worthy vehicle that looked as good as the day it drove off the lot.

That he could use his hands and mind in such a way to make this creation was beyond comprehension to me. This man was worthy of our admiration and respect—the fact is, the human being *is* the work of art.

3 TAKE THE HIGH ROAD

It is important to say: not every culture on earth has a respect for the worth of the individual. All topics in the human rights arena—such as women's rights, domestic violence or world hunger—are built on the foundation that every individual human being has worth.

If you are reading this section and think this is unimportant, you may have discovered why Managing Genius is an elusive aspiration for you.

OK, there will be some annoying people whom you wish would go away. But realize that the same people are at every workplace; just change the names. I realize that some people can fall short of their potential, get distracted and lose their way. However, people are the business. People are our only lasting competitive advantage.

You rarely get to handpick your team and you cannot hire or fire to solve today's problems. Great leaders find ways to successfully work with anyone. *Manage the team you've got.*

So ignore the personal irritants and focus on job-required performance. The show must go on.

People are watching how you treat others. Rise above the everyday fray and show value for people and respect what they can bring to your work group. You should enjoy managing them. You must *like* seeing your employees at your door.

4 SHOWING RESPECT AND VALUE

In an episode of *30 Rock*, Jack Donaghy gives a big smile and says to his manager, "Lemon, I am so glad you're here." Liz Lemon had done nothing specific in her job to earn that praise, Jack just had an overwhelming feeling that gushed to the surface and he expressed it—*you make this a better team.*

In this scene, the boss was looking beyond the present condition and behavior of his employee. For that moment, he was stepping back from asking, *So what are you doing for me today?*

This creates a personal connection based on the incredible worth of the individual, expressing value and respect for him or her.

> People do things not just because they are asked to but because they *want* to.

If you build a core foundation for showing value for people, you will foster trust and communication and give people a reason to stay. People will rise to higher levels of commitment and engagement. People will want to work for you.

However, ignore this chapter, and your employees will slowly pull back and uncouple from you. You may sense a distance or notice that people seem reserved or on guard.

This chapter is not about what people do for you, which is still important and part of the ten essentials for Managing Genius. This idea of recognizing the inherent value in your employees compliments the other chapters and acts as a catalyst for everything else in this book.

This Is Managing Genius

Show Value for People

1 See people as unique

2 See people as capable

3 Have faith in your people

4 Listen with your eyes

5 Involve people

6 "Lovely to see you again"

7 Show a high public opinion

8 Give them grace

9 Individual treatment

10 Room to grow

I realize that we are inundated with special programs and HR initiatives that are designed to build teamwork and an effective work culture. This chapter is different because this is your personal program.

The way that you treat people is a key variable in determining the amount of trust your employees have for you.

What follows are ten simple ways to show respect and value for your employees and coworkers. What follows are some tried-and-true practices that I have observed in Managing Geniuses with whom I have worked.

As you practice these, your employees will follow your lead and your team culture will emerge. This builds long-lasting commitment beyond today's work.

How to use this section

A Managing Genius does these things naturally as a way of life and doing business. Sure, it would sound phony if you were to walk down the hall and tell someone, "I have decided that I will show respect for your skills today." However, becoming aware of and then practicing these ten ways to value people should spill over into how you treat people. Eventually, your employees might think, "I like working for Elizabeth; she really trusts her employees," or "I feel I can approach my boss; he never makes me feel like an imposition."

Here is the trick: make it your goal to pick one item to emphasize each week and eventually these ten ways of treating people will become an everyday practice. Make these second nature . . . like breathing in and out.

1 SEE PEOPLE AS UNIQUE

It was early morning and I had flown all night with little sleep. I was walking through the crowded Heathrow Airport in London wondering how to find my way to a cab.

Suddenly, I heard something amazing that instantly changed the moment for me: someone called my name. It was someone who was scheduled to be part of the meeting but I had not anticipated seeing this person until the meeting commenced. Here in a foreign country, with swirling masses of people moving in all directions, another human knew who I was; it felt surprisingly welcoming and reassuring.

People love to hear their names and they especially love to hear it from their boss. It makes them know what they do is important.

We want to feel like we have a place on earth where we can showcase our unique skills and abilities. We want to believe that someone notices what we do. When we walk away, we can look back and feel a sense of ownership. Our name is on the work.

> People like to hear their names and feel that someone notices their work.

In the midst of everyday work and responsibilities, communicate to your team that you know who they are and you are glad they are here.

2 SEE PEOPLE AS CAPABLE

I was on a backpacking trip in the woods of the Upper Peninsula of Michigan with a fellow employee who was an experienced woodsman. We had the makings of a beef stew in our packs and along the trail my friend stopped to collect mushrooms for tonight's stew pot.

I asked him if he was sure that these mushrooms were safe to eat and whether he knew that certain mushrooms are poisonous.

My friend looked at me with surprise and exasperation. He then got defensive and proceeded to explain to me about the various types of edible mushrooms. He said only a city guy would confuse which mushrooms were OK to eat and which were not.

My challenge to his knowledge left a spirit of distrust between us. Actually, I had no reason to challenge him. I knew that this guy had grown up traipsing behind his father, who had worked for years as a park ranger in this same forest. He also had a master's degree in forestry and when I stopped to think about it, I realized this guy probably could have identified every species of mushroom with ten miles, along with anything else we saw growing or moving within the forest. However, I had to ask that stupid question that challenged his expertise, when a word of respect would have been more appropriate.

Recognize and value what people bring to this team.

This altered our interaction for the rest of the trip. From this point on, he felt the need to explain and justify every decision, defending his credibility at every turn. He had invited me on the trip to show me the wilderness but I had failed to see him as capable.

If you have no reason to doubt an employee's capability; then don't. The more you demonstrate trust in your employee, the more clearly the message becomes that you value him or her.

3 HAVE FAITH IN YOUR PEOPLE

In my early career as a mining engineer, I was working with my boss to develop an annual mine plan that he presents to the entire management group. We spent time holed up in a conference room with maps on every wall and as the development plan took shape, he started talking to me about what to expect during the presentation. I suddenly realized that he was giving me the opportunity to lead the meeting.

He did not make a big deal of it. He did not start coaching me like a parent giving the car keys to a teenager for the first time. He just sat back in his chair and acted like he felt I could not fail.

Faith is a confident expectation that what we hope for will happen.

You see someone's individual potential. You believe in that person and then allow the person to do his or her best. It is an amazing feeling when team members feel they can be trusted to speak for us and handle assets, information, decisions or access to senior management.

Believe people can be trusted with things you deem important and valuable.

When we ask for petty details and treat people like kids, we water down their confidence. We give them responsibility and pull it back in the next breath. We stay in surveillance mode to check up behind their backs or act worried—as if they are about to blow things up.

It felt wonderful when my manager showed faith in me.

4 LISTEN WITH YOUR EYES

At one job, I had a dual reporting relationship.

One of my bosses was a senior director at corporate. Every time I stopped by to talk to him, he would turn halfway in his chair and his eyes would waver back and forth from me to his laptop. He would be checking email and typing short responses as we talked, assuring me, "Don't worry, I'm listening," "Keep talking, I just need to quickly reply to this."

In contrast, my other boss was the chief technology officer of the entire company. He had a far greater realm of corporate responsibility, reporting to the CEO and overseeing a few thousand employees nationally.

The people in the room are your priority at this moment.

If I stopped by to ask a question, he would visibly push his laptop to the side and turn in his chair to face me. "How can I help you?" During those few minutes he was completely focused on me, listening with his eyes. He would pick up his journal and take notes, showing me that he was paying attention to what I had to say.

If you ask people what they want from you, it doesn't matter what they tell you in that moment—in their heart, they are probably thinking, *just listen to me.*

It is that message that permeates our growing up and our work experience. We wish people would listen to us.

Do your employees feel that you give them your full attention? Do you show sincere interest in what they have to say? Do you value them for their ideas and perspective?

Try these techniques that show listening:

- Give amazing eye contact. You listen with your eyes. Turn toward the individual, lean in and squarely face her. Put away your smart phone or turn your computer screen away.
- Paraphrase back why you think they came and what will happen after they leave. This will show that you were listening and participating.
- Ask questions that draw out the subject matter.
- Wait to hear the "period" at the end of the sentence. Do not impatiently cut them off. Let them finish their sentences.

5 INVOLVE PEOPLE

We want to feel like real players on the team. We love to work where we feel included and share decisions and responsibility.

> People love to work where they can become real players.

One of my first professional jobs was at an open-pit mining operation. Eventually I was given the job of blasting engineer, where each week I designed a blast that was the size of a city block.

It was quite a detailed process that culminated in shutting down all mine operations during the lunch hour on a set day. Even the local school had to keep the kids inside.

After we carefully orchestrated the process that closed down the mine and brought everyone into a safe space, the blasting engineer went through a sequence directing the entire operation via radio, culminating with turning the detonator to execute the final blast. It was a weighty moment but after all, I had been trained to do this.

How would it feel if, after all that planning and operational execution, I was *not* trusted with the detonator?

On the other hand, I have had managers for whom I did all the leg work to complete a project, only so they could present the final report. Another manager would redo the slides so it looked like she did the work. Then there is that "we" word that sounds like we worked together.

It shows confidence and trust in people when you allow them to stand up and present research or make decisions to spend money.

"LOVELY TO SEE YOU AGAIN"

Check your body language and facial expressions when you run into your direct reports. Do you immediately think of problems? *OMG, here is another one of those whiny employees to waste more of my time.* Of course you wouldn't say this aloud. This is the kind of attitude people can see on your face.

You should enjoy managing your people—you like seeing them at your door. Give your people the best of yourself:

- Reply to emails from your team first. Everyone deserves a good measure of respect and courtesy but serve your own work group with extra expediency. You will also build respect when people see how proactively you act for your employees. It sets a precedent that we have each other's back.

  Your direct reports should get the best part of your day.

- An important place to connect with your employees is in meetings. Walk into the room with planning and foresight and act like you want to be there; this is the place to be.
- Master the art of conversation. Even if you are not all that good at conversing with people, excel at continuing the conversation. "I have been thinking about your aspirations to learn project management skills. I found a company training class you might be interested in; tell me what you think."
- Finally, I love the phrase *per your request*. It is a powerful statement to give people what they ask for. The most powerful email to send people has *Per your request* in the subject line.

7 SHOW A HIGH PUBLIC OPINION

Public praise awakens curiosity in others and makes people look expectantly to see what your people are doing. Become a spokesperson for your team. Make sure you learn what your people do best and how you have seen them succeed. Give credit for work your people have done and share their successes with others in the company.

Believe in your people. Talk up your people to your boss and to others in the company.

Communicate what they do above and beyond, not that they make it into work most days. The subject should be noteworthy.

Endeavor to make your words consistent. It will not work to go to lunch with a colleague to express doubt or dissatisfaction and then meet with that same individual later to support his or her career aspirations. Your words will catch up with you.

Avoid gossip with others outside your group, where your words about individuals have a chance of getting back to your group. Whoever is listening to you complain can easily imagine you complaining about them to someone else. This is a sure way to destroy the trust and mutual support you have built with your people. On the other hand, people will brighten when they hear your words of praise and support to management and others in the company.

See your words as bouncing around the company.

8 GIVE THEM GRACE

Laura was an engineering manager in our company. On occasion, she would come to my office to confide in me when she received new job opportunities outside the company. She liked to pick my brain on the pros and cons. These were all exercises in exploring the possibilities without ever making the move to leave. She had a strong desire to continue working for her boss, Nathan.

Finally, one day I asked her what Nathan had done to deserve such loyalty from her. She gave it some thought and then she shared a personal and poignant story from several years ago.

Laura had developed a product business plan based on a spreadsheet analysis that she had personally developed. She is a spreadsheet geek; she thinks every business decision deserves a spreadsheet. However, one time she made what she called an "incredibly stupid, embarrassing, boneheaded mistake" in one of the cells. She missed one parenthesis that caused the whole spreadsheet to blow up.

> Demonstrate that you want your employees to succeed.

She felt compelled to go to Nathan and "fess up," showing him how her stupid mistake had cost the company well over $100,000. She was totally humiliated at her mistake and she was ready to accept the consequences.

What happened was Nathan used it as a learning experience for Laura. No one ever heard about this mistake. Nathan never brought it up again, not even in jest. It is as if it never happened.

Nathan found a way to move money around in the budget to cover what he called his "exploratory surgery"—actually he held off hiring for an open position. He and Laura absorbed some extra duty through the end of the year to cover for the open position.

Nathan did tell Laura with a smile, "Why would I let you go after I invested $100,000 in your training?" Nathan knew how to give his employees grace and allow people to learn from their mistakes.

People need to feel reassured that they are on a broad road with some room for learning from mistakes. They have a manager who stands with them and positively supports their occasional miscue.

You should decide how you will respond to mistakes. First, build trust that you are seeking learning, not a personal vendetta. Clearly define the mistake in an open and gracious fashion. Problem solve what happened and what will be done next, like a simple check system.

For closure, communicate how you will deal with Laura's mistake.
- You will not dwell on this issue.
- You will not bring this issue up again or use it against her.
- You will not talk to others to rehash or replay the gaffe.

Look for opportunities to give grace while maintaining accountability. As you allow people to learn from their gaffes, it will feel safe to bring issues to the light of day. People will not worry about making stupid mistakes.

The trick is to know when and where you can give people the opportunity for a second try and where perfection is required. Talk through the difference upfront and share your expectations. For example:

- Missing a couple free throws is part of the game and your player will continue to enjoy your encouragement and support.
- Landing a $20 million fighter plane on a carrier deck does not allow for do-overs.

9 INDIVIDUAL TREATMENT

People will rise to higher levels of participation and commitment when they believe someone recognizes their individual skills and work style. Not all individuals respond in the same way and at the same speed, yet they still get the work done.

Recognize the differences in people and appreciate their personal preferences.

It demonstrates value when people realize that their boss recognizes and respects their individual style. What you give people is patience.

You consider how they uniquely make decisions—some may need patience to gather data and make a careful analysis, while others may thrive on fast pace and shooting from the hip and so do not need that extra time. Some prefer to think aloud, so you give some space to facilitate this, while others may prefer working through things first and then talking after they have had time to think. Some like working independently, while others love group interaction. You can recognize this and show the patience to work with different folks, different strokes.

Get to know how your people like to work and what brings out their best. For example:

"Pranav, I know you like to have some processing time, so how about we meet again after lunch to close on this decision?"

10 ROOM TO GROW

Leave the space for your people to try things, make mistakes and figure things out for themselves.

Jill C. Bradley-Geist and Julie B. Olson-Buchanan are the authors of a journal article entitled "Helicopter Parents: An Examination of the Correlates of Over-Parenting of College Students." Both are management professors at California State University Fresno and they detail how over-parenting can actually ruin a child's abilities to deal with the workplace.

"While parental involvement might be the extra boost that students need to build their own confidence and abilities, over-parenting appears to do the converse in creating a sense that one cannot accomplish things socially or in general on one's own," write the authors.

> Step back and give opportunity for people to do things for themselves.

The authors found that those college students with "helicopter parents" had a hard time believing in their own ability to accomplish goals. They were more dependent on others, had poor coping strategies and didn't have soft skills, like responsibility and conscientiousness.[1]

It is Managing Genius to hold back and let people ask for help. Even then, be slow to charge in to rescue them.

When you give a suggestion, try to sound like you are reminding them of something forgotten, like a casual omission. "You'd probably come up with this yourself but the next time you might want to …"

Cling to the idea that smart, motivated people will eventually find the right solution to any problem, if only they had enough time to think about it.

Not every idea needs to come from you. It is a wonderful feeling to see your people taking the initiative. "I know how you think and what you would want, so I went ahead and made the decision for you."

---

1   Amy Joyce, "How Helicopter Parents Are Ruining College Students," *Washington Post*, September 2, 2014.

Discover Your Managing Genius

- You believe that every individual adds value to the business. In fact, our employees *are* the business and the real reason for our success.

- We may lose competitive edge in technology, services and products. However, our employees will remain as our primary competitive advantage.

- Show respect and value for people independent of their job title or performance.

- There are 10 simple ways (page 210) to Show Value for People. These will build long-lasting commitment beyond today's work.

- People will follow your lead and want to live out the team mission. They will do things not just because they're asked to, but because they want to.

- Consider how this one element serves as the catalyst for everything you do as a Managing Genius.

- Role model this group norm and pump it into the air at work.

The Adult Way

Manage in ways that encourage mature and responsible participation

Big Idea

A Managing Genius leads and builds an adult-minded work culture that is based on maturity and personal responsibility. Adult attitudes and behaviors are the key ingredients that drive every aspect of a high-performing work culture. Fostering the Adult Way is do-it-yourself team building.

My rookie year, I was very immature.

—Dennis Rodman, former NBA basketball player

I know that in my past I was young and irresponsible—but that's what growing up is. You learn from your mistakes.

—Lindsay Lohan

Kill my boss? Do I dare live out the American dream?

—Homer Simpson

Life's a lot more fun when you're not responsible for your actions. Why should I have to work for everything? It's like saying I don't deserve it!

—Six-year-old Calvin in the *Calvin &Hobbes cartoon*, Bill Watterson

The thing is, Bob, it's not that I'm lazy, it's that I just don't care.

—Peter Gibbons in the movie *Office Space*

I realized that I'm searching for what I really want in life. And you know what? I have absolutely no idea what that is."

—Barney in the TV series *How I Met Your Mother*

💡 Important to Know

As I work on this chapter, I sit on an airplane next to a Senior Manager for Cisco who is in his twenties and exhibits amazing maturity and wisdom beyond his years. Then I read that Donald Trump is again considering a run for President. Let me set the stage that *The Adult Way* is all about maturity, not age.

Managers can get caught up in a rolling sea of employee drama. Without an ability to take the lead in this area, you may experience a challenging voyage filled with the ups and downs of individual issues and feelings of entitlement.

Drivers of an Adult-Minded Culture

1 Understand childish ways

2 See work through adult eyes

3 Avoid "parenting mode"

In my experience, a Managing Genius has a knack for creating an even-keeled sailing ship with a surprising absence of employee drama. I can attest to this, as HR is in a unique position to see behind the scenes.

So what is the secret? In this chapter I have sought to answer the question: "Why do great managers have far less employee drama and team dysfunction? Why are their teams more cohesive and cooperative? "

There is something intrinsic within the team culture of any Managing Genius—his or her people are responsible, respectful, reliable and resilient.

When I look at all those people descriptors, a simple truth emerges: the secret ingredient behind a high-performance team culture is adult attitudes and behavior.

Consider that there are often outward indicators of an internal condition. This is like saying that you often see graffiti in higher crime areas of a city. Said the opposite way, you would be surprised to see graffiti in a safe, well-managed neighborhood. The graffiti is an outward sign of a higher crime area. The lack of employee drama and an entitlement attitude are an outward signs of a well-managed team.

Conclusion: adult behavior drives every aspect of work culture. So from my study, I have coined this phrase: The Adult Way.

I suppose that we need a cool-sounding, lofty name like *adultus interruptus*, so the leadership gurus can write a book or create a special program. However, I want to get you thinking "simple." We often search for a magic key for effective team culture. We look for special programs with special names that need third-party experts.

The Adult Way is an important element that works with the rest of Managing Genius to create a stronger team culture. You can own this yourself. This is within your power and ability to manage. There is no need for special programs or outside help.

First, I need to get you thinking in new ways. Then I will give you some ideas of how you can create an adult-minded team culture. Start here: three items lay the foundation for fostering an Adult Way-oriented culture.

1 UNDERSTAND CHILDISH WAYS

1 Corinthians 13:11 says, "It's like this: when I was a child I spoke and thought and reasoned as a child does. But when I became an adult my thoughts grew far beyond those of my childhood and now I have put away the childish things."

We know from experience that attaining a certain age certainly doesn't mean childish ways are completely abandoned. As you read this chapter, consider that a few weeds can spoil the whole garden.

In My Annoying Boss (page 225), you see snippets overheard at a local Starbucks. When you listen to conversations like this, it is important to keep in mind that *this person is someone's employee.*

However, her boss may not see these emotions displayed so transparently on the job. These attitudes and feelings often play in the background until they surface as emotional responses to stress and conflict.

Some employees may fall back to a default response when they are having difficulties working with their manager. It's basically a variation of youthful patterns of how we learned to respond to authority, conflict or the hassles with getting along with coworkers.

We also learned along the way what works for us to get our way or get someone's ear. These responses can become deep-seated and involuntary, just waiting to get expressed to your coworkers and boss.

My Annoying Boss ...

She is such a micro-manager. She nags me to be at my cube by 8:00 a.m. She has no idea how tough my commute is. I can barely get dressed and do my makeup to make the first bus. I always text her when I am on the second bus, but that is not good enough for her.

She is always on me for something. You should hear how people talk about her. I try to avoid her when I see her.

Last week was the last straw. She passed me by for a promotion. What is she thinking? I have a college degree. I have worked here almost three years.

I have a mind to go to HR and tell them what's going on.

Hey, we need to go; I'm late for her meeting. But first let me buy her a scone. That will keep her wondering.

This story illustrates some of the common, childish tactics that I have observed throughout my HR career. It is important to understand these behaviors, so you can recognize them and deal with them in real time:

- **Dismiss authority.** What right does my manager have to say that to me since she has defects and flawed thinking? It proves I can ignore her and challenge her authority.

- **You are not worthy of my respect.** Dismissive behavior can move into contempt of you personally. This elevates the complainer to a superior position, "I am better than you, I know more."

- **Triangulate.** Most of the time your employees will not challenge you to an arm-wrestling match where they have to look into your eyes. Instead, they will play out their disappointment and frustrations with a third party to see if they can get this other person to fight their battles for them or at least validate their feelings. "I have a mind to go to HR and tell them what is going on."

- **Physical Avoidance.** People learn to agree with you to get you off their back, even when they have no intention of following through. It is much easier to give meaningless head nodding or use questions to deflect the conversation. Later, they do everything possible to stay out of sight and out of mind: "I avoid her when I see her coming."

- **Excuses galore.** Your frustrating employee was once a teenager who was not at fault for her math grade because the teacher lost her homework. When she was in college, she often ended up asking around the dorm to find someone who took notes for the class she missed. Today she is saying to you, "Oh, I thought you meant *next* Tuesday, not this Tuesday." "That's not my job."

- **Living in the moment.** There are two kinds of people in this world: future-thinking and present-minded people. A present-minded person becomes consumed with the immediate pay-off. The future-thinking person is able to delay gratification to focus on a better outcome somewhere down the road.

- **Whining.** "It is all about me and what I need." So the way to get you to focus on the person is to get emotional—even cry—so the world can "stop and acknowledge me." We operate in different ways and respond to stress in different ways. Some are blamers, complainers or whiners.

- **Entitlement.** This is the most common form of employee response you will face. This is where people believe that they deserve something. They say,"You owe me" and so your management prerogative slips. You become an administrative manager who balances pressing business issues with past-given entitlements.

> **The Entitlement Continuum**
> - You give something
> - Employees respond with gratitude
> - Next time, did you forget? We were expecting it
> - So you give it again. This comes across as nothing special, just obligation
> - HR creates a policy or program
> - What else will you give me?

This is the *raison d'être* for HR departments where they see their role as oversight to maintain equity and fairness. While consistency and shared experiences should be defining hallmarks of a work environment, you must be careful not create a culture of personal entitlement.

A story: One year on the Friday before Memorial Day, our CEO sent out an unexpected email around noon giving everyone the rest of the day off with warm wishes for a safe and wonderful holiday weekend. People were happy as they packed up early to go home.

Then, as the next holiday approached, some employees started coming by or emailing me to ask, "Are we getting a half day off this Friday?" As they waited, the mood became sour and emails started flying. "What is wrong with management? Last time we got a half day off before the holiday. I was planning on this time off."

Eventually, the situation became a source of disappointment for some (though, interestingly, not all) of the employees.

2 SEE WORK THROUGH ADULT EYES

I was at a light manufacturing unit and I noticed a handwritten note by the time clock. It must have been written by a crew team leader:

"This is a business! Find some work to do!"

I was impressed with this crew team leader's attempt to set an adult bar about how people think and act about the work. This is a real business. We serve customers and people are counting on us. We are here for a reason. We must all participate and take responsibility.

There seems to be ambivalence in today's culture concerning what it means to reach adulthood, where we embrace personal responsibility.

We postpone or avoid real careers that demand sacrifice, hard work and starting at the bottom. It's easier if we just live with our parents, postponing commitments and live our lives Online. It is noteworthy that over one-third of the millennial generation is still living in their parents' home.[1]

---

1 Richard Fry, "In Post-Recession Era, Young Adults Drive Continuing Rise in Multi-Generational Living," Pew Research Center, July 17, 2014.

So there is a good chance our Starbucks complainer may still be living at home and still blaming her parents for her frustrations. In college, she only had to worry about grades and social approval. Up until this point, her authority figures never bailed on her no matter how she treated them. She cannot get kicked out, just coddled.

Now she wants her boss to respect her, give her autonomy and let her be involved with weighty decisions because, in fact, she did get a business degree from Pepperdine University.

No one has prepared her for the adult business world where the stakes are suddenly higher. She may not realize this but her "stupid" boss represents the company and carries her salary in her budget.

Millennials sometimes do not look at authority and companies through adult eyes or with a lens of reality. They can blame the boss or company for how they feel. They feel like a victim. They think real life is depicted in TV shows like *The Mindy Project* or *How I Met My Mother*.

> Early professionals may prefer to be judged by promise and potential, instead of by accomplishment.

In my early career, I worked for Doug, a tough-minded boss whom I did not know at the time was a Managing Genius. Many days I went home feeling discouraged over another round of tough-love feedback. Of course, I was learning a hundred lessons along the way. Wisdom does not always come to us in the present moment.

One time I explained something I had done and Doug broke in to ask a "tough-love" question, "Will there ever be a time when you stop defending yourself?" When I shared my feelings over some disappointment, Doug responded, "Why does everything have to be about you?" During a pay discussion, Doug jabbed me with, "Why do you feel so entitled?"

I came to realize that Doug would not be asking me those things if he did not see potential in me. That was what he was doing to get me ready to accept greater responsibility—to grow up. It was a gift that only an adult-minded person could give me. If I could only embrace it.

3 AVOID "PARENTING MODE"

Esther is the CEO of a financial services company. We are sitting in her executive boardroom talking about her management philosophy. She begins to teach me what is most important to her.

She proceeds to share her wisdom, "I believe that leaders nurture the people who work for them. I want to take the time to understand and support my employees' aspirations. I want to see people thrive and succeed and I do that through affirmation and encouragement."

"You assume a huge responsibility when you decide to become a people manager. You need to look after them and keep them on the right road. You need to defend them and create a space around them where they can grow and mature."

"I feel a huge satisfaction in seeing my employees get established and advance in their careers."

Esther pauses, looking at me expectantly to hear my thoughts.

I reply that there is nothing wrong with her leadership approach. However, she can't call this managing people. It sounds to me that Esther is actually "parenting" her employees.

What is parenting mode?

Understand that a common *default* managing style is to parent people. Why not? We all had parents and many of us are parents. It is tough to switch gears as we move between home and work.

Parenting
- Look after
- Defend
- Care for
- Nurture
- Protect

You get one of your kids out to the school bus and drive one to preschool, all the while instructing, guiding, cajoling, refereeing and micromanaging the household. You are managing a ton of details like food, laundry and schedules for everyone.

Then you come to work and try to switch gears, leading your 32 employees. It is easy to unknowingly slip into parenting mode.

We all bring baggage from family upbringing and our community. This influences how employees may respond to authority, deal with conflict or express themselves to get what they want.

Some households learn to express themselves by raising their voices with emotion and enthusiasm. To others, this may seem forceful and argumentative. Others are more reserved or formal in their communications, which to some comes across as passive.

Some cultures are patriarchal or matriarchal, while some people grow up in broken homes with different parents coming in and out. Some have a Tiger Mom, while others have parents who let the children fend for themselves.

Your employees also bring baggage from their previous bosses and work experiences. Working for that demanding, manipulative manager has made some distrustful of strong authority figures. As a result, they may hide information and act defensive to feedback.

Unfortunately, these emotions and negative behaviors usually surface unexpectedly—often when your people are facing stress or conflict. Don't you wish that employee "special care instructions" were written out in detail, like the special care instructions on your sweater?

EMPLOYEE CARE INSTRUCTIONS
- MAY BRING BAGGAGE
- MAY RESIST AUTHORITY
- AVOIDS CONFLICT
- NEEDS THE LAST WORD

It is just as important to reflect upon your own background. You may have a propensity to be a "hands-off" manager because your parent was absent. You may be a nurturing manager, reflecting the warmth of a caring caregiver. You may think you are decisive about your managing approach but in fact you are actually just following a well-established script from family and previous jobs.

It is important to establish the working relationship that you want with your employees. Do you want them to be fans, friends, followers or family? Will you manage them with professionalism and objectivity?

It is never all or none. You can treat people differently based on the needs of the moment. Empathy is a great thing but too much can easily turn into sympathy as you get enmeshed in the personal details. It can turn us into an "over-nurturing" caregiver without realizing it.

Signs that you are parenting versus managing

Left unchecked, a parenting style can "dumb down" your group to the lowest common denominator. You can find yourself catering to the "neediest" individuals in the group. You may have the best of intentions but it stirs up entitlement, game-playing and drama—not a good combination for an effective adult work culture.

Moreover, you will find it difficult to make objective decisions and exercise judgment over your individual employees.

> Some people have a need to feel special and seek attention.

Important to note that this may not be your everyday practice. We all have *default managing styles* that can spring up under stress or pressure. In turn, your employees have their own learned behaviors that can spring up unexpectedly.

Here is a fly-over of parenting mode:

You feel responsible for their careers. Remember, it's not about what *you want* for people, it is what *they want*. Have they voiced their desires and goals to you? Let people take responsibility for their own careers. This not to say that you don't help your employees reach their goals but they (not you) have to create their own career aspirations and decide where they want to go.

You have to maintain a happy family. I hear CEOs using this phrase to convey the congeniality and mutual commitment in their work force. They say with pride, "We have a family work culture."

The word "family" means many different things to different people. Most families are dysfunctional in some way and family members often make accommodations. Most of the time it somehow works out.

Remember that parenting is unconditional. Managing people in the workplace is conditional. Be careful not to mix up the two scenarios. Parents are required to parent their children, whereas the business world is based on "if"—If you come to work every day and if you perform in an acceptable manner, you will get to keep your job.

You nurture people. Top of your to-do list today: "Fix Jeremy." Have you ever worked hard to bring back a meandering employee? Did you believe with all your heart that you could turn around that wayward employee?

Jim is timid, so you praise him whenever he exhibits courage. You nudge him to take more speaking opportunities.

You think Susan has a tendency to be moody, so you encourage her daily. Every few months you give her a book that you think she will like. Did they ask for help?

We all get the opportunity to manage "special people" who constantly demonstrate childish ways. In fact, there are people for whom nothing in this world will ever be right. But there you are, thinking, "I will change this person."

> Empathy can turn people into "projects" where you feel compelled to "fix them."

We assume that people want to be like us and will, of course, choose to demonstrate the like-minded character traits that we value. "Do you understand how much knowledge and experience I have to share with you?"

Empathy can turn people into projects.

Jeff is a young man in his twenties who needs to pull it together. Celia thinks, Jeff is really a good guy at heart—just a little misunderstood. She decides to take him to lunch soon. She knows she can turn him around and groom him for better things in the future.

You talk down to them. We drop the kids at school and sometimes we forget to switch modes with our employees.

I was observing a customer service director as she talked with her work group about a list of details. I noticed that she ended every sentence with, "OK?"

"We need to hand in our time sheets no later than Friday COB, *OK*?"

"C'mon, this month I need your sales reports on time, *OK*?"

"Next week's meeting will be at 10:00 a.m., *OK*?"

She went on to oversell anything she needed with hyperbole. "If we don't turn this around we could lose our jobs!"

Then she used a *special voice* when trying to share directions or expectations with her people, "I mean it this time, guys. You need to get your budgets in on time."

You bail them out. Jack needs your quick help. It's 5:45 p.m., and you're gathering your stuff to go home. Jack calls with an urgent request: can you lend him a hand on a spreadsheet that is due in the morning?

How many times do you or others on your team get asked to bail out someone because he or she has failed to think ahead? I call this "rescue."

> We have Bruce Wayne syndrome. We feel the need to put on a cape and help people out.

Don't confuse this with supporting a teammate when something unusual or unexpected comes along. Adult-minded employees mutually support one another.

A rescue employee seems to asks for help continuously from you and teammates. This may get voiced by sharing frustration or helplessness over an obstacle or roadblock .

The important question: Do you like bailing out your employees? Does it make you feel needed? Your rescues may be perpetuating the negative habit. Adults are able to "do for themselves."

Surveillance mode. Observe this at your next multifamily picnic. Some parents are oblivious to where their kids are in the park; others watch their kids' every move like hawks. Still others have a sixth sense of where the kids are—the intuition of knowing without watching.

However, we need to switch gears when we come to work to get ourself out of surveillance mode. You can do this only if you are able to withstand emotional distance and give people trust and the space to make mistakes. Adults will want elbow room—some more than others—and will not want to be watched or followed.

You try to understand your people. A common theme in the best-selling leadership books is that a good leader is adept at reading and understanding how their employees are feeling. You can read their demeanor and actions, so you know how you can provide the best support.

How about the flip? Adults keep the people in their lives informed on their emotional and physical location. People do not have an inalienable right to keep their manager in the dark. Adults do not keep you guessing.

This Is Managing Genius

Everyone searches for the magic key for creating a team culture with high morale and shared participation. Actually it is quite simple: adult behavior is the one ingredient that drives every aspect of the team culture.

The Adult Way

1 Understanding
   Adult Participation

2 It starts with you

3 Cultivate an
   adult-minded culture

4 Get people in the game

5 Fool-proof your team

In this section I have provided a simple, boiled down summary of the basics of adult behavior.

Your leadership will prevent a few individuals from pulling the group off-track. The Adult Way is the foundation for a fully-functioning team culture.

This is do-it-yourself team building that is within your power and ability. There is no need for special help, approval or fanfare. In time, your best employees will drive this with healthy peer pressure.

Sounds simple, but this is a game-changing paradigm shift.

1 UNDERSTANDING ADULT PARTICIPATION

This first section defines and describes the seven elements of adult participation. The Quick Guide (see page 239) is a one-page summary of attributes that should define team members. This is what adult-minded people look like. This is the basis for how you connect with your employees. Take the lead to infuse this in meetings with your boss and colleagues.

As you develop a strategy to implement The Adult Way, make it fun and light-hearted. Teach the principles and talk it through as a group, allowing friendly banter. Share your own embarrassing moments, "I realize now that I responded to that crisis in an immature way. Next time I want you to call me on this."

Let your team share their frustrations with immature acting people with you—if not you, they will talk to someone. Make sure the sharing is not gossip. Do not use names to point out undesired behaviors.

1. Responsibility

In the popular young adult book *The Hunger Games,* we meet Katniss Everdeen, who as a young girl sneaks outside the fence to hunt in order to feed her family. When Katniss's sister Prim is chosen for the fight-to-the-death contest, Katniss volunteers in her place. Katniss is taking responsibility for her family and she faces real consequences.

The superhero Spider-Man, created by Stan Lee, learns this lesson from his uncle: "With great power comes great responsibility." Peter Parker, Spider-Man's alter ego, shares, "You say you don't want the responsibility? Guess what? People like us ... we don't get a choice."

Responsibility is more than just an interesting idea or job task. It means we take personal ownership for the outcome and have skin in the game. If we share responsibility with others, we commit to getting along with them and finding positive ways to work together.

People who fully experience the realities of why we are here and what is important will care more about the outcome. If they share in the consequences, they will feel commitment and ownership.

2. Respect

Ordinarily, you will not see people show disrespect openly where you can readily deal with the criticism. It will most often come in the form of persistent whining behind the scenes or to a third party, such as HR.

Today email, texting and social media are amazing tools for increased productivity. Unfortunately, they are also remarkably efficient for spreading disrespect and a greater level of "uncontrolled" free speech. Employees can easily circumvent their bosses and make their opinions into trending tropics.

In one marketing company, an employee posted disparaging comments about the senior managers in his company. Most people reading this would wonder why he is posting his opinions Online. It is important to remember how easy it is to spread "non-thinking" disrespect and at amazing speeds.

Adults maintain a healthy respect for the business, the team and the leadership. They would never disparage colleagues.

3. Reliability

Reliability speaks to follow-through. Managers have good reason to rely on their employees because they carry their weight, contribute to the team and their word can be trusted.

In the movie *Cold Mountain,* Nicole Kidman plays the character Ada Monroe, who has been raised in a genteel household where she was pampered. Her character at the start of the movie almost seems like a fragile, porcelain doll. However, through the hardship of the Civil War, she acquires the skill and experience needed to become a reliable contributor to the farm. In one telling moment, Ada says, "This thing is about the first thing I've ever done that might produce an actual result."

We need to reach a transformation in our career where people can count on us for an actual result. Adult-minded people keep their promises.

4. Resilience

Resilience is the capacity to overcome adversity and withstand stress and snafus. When you have resilience, you are optimistic in your ability to solve problems because you have a history of getting things done.

In the movie *True Grit,* the character Mattie Ross is a fourteen-year-old girl who leaves home and goes off in the middle of winter to find her father's killer. The story is about people with resilience, thus the title—they have the grit needed to finish.

Another story of reliance is the story of Louis Zamperini, who competed in the Berlin Olympics in 1936. When World War II began, Louis was an airman whose Army Air Force bomber crashed into the Pacific Ocean. After a record-breaking forty-seven days adrift on a shark-encircled life raft, he was captured by the Japanese. His story of the POW experience shows his endurance and unbreakable spirit.

The opposite of resilience is to act helpless and come across as a victim. Watch how different people respond to natural disasters such as a hurricane or flood. Some communities demonstrate a resilient nature, where people step up and get things done for themselves, their families and their community. There are others who passively wait for the government to rescue them.

5. Self-control

We often give youth a voice when what they really need is to learn to restrain themselves and participate fully in the present moment. To successfully work together, people need to learn mature restraint. Social graces and manners are founded in self-control. Self-control is closely tied to respect.

In every group meeting, you can spot the people who lack self-control. It is the guy who loses concentration and begins to joke around when you want everyone to stay focused. It is the woman who looks distracted and starts talking with people around her. Someone else is playing with his phone...."Sorry, this is an important text."

Another form of self-control is what Professor John Medina of the University of Washington calls "self-calming." That means adults need to have the ability to settle themselves down when facing problems. He believes that this trait starts in early childhood when children eventually need to find ways to calm themselves.[2]

Unfortunately, parents often feel they are responsible for calming their children down. So later in life, do children's managers need to take over this responsibility? This does not sound like a Managing Genius to me.

Adult employees cannot act as fully functioning team members unless they can show the self-control to decide how, when and to whom to express their emotions.

6. Giver versus taker

Every profession has its own particular jargon. In the circus, *cherry pie* is the slang for the extra work—outside their normal job—that circus people do to help the show.

Thus, at the circus you might have heard, "Cherry pie on the big top canvas." Everyone would understand this as a general call for all available hands to help load the tent canvas.

---

2 Dr. John J. Medina is a developmental molecular biologist and a professor of bioengineering at the University of Washington School of Medicine.

Are your employees willing to pitch in according to the needs of the moment? Can they balance their own individual desires with the needs of the circus?

Adult-minded employees are very aware of others' needs and have an ability to give help and support. Left to their own way, people may only volunteer with a "what's in it for me" attitude—where they get personal recognition, visibility with top management or the chance to pad their resumes.

If you leave "cherry pie" out of your managing equation, you will manage a group of individuals who may begin to focus on entitlement, pecking order, seniority and status. Selfish people often display these behaviors:

- Most discussions come back to their personal status or desires.
- They are concerned with their personal gain regardless of another's expense.
- Have an exaggerated view of themselves and their jobs.
- They act superior by comparing and dwelling on the deficiencies of others.

7. Open Sharing

A huge contributing factor to team dysfunction is a lack of complete communication. For a variety of reasons, people may choose to share partial stories and withhold necessary critical information. When that happens we are left wondering, trying to piece together clues to figure out what is going on.

Adults need to keep the people in their lives informed about their emotional and physical location. Adults do not keep you guessing. Adults will keep you informed on what is important for team business.

To avoid getting caught, kids will bend the truth and duck to hide. Adults can stand up to observation and believe in full disclosure. They deal with reality, facts and truth—even if it may not be personally beneficial.

Adults speak "grown-up." Direct communication is required with no third party triangles or side angles. There are no private conversations with favorite folks.

Attributes of Adult-Minded People

1. Responsibility Take personal ownership.
Willing to "do for themselves."

2. Respect To you, team members, authority,
company assets, rules and policy.

3. Reliability Trust that is earned through sustained
follow through and promises kept.

4. Resilience Staying power and endurance.
Appropriate seriousness and presence.

5. Self-control Ability to calm down and focus on
a task. Self-discipline to persist.

6. Giver vs taker Show empathy for others. Give help
where needed without being asked.

7. Open Sharing Stays in the light. Speaks directly
without guile. Open to feedback.

2 IT STARTS WITH YOU

From my experience working with great managers, I have found that they are always flying above the everyday office politics, gossip and drama. Here is how they do it:

A Managing Genius does not respond to every person who pulls on his or her chain. It is interesting that we read in the written accounts of Jesus Christ, that he often frustrated the religious leaders of that day. One way was by choosing not to respond to their questions that were seemingly asked to corner him.

Jesus did not ignore them as much as he was staying on message by redirecting them. He focused the discussion back to the heart of the matter, rather than addressing every side issue that got tossed his way.

My favorite quote from Jesus, as he speaks to a group of naysayers,

"Here is how I describe these people. They say,
'We played the flute for you and you did not dance.'"

This is important—imagine people playing a flute and expecting you to dance to their questions or special requests. Managers who aren't clear on where they are going can easily get sidetracked by anyone who plays their flute. Ignore the impulse to dance to their immediate desires.

The quotation also shows that the local religious leaders wanted Jesus to be something he was not and make him do what he was not intending to do. If he gave in to their whims, he would never satisfy them no matter what he did or said.

This is how managers become reactionary and defensive, eventually losing confidence and respect.

Be aware of how you *respond* when people "play their flute." You need to break the conversation loop and remind people "why we are here."

Sometimes the best method is to do what Jesus did—just ignore the question and proceed on with your original agenda. This sends a strong message, without words, to everyone within earshot. The point is, the message you deem is important is being discussed.

A Managing Genius is a "self-controlled" leader. I observed one group director who seemed to leave his employees in a cloud of turmoil and anxiety as he pushed through his undulating agenda. I would describe him as a man of "abrupt transitions."

His people became worn out and fatigued after spending time with him. This managing style stirred up negative emotional responses. Understand the difference between a sense of urgency and a rushed, furtive style that gets people jumping from one topic to another in an unplanned manner.

People will respond to the tension in the room. A fire-fighting mode wears people out. They will move away from ambiguity and uncertainty.

It is a universal character trait in Managing Genius to be able to rise above the chaos, establish calm and refocus the team.

Keep your "game face" on. Reset the conversation back to the original reason we are here. This only works when you step up and take control.

A Managing Genius stays above the colloquial drama. You cannot stop people from sharing gossip or playing out the latest office drama. In fact, if you stop to lecture or chide people, you may come across as the nagging parent.

But you can control you.

Do you try to act like you are "one of the gang"? Do you participate in laughter at someone else's expense? Do you share gossip and teasing banter? Attention becomes a powerful elixir for managers to dispense.

Someone comes by your office to share the newest story and, of course, they ask if they can shut the door. Do not get sucked into third-party gossip or the latest trending topics. (Keep the door open.)

You have the power to redirect the conversation, or you could choose to just ignore and not take the bait. You will be amazed to see how your actions will serve to quench the workplace drama.

Bottom line, you should never participate.

3 CULTIVATE AN ADULT-MINDED CULTURE

In my first job out of college, I worked as an engineer at an open-pit mining operation in the Upper Peninsula of Michigan. An everyday complaint, even within the management ranks, was when we were forced to wait for the long and winding railroad train. The train shipped final iron pellets to the Lake Superior docks and then on to east coast steel mills.

Specifically, we would bitch when it happened to block the road at a shift change. Just when we wanted to go home, we'd be stuck counting the rail cars.

One day, my boss overheard me whining about the train. I remember his words very clearly: "When I have to wait for the train, I see my paycheck in those loaded rail cars."

This was an adult response and truthfully I feel chagrined at my attitude even now.

In looking back on my work experiences, here are some ways that I have observed Managing Geniuses cultivate an adult-minded team culture:

You set the tone

How do you talk about the company? Your boss? Senior management? Do you carry around a sense of entitlement? Are you a whiner?

Your employees will follow your positive words and attitudes or will be happy to take your lead and complain with you as well.

Do not let your work world squeeze you into it's mold.

Teach and discuss a healthy, adult-minded respect for the business, management, products and services and customers. The trains block the main road because they deliver products to our customers. When our network is slow, it means we have more customers Online ordering our products.

"We are working late to make these extra shipments because sales have peaked—that is job security."

"We're doubling up in office cubes because our growth is outstripping space. This will create more opportunities for everyone.

Sometimes it also works to just not say anything.

In the old days of the police band radio, swearing was not permitted, so dispatchers would say, "Go to this address to deal with an "Adam Henry" (note the initials). If the CEO is an Adam Henry, it is not your problem. One way to deflect the negative words is to say, "I cannot change the CEO but I can change me. What could I do to be a better leader?"

Maintain "adult conversations" with people

We need to avoid sounding parental, chiding people or chewing them out. It can come across that we are talking down to people in condescending ways. If we do this we might unknowingly create a non-adult response from our employee.

Note that when my boss corrected me about the mining train, he shared it from the perspective of "here is how I think," not telling me how I should think.

Yet, here I am writing about the story—*it is still a vivid memory.*

Manage the drama

When pressured, people sometimes tend to revert to the immature ways learned in their upbringing and past jobs.

You are the chief spokesperson for what is happening on your team. Speak up when you see non—Adult Way behaviors being exhibited.

Remember that your "non-managing" speaks loudly. In these moments of stress, remember that nobody knows your team better than you do. You can manage the drama. Give a simple reminder or a lighthearted word of encouragement. You might simply point people back to the matter at hand. Remind them *why we are here.* You can also show an adult-minded example to help people reset. Show your team how to work through stress or disruptive drama.

Coaches call a time-out when the momentum of the game shifts dramatically. When team drama rises above the level of distraction, regroup your team to reset the agenda.

Bring discussion and drama to the group level

You can make great strides toward creating an adult culture by using the power of the group meeting. Bring immature behavior into the "light of day" in a gracious but clear way. This will use peer pressure to form joint expectations and reach shared perspective on the issue.

Individuals will forego immature ways when surrounded by adult-minded peers.

When someone has strong feelings about something, chances are others feel the same way. So it's best to talk about it as a group. Whiners prefer to make their case privately in the judge's chambers. Who wants to make their case in the open courtroom to the full jury?

Guide your team through times of stress

In the *Wizard of Oz*, we see a small team of unique individuals who work together to reach their goal. They are quite plucky as they press ahead but they do face the occasional stress of the unknown. For example, they get a bit frightened right before they meet the cowardly lion:

"I don't like this forest! It's dark and creepy!"
"Of course, I don't know, but I think it'll get darker before it gets lighter."
"Do you suppose we'll meet any wild animals?"
"We might."
"Animals that eat straw?"
"Some, but mostly lions and tigers and bears."
"Lions! And tigers! And bears!"
"Lions and tigers and bears! Oh, my!"

The important point is that some issues can loom large when individuals collectively weigh in to add their fears to the conversation.

You should step in as soon as possible to defuse the unfounded fears. You do this by bringing special issues and problems to group meetings to take away the mystery and suspense. Turn issues into manageable action items and get your team moving forward down the yellow brick road.

You can be the voice of reason. We must all take responsibility and recognize that our jobs come with stress and tension. Every job has its ups and downs, mundane parts and difficult people. Jobs, pay and status may not get better.

Be aware that stress and obstacles can unnerve your people and bring out a rash of childish behaviors. Stay aware of what can interfere with your team's ability to do its job. Watch for annoyances or distractions that cause people to slow down, mentally check out or worry.

You are not there to hold their hands. Just call a time-out and redirect people toward what they have been trained to do.

Give attention to adult participators

It can feel like we are managing within the *Seinfeld TV series* where the characters were driven largely by self-interest. We keep watching *Seinfeld* and begin to think it is normal for adults to think that way.

Make sure that the Adult Way shines brighter.

Do not reward "*Seinfeld* characters" with unwarranted time and attention. Instead, show value for individuals who have an adult-minded attitude and show a willingness to do whatever it takes for the good of the team and customers. Praise people who put others first without being asked and do the right things without being watched.

Do not jump in to save people or pamper them

Advice columnist Ann Landers wrote, "It is not what you do for your children, but what you have taught them to do for themselves that will make them successful human beings."

During one college summer, I worked on the grounds crew at the Wisconsin State Fair. One day, in the middle of the shift, it started pouring rain. I remember looking at my boss, expecting him to stop the work and take us inside.

My boss took a box of garbage bags and showed us how to punch out holes for our arms and heads to make makeshift raincoats. Our boss worked with us in the rain until the job was finished, at which point we were thoroughly wet and cold—and I lived to share this story.

Children have a difficult time seeing how extra effort and working through an uncomfortable environment translates into customer satisfaction. We may treat employees like porcelain dolls on a shelf. When that's the case, people do not get the experience of working through to the finish, even if it means finishing in the rain.

Work is what it is. The writers and pundits tell us that routine and repetition is bad for the human spirit. We worry that people will get bored and expect things to change for the better. But everyone's job has boring, unpleasant parts that they have to power through.

Let people to work through the difficult parts of their jobs:

- **Do not be too quick to rescue.** The key concept to learn is the difference between "it's hard to do" and "I can't do it."
- **Let them make mistakes.** Experience is the teacher we feel most comfortable with—that's how you've learned things in your own career.
- **Let them face reality.** Don't sugarcoat things. If your employee drops the ball and disappointed a key customer, let him personally make the phone call to discuss the mistake.
- **Let people work through things.** People need to learn how to effectively deal with setbacks and hurts. Provide a supportive work environment where everyone can find the space to learn from their mistakes.
- **Things may not get better.** This is sometimes the reality in the workplace. Some things are just not under your control.

It is a specious logic in American business that things must change for the better—if employees work hard and put in their time, they will reap the good life and have it easier. We expect that pay will keep increasing and benefits will get better. In reality, jobs and work status may not improve.

Adults need to live with unresolved issues, unanswered questions and partial information.

4 GET PEOPLE IN THE GAME

Every *individual need* does not upend the organization and team. A Managing Genius knows that there are many factors in play at any one time. They can *balance* the needs of the customer, organization, team with the needs of the individual.

Keep moving forward

At a paper-making facility in Oregon, we experienced frequent petty team issues and grievances that pulled in the shift supervisor. One group that was a "frequent flier" for grievances was the dry end crews where the final paper was rolling on huge rolls that shipped to customers.

What was happening was at the dry end of the machine the paper had to be restarted and rewound every twenty or thirty minutes. This left the a crew at the dry end with lots of idle time. You get the picture.

> **Manage your team to balance four needs**
> - Customer
> - Organization
> - Team
> - Individual

You will experience less employee drama when you keep your team moving forward. Your active leadership keeps people focused on what is important.

Idle time is a great opportunity to take your eye off the ball and start thinking about things that are not related to doing the very best job possible today. It gives people the opportunity to take inventory and find things that are wrong.

Give responsibility, not parenting

You establish an adult-minded work culture by the way you deal with problems. If you let people plop problems onto your desk, you may end up owning the problems and holding people's hands to get their work done.

Raji comes into his manager's office three weeks before the software project is due and asks for help. Raji was given this project six months ago and this is the first he's said anything. By dropping this on you, he could be subtly involving you with the problem to try to get himself off the hook.

Karen is asking for your help with a complicated spreadsheet that she has been using to project plant inventory. Today, she found an error in one of the cells and needs your help to make sure the spreadsheet is right. So, has inventory been wrong for three months?

Look for the right messages: "I made a mistake," "I was wrong" or "I have to solve this and need your help."

Managing Genius is 100% pure adult participation

You do not eradicate childish behavior in your group through proclamation or programs. You make this happen by showing people a manager who knows where the group is going. You are fully engaged and create momentum and action. You give people a work system that keeps the team moving forward.

Master the art of managing people and you will keep people mentally "in the game." Every chapter of this book will promote adult thinking and responsible behavior.

5 FOOL-PROOF YOUR TEAM

The Wisdom of Bart Simpson ...
Bart: *I am through with working. Working is for chumps.*
Homer: *Son, I'm proud of you! I was twice your age*
when I figured that out.

Any group can have that "special employee." This one person annoys virtually everyone and sucks the oxygen out of the room.

We will always have challenging work relationships that take extra effort. We will not "click" with everyone. *Then there are fools.*

Proverbs 13:20 says, "He who spends time with wise people will become wise, but the companion of fools will suffer harm."

Fools are special people who require special handling. They were the class clown, college party animal and now the center of attention on your team.

So you come to my office once again to share your exasperation. "This person is truly an flaming idiot." I ask, "Why is he still here?"

It surprises me when a manager lets a fool hang around. Why do we continue to manage around Homer Simpson?

Here is a strategy for "fool-proofing" your team.

1. **Identify them.** *Say their name.* When you ignore the "elephant in the room," you leave the issue twisting in the wind. It is a major step to simply identify fools. "You are wearing me out Jeremy. We do not need a class clown on the team."

2. **Do not participate.** We become mildly amused and ask for more details. We laugh at their jokes and get sucked into asking for more details about the latest gossip. Never do this. Take the high road and learn the art of ignoring. Remember, *it takes two to dance.*

3. **Let peer pressure work.** Fools like to operate on the fringes. They walk the halls to find people with time on their hands. They use email to keep people entertained. Bring fools into the center of the team—people will think twice about their immature behavior when surrounded by adult-minded peers.

4. **Step up to make tough decisions.** In my HR experience, it seems that people managers are more likely to deal with objective, poor job performance rather than subjective, foolish behavior that has a clear negative impact on the team. Managers need to see that keeping a single foolish person around can have a greater

> You need to let your special employee go work for your competitor where they can serve as their special employee.

negative effect than several individuals with poor job performance. You need to be ready to make tough decisions to deal with fools on your team. "Derek, your behavior continues to have a negative impact on the team..."

Discover Your Managing Genius

- Adult behavior is the one key ingredient that drives every aspect of work culture.

- Employees bring established behaviors from their upbringing or work history. This affects how they respond to authority, deal with conflict or express themselves to get what they want.

- Managers sometimes default to "parenting" their employees. A parenting style will encourage entitlement, emotion or game-playing. This can give a few people undo influence and dumb down your group to the lowest denominator.

- A Managing Genius leads and builds an adult-minded work culture that is based on maturity and personal responsibility.

- Fostering The Adult Way is "do-it-yourself team building." This is a game-changing paradigm shift.

Individual
Approach

Fine-tune your managing
approach to the
differences in people

Big Idea

See your employees as individuals. Recognize their unique desires and abilities so you can manage to bring out their best. This insight allows you to fine-tune your managing approach to the situation and individual. In turn, this creates a culture based on performance over entitlement where individuals can shine.

We all have different parts to play, Matthew. And we must all be allowed to play them.

—Lord Grantham, *Downton Abbey*

In this galaxy there's a mathematical probability of three million Earth-type planets. And in the universe, three million galaxies like this. And in all that, and perhaps more . . . only one of each of us.

—Dr. McCoy, *Star Trek* TV Series

Welcome to the world. Everyone's different, everyone gets treated differently.

—Dr. Gregory House on the TV series *House*

Liz Lemon: *You think you're better.*
Tracy Jordan: *No, I just think I'm different, in a better way.*

—*30 Rock*

Important to Know

My undergraduate degree was in mining engineering. It seems now like an curious career choice but at the time it made perfect sense. In any event, I am thankful for the amazing work experiences in a industry loaded with history and heritage.

One summer, to get real experience during college, I worked as a hard rock miner in an underground silver mine near Wallace, Idaho.

Something you would only know if you worked underground, down in the dark depths of the mine, every worker is referred to as "Buddy." Imagine working where it is pitch black and every person is wearing a hard hat with a head lamp. Unless you are up close, it is impossible to recognize anyone.

"Hey *Buddy*, can you give me a hand?"

Up on the surface, where we manage in the light of day, thankfully we can see the individuals whom we work with. Employees are not nameless and face-less workers whom we treat the same.

An essential element of Managing Genius is to see your people as individuals and recognize their unique desires and abilities. This chapter is a new way of thinking where you see the "trees in the forest."

How to See Your Employees as Individuals

1 Each individual has their own story
2 Should we treat everyone the same?
3 Make "discriminating" decisions
4 Fine tune your managing approach
5 Allow individuals to shine

1 EACH INDIVIDUAL HAS THEIR OWN STORY

I sat in the back of my daughter's fifth-grade class and watched with awe as the teacher skillfully managed the room filled with kids who were bubbling over with energy and enthusiasm. The teacher was a master at orchestrating the controlled chaos, keeping the class moving ahead with a guiding hand and a gentle heart.

As I watched her manage the classroom, I became aware that the class was actually filled with twenty-five unique kids, each with different personalities and individual abilities. The room was riding on the top of a rolling sea of self-interest, ability, attention span and physical needs.

Later, this teacher displayed the true level of her teaching skills when we debriefed on the class. She was able to go through the entire class by name and talk about their individual qualities.

What I learned that day was that *good* teachers can manage the classroom to get through a lesson plan but it takes a *Teaching Genius* to see the class as twenty-five individuals brimming with personalized needs and desires. You can see that each kid has a unique story.

It is Managing Genius to see the individuals in the room.

In the same way, it is Managing Genius to pull together a dissimilar group of individuals who each have personalized motivation and desires.

Individuals will feel a greater sense of job satisfaction and commitment as they see that their boss is not using a cookie-cutter leadership approach. People are unique:

- They go home to different family situations, varying financial status and a wide range of living conditions and social connections.
- People want different things from their jobs. Some are motivated to pursue career advancements, while others may keep their jobs at arm's length to focus on their families or recreational passions.
- People can get bored or their family situation calls for more pay.
- Jobs, technology, customers and the work landscape are constantly evolving. The match between the employee and today's work can drift or fall out of sync.
- As managers, we mistakenly assume that our employees want the same things we do. We expect them to dive into work with the same enthusiasm and commitment that we feel.
- Human nature is capricious. People can be different at different times of the day. People may get distracted or have selective memories.

Effectively managing a team of people in this undulating sea of individual change requires a different way of managing.

2 SHOULD WE TREAT EVERYONE THE SAME?

A Managing Genius recognizes the individual uniqueness and contributions of the individual. You endeavor to treat everyone consistently and even-handed but not necessarily the same.

This is easy to say but tough to manage. People may want to feel unique, as long as they come out on top in the comparison. If others are treated better, you get reminded it is your duty to treat everyone the same. In fact, they may complain that you have no *right* to differentiate between employees.

At the root of this attitude are three common entitlements: seniority, loyalty and fairness. These give employees the notion that he or she has a right to a particular reward or benefit and this right trumps your management judgment and discretion.

It is important to spot and understand these entitlements:

Seniority is a strong emotional feeling whereby you think job tenure gives you special privileges. Most people have an expectation that they should be served before the people standing behind them in line. However, in today's environment of rapid business changes, frequent changing of jobs is commonplace. Therefore, the static idea of seniority may not be such a good business driver. For example, individuals who have taken risks to seek challenging new responsibilities are more esteemed than someone who held their spot on the org chart for ten years.

Loyalty drives us to make current decisions based on past relationships and performance. "I've always been here for you," "I've never turned down your request to work overtime." The message "you owe me" is strongly implied because we have a special relationship that trumps current events.

Fairness is fueled by comparisons: "You gave the last training opportunity to Sonja, so I get to go this time." This forces you to view fairness as if the scales are sitting on your desk and you must weigh each decision to keep the employee balance. However, fairness is something to be achieved over a long time period.

3 MAKE "DISCRIMINATING" DECISIONS

There is nothing wrong with choosing to appreciate a person's seniority and valuing their loyalty. Just be aware that employees may to try and *force you* to make decisions based on entitlement.

It is your job to make decisions to pick someone over another based on the needs of the business. Discrimination is the ability to show the careful judgment that allows us to recognize or draw fine distinctions between people. This demonstrates your character strength—you are astute, judicious, perceptive and selective.

Stacey needs an employee to travel to Boston for a week, This person will meet with a vendor and train on a new software package. After the week of training, this person will serve as project leader for implementation of the new software release across the company.

> Make discriminating decisions based on business needs and individual performance.

As it happens, Stacy hired Thomas last year specifically because of his previous experience with this new software. He had worked for ten years at a nationally recognized consulting company that specializes in software implementation and training. He has paid his dues to develop his skills, constantly traveling to customer sites to do projects, developing valuable experience. Looking at the current needs of the company and her team, Stacey has determined that they need this software implementation done right the first time. She decides to send Thomas to Boston.

However, word soon gets out that Thomas has been chosen for this special assignment and the cool trip to Boston. Kelly, another software engineer, is at Stacey's door demanding an answer. "It's not fair—it is my turn." Stacey looks down and sees two new emails from people who also want time with her to discuss this decision. Stacey is thinking that by now someone must be talking to HR or her boss.

Employees are suffering through feelings of entitlement, which generates discussions of comparison and feelings of envy. It is unsettling to experience envy and it can cause an employee to feel insecure, like he or she is out of personal control. We tell ourselves that the success of another person is a matter of luck or connections. We turn to entitle-ment based behaviors to get back in control of the situation.

It is Managing Genius for Stacey to make this tough decision. This is what managers do—they make decisions to pick one person for this assignment, that person for the next. When you say yes to one person, you say no to everyone else.

Stacey's decision to pick Thomas was a business decision based on both current events and future needs. Stacey has determined that Thomas brings a high desire and skill to the organization, which she is anxious to put to good use for the business. Her decision was a legal discriminating decision based on the objective needs of the business.

In fact, her other employees knew about this new software purchase over a year ago. They could have taken it upon themselves to learn the software and make themselves more competitive.

> At the heart of everyday business managers make manual interventions using judgment and discretion.

Seniority is an easier option—you only have to hold your place and then lobby the powers that be—my boss, his boss and HR—to intercede on your behalf.

It is important to watch what you say at this moment. It is common to seek appeasement in the present moment and promise something for the future. "Don't worry, you will get your chance on the next one."

However, in a burst of Managing Genius, Stacey smiles and calmly replies to Kelly, "I don't remember telling you things would be equal around here. I need to make tough decisions for the good of the customer, the company and the team."

"Thomas chose to get more training on his own time, and this makes him a more valuable employee for this project. You can choose to upgrade your own technical skills so that you will be competitive for these opportunities in the future. But that is your responsibility."

"Now, speaking of responsibilities, where are you with the project that's due next Friday?"

4 FINE-TUNE YOUR MANAGING APPROACH

Steve was a project manager for a construction company that built strip malls. Steve has been a top performer for ten-plus years.

His company won an unusually large, mega-project to construct a shopping mall. Steve was thrilled that his boss gave him the opportunity to step up and manage a project of this scale.

As it turned out, the project required a different set of management skills. It was highly complex with a much bigger budget. In this project, he got work done through direct reports and he spent more of his time leading meetings.

> My manager is the only one in the company who totally understands the work that I do.

Steve found out too late that he was in over his head. The project fell seriously behind schedule and the cost overruns loomed large. Eventually, his boss stepped in midstream "to save the project." As Steve shared whimsically, "Someone's head had to roll, so they fired me."

Consider this: Steve would have benefited from an *individualized managing approach*. His boss assumed that Steve could transition up to a mega project because of his previous success with smaller projects.

His boss failed Steve by taking a hands-off approach. His boss should have coached him in the new role, not just throw him into it. New jobs and situations call for extensive front-end communication to identify what is different and how to get started well. He should have set up automatic controls, just as commercial airplane has warnings if the altitude drops.

Important to note, people may not admit up front that they cannot do something. If you ask someone if he or she can drive a manual transmission car, you may hear yes, followed by the sound of grinding gears. You want people to feel comfortable saying, "I really want to do this job but I think I need some help with this aspect."

It is Managing Genius Pay to make sure your people are able to succeed. Hands-on or -off is a situation specific decision.

5 ALLOW INDIVIDUALS TO SHINE

There is the story of the elementary school that has eliminated letter grades for academic achievement. Now they use a three-tier system: Achieved Excellence, Close to Excellence, Pursuing Excellence.

We are told competitiveness is wrong, so we reward participation, trying hard and good attitude. *Every kid gets a trophy.*

In the workplace we are careful to not draw attention to a star performer. People may challenge your judgment or focus scrutiny on the exceptional performer in order to bring them back to average.

So we chase cooperation, freedom and team spirit. Give everyone a chance. Later, we may think our employees seem unmotivated or uninterested but actually they are thinking, "Why bother?"

Real achievers want someone to take notice of their achievement when they work harder than others or when they differentiate themselves and move out from the pack. They want to see rewards for their individual effort. They want to be recognized for their creativity, extra effort and quality work. They speak through their work and they expect someone to select them for promotions, additional responsibilities, access to senior management and assignments that enhance their career.

> A high performance culture only exists where individuals can shine.

It takes a manager with significant skill and courage to single out and reward top performers. It isn't always easy but it will pay off as you create a culture of *performance* versus *entitlement.* It will also allow individuals to feel a greater sense of job satisfaction and commitment as they see that their boss recognizes their individual uniqueness.

In the movie *Princess Diaries,* Mia Thermopolis says, "My expectation in life is to be invisible, and I'm good at it." Under-performing people want you to treat everyone the same so they stay invisible.

If you do not distinguish worthy individual employees, you make them invisible until the day they leave for a better job opportunity.

This Is Managing Genius

All of the "Important to Know" items above are indeed important to know. However, one of them deserves extra attention simply because getting good at this skill can have a significant impact on your personal success as a manager. Fine-tuning your managing approach to the individual differences in people and the specific situations they find themselves working in is an essential found in Managing Genius.

Managing Individuals

1 A simple diagnostic tool

2 How to manage individuals

To get good at this, you need to have a simple diagnostic tool to help you establish a relevant perspective as to how the individual fits into the present situation. When you are able to do this, you will be able to establish a team culture that is open and willing to address individual differences in desire and ability. This will create a culture defined by individual performance versus group entitlement. All team members are valued while excellence is acknowledged and celebrated.

1 A SIMPLE DIAGNOSTIC TOOL

At this point in *Managing Genius*, I want to improve your vision for seeing the individual trees in the forest. This will enable you to adjust your managing approach to the situation and individual.

What follows is a simple template for seeing individuals using two factors: desire and ability. The template helps answer the general questions, Is the employee motivated? Does the employee have the skill set to do the job?

Just as importantly, you want people to self-manage. Teach them how they can self-assess in regards to how they think and feel in these two important areas. When you build mutual trust, you will be able to have these kind of conversations.

DESIRE

Do they *want* to do this work?
People may waver in motivation or confidence. Check in early and often.

ABILITY

***Can* they to do this work?**
Jobs, technology and business needs change. Look for gaps.

DESIRE

A friend asked me to talk with his high-school-aged son. For years, this young man had shown promise as a talented football player. However, he abruptly decided not to try out for the high school team and his father was disappointed with his son's decision.

Ultimately, many parents struggle to understand when their kids do not share the same desires they do. As parents, we wonder why would my child would give up on the team (or choir, or musical instrument, or whatever) when he or she clearly has the skill and ability?

One day I had the opportunity to drive the student home from school, so I asked him about his football decision. He showed personal insight and maturity by sharing the basis for his decision. "I like the sport," he told me, "but I just got tired of getting hit. The physical contact is not fun anymore and I just can't get my heart into the game." He had lost his *desire* to play the game.

Desire
- Motivation
- Mental willingness
- Emotional readiness
- Personal confidence
- Aspiration
- Ambition

When you talk with an individual about current work, ask whether they have the heart for this work? Is their head in the game? When things get tough, will they have the mental toughness and enthusiasm (desire) to carry them through the uncomfortable or painful parts?

Anything with a satisfying reward or product requires a process that you complete before you reach the finish line. You will need to practice, develop proficiency and put in the required sweat equity. You cannot motivate people or push them through this; they have to want it.

It is important to know your employees:

People will waver in desire. People will feel emotional ebb and flow due to many different factors. For example, Susan is totally committed to you and the business and until recently she has been an employee you can count on. However, her performance has lately become spotty and incomplete. She finally shares with you that her preschooler has started crying uncontrollably every day when she drops her off at day care. It's no surprise that her head is not in the game.

Confidence is often tied to people or places. I mentored a senior manager whom I thought was a skilled speaker. But when she got a great opportunity to speak to the senior team, I was surprised to see how she struggled and stumbled. Something to consider: Confidence can be tied to your mentor in the room, speaking to familiar faces or playing on the "home field."

We do not always know what we want. Individuals may not understand what they want. This is especially true when they have had limited work experiences. Their vision is limited to what they have previously seen and done.

If I can do it, they can do it. We often transfer our own personal assessment of our abilities to others. We think it is easy, so we may not take the time to understand how the individual looks at the work. Does she want to do it (desire)? Does she feel capable (ability)?

People don't always desire what *we* desire. Maybe you left home and worked part-time jobs to get that college degree and then started up the ladder to pursue increasing levels of responsibility, professional skills, knowledge and status. You decided to forego family ties for now.

You just cannot understand why the employee sitting across the desk from you is not willing to show the same tenacity. How can he be content to just do his job for forty hours a week and then go home, never to read an email at night, never to think about what he should do first thing tomorrow? Your priorities may not be your employee's priorities. You don't judge priorities—you just make decisions based on desire and ability.

Processing time. Sometimes people may have a desire to do the job but they need some time to process the opportunity and make the next move. Give people a break to catch their breath. It is a special skill to think fast in the moment and be able to make a decision in a heartbeat.

Finding desire. You can ask thought-provoking questions to help people see for themselves what they want to do. In the end, people need to make their own decisions and decide if they want to step onto the bus.

 ABILITY

It is human nature to say you can do things, only to find out later that the task was over your head.

When I worked as an engineer at an open-pit mine, I found myself in the middle of a labor strike. All of the hourly employees were gone at the end of the declared shift. The employees simply turned off their equipment and went home.

Management was tasked with moving all the mobile equipment to one place near the shops. I was riding with the general manager and he pulled up to a Caterpillar D-10 bulldozer at the bottom of the pit. He asked me if I could drive it up to the shops. I had operated farm-driven tractors as a kid and I was certainly not willing to admit my skill gaps. However, a D-10 is a massive piece of equipment weighing ninety tons and having an eighteen-foot blade.

Ability

- Competence
- Skill
- Aptitude
- Knowledge
- Training

As he drove away, I felt a wave of fear and anxiety. It took me twenty minutes just to get it started. Although it turned out well that day, I probably should have admitted that driving such a large vehicle was out of my skill set.

Use *ability* as the second simple diagnostic guide for helping you use your individual approach. People may have *desire* (enthusiasm and motivation) to operate a D-10 dozer but they may lack the requisite training and skills to do the job.

Of course ability works *with* desire—I was eager to please and appear skillful but at the same time I was fearful of showing a lack of skill. Should I really have been trusted with this job?

Recognizing ability is essential:

Know that competence may not readily transfer from one job or project to another. If you have successfully managed a team of twelve on the manufacturing floor, does that mean you can manage the entire 150 person operation for a shift? If you are able to present to a group of eight engineers in a meeting room, does that mean you can stand up before the entire work force and introduce a new process?

Of course, the answer to both questions is: not necessarily. Do not assume that competence in one area under a certain set of circumstances automatically translates to the next situation. Begin your decision about capability transference with a candid conversation with your employee. Give him or her the ability to be honest and opt out if necessary. It may be much better to do that now rather than later.

Don't assume that credentials and work experience make people capable of the task at hand. On my first professional job, my boss assigned me to build an environmentally correct, state-certified catch basin for an existing oil storage tank.

First, to be fair, I had just earned a degree in mining engineering and this was a civil engineering-type job. I learned later that there was a long list of design considerations, including correct construction materials, state regulations, approval process, safety factors, temperature and weather considerations. I remember my impatient boss finally taking back the work and chiding me, "What did they teach you in school?" (This boss is not on my list of Managing Geniuses.)

In the same way, we see the MBA on someone's resume and assume that he or she must know how to read a financial statement and how to create an annual budget. After all, she can solve a problem on our shipping dock, so surely she can solve the inventory issue involving international shipping. The work is so similar, right?

Ability may be situation-specific. Consider the weight of the job and the individual or team's readiness to handle it alone. Understand that there is work that calls for a more micromanagement-based approach. The trick is to pick and choose those few critical items where you need to provide more oversight and some milestone reviews. It will help your group to identify these in advance so they know what to expect from you.

For example, trail-blazing work is different from repetitive work. Is this a new project where they'll need to show craftiness and the ability to jury-rig a new system? Some people do well facing stress and thinking on their feet, whereas some break down under the pressure, even though they're seen as highly capable and motivated.

For example, in a new technology startup, we hired our first hardware test manager and showed him the empty room where the lab would go. We presented him with a budget that included money to build the lab out. What a dream job. He quit the next day. Some people love the idea of building out a new lab, while others feel overwhelmed.

> **Some situations require "micromanaging"**
> - Mission-critical
> - Multiple players and shared responsibility
> - Broad impact on group
> - High visibility
> - Big-ticket financial
> - Key customers
> - Startup work

Another example where it is important to check for ability is when we must depend on others. Individuals may feel that they have the ability to do the work but in the company, they face the inabilities of others.

So they hit a roadblock because they are dependent on others for a shared contribution. This is a great situation for a manager to engage the employee. "Are you aware that you will need to depend on the X department in order for you to finish this work? Can you effectively interact with them for needed resources?"

Individual Contribution = Desire + Ability

Consider the sequence for teaching my teenage daughter, Annie, to drive a car. She started from the doubly precarious position of low desire + low ability to operate a motor vehicle.

Annie wanted to achieve the status and enjoy the freedom that comes from driving but on her first day behind the wheel, she had a low desire. Annie looked pensive and tentative. Driving seemed like a daunting task with too many skills to learn.

This was a situation that calls for "micromanaging." She needed encouragement and step-by-step coaching to get her started. Would you hand the keys for the car to your teenager and say, "I am a hands-off parent, so go for it, you can do it?"

After a short while, Annie got over the early jitters and thought she really knew what she was doing. Her desire was high, which was unfortunate because her skill was still low. "I think I get it." The driving instructor, however, can see all the things she has not yet mastered.

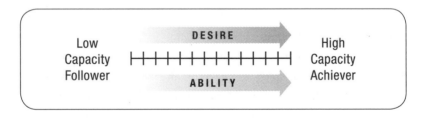

I could have made the mistake of thinking Annie was completely ready to be on her own, simply because she exhibited the *desire* to do so. *But she didn't know what she didn't know.*

In time, new drivers grow in their abilities. However, they will likely, from time to time, lower their mental guard. Their emotional awareness may waver. They may get careless or mentally distracted.

When you step back and look at the overall learning process, you realize that people do not lose the abilities they gained from their driving experience. Generally, their physical ability to drive a car will not be diminished. However, their mental or emotional state can vary and they may not always pay attention as they should when driving. You learn about the dangers and hazards of cars through driving experience and we hope and pray that the required learning and skill will come without incident or injury.

The interaction between desire and ability. In the past you may have wondered if a job assignment was right for an individual. Every manager has a story or two about people they have moved into a job and it did not work out.

You need a simple way to determine a person's likelihood of success when it comes to a job change or a new assignment. The chart on page 266 is a continuum that will help you make that consideration.

At the left of the illustration, you have people I term "follower." They will usually be enthusiastic about the new job but at the start they may feel unsure or need to gain confidence. Be aware that these people may need more individual attention.

Moving ahead. On the right side of the illustration, you have seasoned employees who have both desire + ability. This puts them into a position where they act independently and totally own their job responsibility. Important to note, people on the right of the continuum should get more trust and shared leadership. These employees have earned the right to more autonomy.

Use the chart as a simple guide for discussing whether a job is a right fit.

Desire and ability can fluctuate. The reasons may not be transparent or readily shared. It is a positive thing when employees can at least let you know that they are hesitant to jump into the newest assignment. Then, you can discuss what they are thinking and figure out next steps.

Desire is more apt to shift up or down due to personal issues such as family matters, distractions outside of work, feeling tired or sick.

Ability is a more step-wise growth—once you acquire a skill you retain that skill unless there is a technology or job change. For example, once an accountant knows how to close the monthly books, they get it.

This section gives you a simple tool to determine whether your employee can take on a new responsibility. In fact, print out this illustration and use it as a everyday discussion guide.

2 HOW TO MANAGE INDIVIDUALS

Use the chart on the next page as a guide to managing individuals. The key principle is to learn the right time and place to ask questions to check in with your people.

Interview your people and know what they do. At one technology company, we were forced to cut expenses across the board. The senior team worked in a closed-door meeting room to come up with the list of surplus staff.

On Monday morning after the layoffs, our CEO charged into my office to impatiently complain that he had not received his daily business report. I explained that on Friday we had laid off the person who did that report for the senior team. She had been deemed as "nonessential in the process."

He looked at me, dumbfounded and I realized he had no idea who created the report that he read daily. As far as he knew, the report just magically showed up on his desk.

> How can you treat people individually if you do not know what they do…or can do?

It was interesting that his predecessor had taken the initiative of walking the hall in order to find and meet the daily report creator and learn a hundred other important details that, when added up, made up the work culture. When his predecessor talked about the report, he would say, "Has anyone seen Christine's report?"

His individual awareness was infectious and every time I saw Christine, I'd also think of her report and how it contributed to the business. A Managing Genius can put names on the work. Individual recognition has a way of spilling over into the organization, transforming avatars into real people.

People love to work at a place where management takes the time to get to know them as individuals. People will warm up to you and respect you as a leader when you take interest in their individual work.

How to Manage Individuals

Know your People
Know your employees: Understand their aspirations, hidden skills and motivations. Hold casual "interviews" periodically to stay apprised.

Individual Performance
Allow individuals to shine. Motivated people will reach higher if you show that you are willing to reward individual performers, in an objective, fair and unbiased fashion.

Check-in
Hold a "pre-game check-in" to ensure that individuals are ready and available. Ask people to keep you apprised of changes. Look for a natural check-in point to update.

Managing Approach
Do not use a one-size-fits-all managing approach. Fine-tune for the situation and readiness to do the job—whether hands-off, micromanage or somewhere in between.

Selection Decisions
Use desire and ability as a guide for matching people with internal jobs. Interview internal employees to ensure internal staffing decisions are based on desire and ability.

Coaching
Teach people to think about their career aspirations using desire and ability. This gives a simple guide for individual development meetings.

Build Trust
Give individuals a safe place to privately share how they see the work. Keep these conversations separate from selection decisions. Openness works both ways.

Here are a few more ways to get to know your employees that I observe in Managing Geniuses. They sound simple and ordinary but they are effective in developing a work culture that recognizes individuals:

- Memorize names and faces.
- Continue to interview your employees once, twice, three times and maybe more. Your employees at all levels are developing and their desires and aspirations are changing.
- Keep prior conversations going—circle back on what was shared last time and then add to the conversation.
- Slow cooking. Some people are slow to let down the walls. With some people, you know all their dreams and problems in ten minutes, while others will keep their cards close to their chin for years.
- Talk about work and the business. There's no need to play counselor or solve their relationship problems—You can guide the conversation by sticking to the "big three": their jobs, what they are doing in the business and their future career aspirations.

Keep a finger on the pulse. It is Managing Genius to pay close attention to changing work situations and how that can potentially impact your employees. Take the time to know and understand the individuals on your team and how they might respond to stressful situations or decisions.

> Your employees will appreciate when you stay apprised of what they are doing.

I remember one Managing Genius starting meetings by checking in on his people. "How is Brian doing in his new job?" "How did Michelle do on her recent trip?" This sounds so basic but it is surprisingly uncommon.

Be sure to look at today's situation to understand how work will get done by deploying the players to get the best outcome. It's easy to miss the fine brush strokes.

Remember that people often get bored, want attention or have selective memories. Jobs, customers and the work landscape are changing and evolving. Readiness can be affected by scale, complexity, technology, customer expectations and many other factors.

Ask people to keep you apprised of changes. Have natural check-in points to update: Are you with me? Can you do this? Any changes I should be aware of? This creates an adult-minded culture.

Coaching and employee development. In the opening story, Scott walked around greeting people with the general question, "How are you doing?" Whereas Holly was able to approach people with an individual perspective of where they were and where they wanted to go.

You want to help people, yet most of us lack the necessary diagnostic skills to access where people are and determine what they need next. You can you do a simple one-on-one meeting with an employee who wants to know how he or she can grow new skills and advance in the company.

To encourage and support personal growth, use *desire* and *ability* to discuss how the person feels about his or her job. Then help set career aspirations and self-development goals based on that feedback. Ask people to self-assess these two factors before individual development meetings.

Keeping up with employees. How can you be expected to monitor the emotional status of ten, twenty, a hundred individuals who may be facing new tasks or experiencing emotional turmoil in their personal lives? The fact is you can't.

Teach people how to talk about the work using the framework of desire and ability. This gives you a simple way to discuss the work.

Important to note, some people are hesitant to share feelings with management about their job. Greater work responsibility means pay and advance-

> Make it easy for individuals to share how they are feeling about their jobs.

ment, so you cannot punish people when they talk openly about how they feel about the next potential job. These are valuable *talking points.*

Once you set the culture, adult-minded people will talk openly and explain how they feel.

Stay tuned to changes in people and their work so you can ask insightful questions, like, "I noticed your hesitancy with taking responsibility for software projects. Would you think it is a lack of desire to be in a lead position or it is that you feel you lack some ability?"

Discover Your Managing Genius

- See your employees as individuals. Knowing what they are thinking in terms of *desire* and *ability* allows you to bring out their best.

- Fine-tune your managing approach to individual and the work situation— hands-off, micromanage or somewhere in between.

- Stay abreast of current events. People, jobs and companies change. You do not manage on autopilot—an individual who was autonomous yesterday may need greater attention today.

- By focusing on individual performance, you create a culture of achievement where top-performing individuals can shine.

- People want to be recognized for their superior effort and contribution. If you treat everyone the same, top performers will lose heart and may look to work where they can receive individual recognition and reward.

Workplace Relationships

Create ways for team
members to build rapport
and community

Big Idea

People come to work expecting a colleague-friendly work community. Social connections at work are a strong indicator of job satisfaction. However, community does not just happen. It is Managing Genius to shape and guide the work culture to create ways to build rapport and a shared community.

Amy: *This is nice that we all get to eat together.*
The guys: *Oh yeah, absolutely.*
Amy: *Can we maybe put the phones down and have an actual human conversation?*
Sheldon: *We can, but thanks to Steve Jobs we don't have to.*

—*The Big Bang Theory* TV Series

Leslie: *Come on Ron, we were friends for 10 years.*
Ron: *We were work proximity associates.*

—*Parks and Recreations* TV Series

Cora: *Are we to be friends then?*
Lady Grantham: *We are allies, my dear, which can be a good deal more effective.*

—*Downton Abbey*

Whatever comes out of these gates, we've got a better chance of survival if we work together. Do you understand? If we stay together we survive.

—Russell Crowe in the movie *Gladiator*

💡 Important to Know

After college Amy moved to Seattle to chase her aspirations to work in the software industry.

Amy grew up in Connecticut and went to college at Rice University in Houston. She has continued enjoy a close relationship with her mother on the east coast, keeps up with her father in Chicago and her two brothers, one on each coast. The family keeps up on social media and regular video chats.

Amazon hired Amy and relocated her to Seattle to work at their south Lake Union location. It was quite an opportunity and she is living her dream. Moving to a large metropolitan area where she knows no one was emotionally tough. Saying goodbye to her college friends, who were launching their own careers in various locations, was difficult as well.

The Workplace Neighborhood

1 Why we come to work

2 We look for social interaction at work

3 Employee morale is tough to manage

4 Define the relationship

She cannot afford to live near work, so she commutes on the Sounder Train every workday. She is on the train at 6:25 am and sits with nameless commuters either sleeping or staring at their laptops. Then she does the reverse trip every night, sometimes catching the last train due to work demands.

She is usually exhausted by the time she gets back to her apartment. She eats a Lean Cuisine while preparing her outfit for the next day. She continues the work day with texts and emails to her coworkers. She checks social media to connect with her distant college friends. Often she falls asleep by 10:30 in front of the TV.

Amy has little opportunity to form relationships outside of work. Her job is her world and she has made her coworkers her new family. There are many recent college grads in her division at Amazon and they get together on the weekends for movies, concerts or to explore Seattle.

Every morning, she walks over to Starbucks with two coworkers for her tall skinny vanilla latte. Lunches are fun times to connect socially with different coworkers. Just recently, she started walking with Tialia, who is a software test engineer from Taiwan.

Recently, Amy started hanging out with a guy from work. David is a recent graduate of Emory University in Atlanta and he also moved to Seattle knowing no one. They have agreed to take it slow and keep it quiet at work but everyone has already figured out that they are an item.

Amy loves her boss, Sarah, who is a thirty-something single professional. She is a Wisconsin native and has a degree from Duke.

Sarah has taken Amy under her wing and coached her through the transitions to the world of work and Seattle. They get coffee every Tuesday morning and have lunch almost every Friday. Sarah provides welcome guidance, encouragement and support.

Amy is proud to work at Amazon. She feels a deep loyalty to Sarah and she feels like her Amazon coworkers are her Seattle family. Sarah brings a sense of warmth and relationship to the department that makes Amy feels at home on this job.

1 WHY WE COME TO WORK

We work to fulfill three basic needs:

1. To meet a primary need for money.
2. To use our abilities and feel needed.
3. To have a place where we belong.

Of these three, the place where we belong—the social community that we find at work—is what provides the most sustained value. Clearly, we are made for human interaction. Workplace relationships have become an essential aspect of our life.

There was a time before the Industrial Revolution that people's residences were also their workplaces, such as with artisans and craft workers in Victorian England. For example, in Charles Dickens's Great Expectations, the central character, Pip, works for his brother-in-law as an apprentice in a blacksmith shop attached to the family home.

The industrial revolution of the late eighteenth and early nineteenth centuries transformed the social landscape. It took people out of their homes to work in centralized facilities. We began to work with tools and equipment that could not be owned by individuals, nor transported back and forth between work and home. Often people walked across town to work in large smoke-belching factories or mines.

The Industrial Revolution also brought a change with how the business was run. No longer did we work directly for the owner. As the business grew, the owners had to delegate surrogate managers to hire, train, discipline and reward the workers for the enterprise. This created intermediary layers in the chain of command and suddenly the boss played a huge role in overall job satisfaction and worker experience.

> For some employees, the workplace is the main source of their daily relationship needs.

Most of us are employed outside the home where we connect with coworkers in the everyday course of business. We connect in unique ways to our job, the people we work with, our company and the leaders.

The Census Bureau reports that about 25 percent of households in America consist of people living alone. We work long hours and experience ever-increasing commutes. We eventually do make it through the rush hour traffic, where thousands of cars are driven by solitary drivers listening to their iTunes play lists. We grab takeout food to eat while we surf the web, connect on social media or sit alone streaming a show on Netflix through our iPad.

2 WE LOOK FOR SOCIAL INTERACTION AT WORK

Robert Putnam writes in *Bowling Alone, The Collapse and Revival of American Community*[1], that people in America were once connected within their neighborhoods, communities, civic clubs and churches.

---

1   Robert Putnam, *Bowling Alone: The Collapse and Revival of American Community*, New York: Touchstone, 2000. Read Chapter 5, Connections in the Workplace. Read Chapter 5, Connections in the Workplace.

Now our highly mobile society leads us to move far from our family and childhood friends. Americans have increasingly disconnected from social structures and bonding relationships in their communities and civic organizations. We hardly know our neighbors and we are disinterested in PTA, church, local politics or other groups that once created a sense of community outside of work.

Putnam writes, "many studies have shown that social connections with coworkers are a strong indicator—some would say the strongest indicator—of job satisfaction."

So we come to work wanting and expecting to find social interaction and relationships. We meet coworkers to trade confidences and to share kindnesses. We look to one another for mutual support and understanding. We drink coffee together and share afternoon snacks, during which we share as an endearing spouse or best friend.

3 EMPLOYEE MORALE IS TOUGH TO MANAGE

Workplace tension can spring from disappointments when employees experience unmet social needs at work. What people want or expect from their boss and coworkers often run in the background as unspecified or silent relationship needs.

Cultural differences that result from a diverse society can present difficult management obstacles. These obstacles can make for awkward work relationships where you need to be skilled and astute to sort through divergent expectations in order to minimize job dissatisfaction.

Eventually, senior management or HR get wind of dissatisfaction from a few of your employees. They eagerly step in to smooth over hurt feelings and alleviate employee dissatisfaction. Soon some expert shows up or they pull a program off the shelf to build employee morale. They are thinking that competent managers keep people happy.

However, when all is said and done, your employees look to you to pull together the workplace as a congenial group that provides us with an overall positive atmosphere.

Millennials are springing up as the core of the work force. In their interview they may ask, "How is the work culture here?" Yet they often want more than they are willing or able to give.

As the manager you are left worrying how to juggle all these fragmented relationships. It seems that there is always something happening in the background. The issue is that this "background stuff" has the very real possibility of affecting things. Not only things in

> It is Managing Genius to cultivate a colleague-friendly work neighborhood.

the background but in real life, daily work issues. People may bring their baggage to today's meeting.

Many of us do not have the social skills to meet every emotional need for our people. It is likely that you will fall short in some way.

4   DEFINE THE RELATIONSHIP

In the TV Show *30 Rock*, Jack Donagy asks his manager, Liz Lemon, to rethink how she views her managing role:

> Liz: *You need to tell Jenna this whole thing was your idea and I didn't know anything about it and that she should be mad at you, not me.*
> Jack: *Oh sure, then we can sit around and braid each other's hair. Lemon, you're a supervisor. These people are not your friends.*
> Liz: *Yes, they are my friends.*
> Jack: *No. They're your employees.*

For any relationship to remain viable and mutually beneficial, you will need to "define the relationship." The Urban Dictionary calls this DTR, so you might say to a friend or romantic interest, "We need to have a DTR talk."

Team leadership should come from you. You need to define the manager-employee relationship and the overall team experience.

Unfortunately, most managers only choose to focus on the mechanics of everyday work and achieving the business goals. They let their Admin or the team social butterfly worry about the birthday cakes and team get-togethers.

Then, of course you need HR to play the benevolent Aunt who gives advice for how you parent the kids. Later, HR steps in with a one-size-fits-all program to increase employee morale.

> Happiness at work? Once you get your employees to like you as a manager, then you can chase happiness.

When your manager-employee relationship is left undefined, you risk developing different levels of affinity with different employees. Your work group will develop their own inner circles, with a small group of people feeling left out and standing at your door looking for extra attention.

With diverse work cultures, this is a recipe for dissatisfaction somewhere in your work group as people miss one another in the exchange.

All this is to say, you need to decide how you will define your role within the context of the social community of your work group. Left to drift, your managing role may become defined by others.

These common questions often "define the relationship":

1. Do you like me?

Getting employees to like us is an uphill challenge. People's emotional energy and attention span will ebb and flow. People bring to work varying desires and sometimes undeveloped social skills. In fact, getting people to feel anything on a sustained basis is virtually impossible.

Your employees are a primary concern for you but the feeling may not be reciprocal. They bring their own personal desires, often secret or undefined and they may want from you what you cannot give. This can change without notice, leaving you to solve the mystery of what they are thinking and how to retain their commitment.

It is interesting that for all the concern we give to how employees feel about us, the relationship is never quite reciprocal. You can spend considerable time worrying about how they feel about you and their job, making sure you do everything possible to ensure they stay with the organization. They, on the other hand, can you give their two-week notice or even walk out the door this afternoon.

When we want people to like us, we often chase "niceness." The safe manager is a really a nice person who leads with positive affirmation and gets high scores on the annual employee feedback survey. HR is often in the position to determine managing skills based on the absence of problems or complaints.

2. Are we friends?

Managers usually have a vague idea that you're supposed to keep a business-first focus and hold back on the personal relationships with the employees. We blur professional and personal boundaries when we develop too-close friendships with individual employees. This interferes with our ability to make objective decisions.

This is the Liz Lemon thinking. However, is Liz really friends with her employees? Our true friends have access to all areas of our lives and *we keep moving the relationship forward* to unfold those areas. This means we keep turning over new cards that display our feelings and aspirations. Usually, there is no holding back.

At work we drift in and out off working relationships based on current events. It is like a basketball coach bringing in good ball handlers or three point shooters as a game-winning strategy. At that moment the coach is not hand-wringing over how players might feel.

Is this a committed mutual relationship or is the basketball player just looking for more playing time to build up their statistics?

3. Are we family?

I get nervous when I hear a CEO say that their work culture is like "family." How many of us came from fully functional family units?

In fact, today's diverse work culture brings many definitions of the word family. This is one more example of where we use a sentimental word to describe a desired work culture.

Remember, in a true family, you are a member no matter what. There is no "if" in a family: if you discover something about a family member and don't like what you see, that person is still your family.

However, relationships in business are based on *if*—if you continue at an acceptable performance and behavior level, if you play well with your coworkers, if you respect the company and our customers, you will get to stay here. This is a job, right?

4. Are we having fun?

Jerry Seinfeld said in one of his comedy routines, "There is no such thing as fun for the whole family."

Fun is really difficult to play out with a diverse workforce. Yet we try to increase morale through "redemption activities", where we try to release employees from their workplace burdens and tension. We think that team building is an activity to take us away from our jobs.

Yet, it is a moving target to try to control team spirit, personality issues and chemistry. They are people, right? You cannot make people feel happy and truthfully, *most of us lack the fun gene*.

5. Who will define the relationship?

It is Managing Genius to take ownership for the workplace community.

Too often managers look to HR or special programs to manage the work culture for them. But managing people is a local event—you own the "final 50 feet" in the Company.

Community does not just happen. It needs guidance and pruning.

You are in the best vantage spot to build your team environment and keep your team close during real work and everyday events. You know the people and understand what they are facing.

You will earn respect when you take an active and everyday role in building and maintaining a vibrant colleague-friendly work neighborhood. It is Managing Genius to develop a do-it-yourself philosophy for your workplace. You gain power when you become a hands-on manager who is adept with everyday team operations.

You have the best seat in the house.

This Is Managing Genius

The goal of this chapter is to show you how you can build a workplace community and create a work environment for your employees based on professional and positive work relationships.

I want your team to see you in the center of team operations, so they see you taking ownership for the working relationships within your work group. This is how you keep the right balance: stay friendly without focusing on friendship. Manage in ways that creates affinity and common threads.

What follows are simple ways that you can manage the shared employee experience. Take the lead to define the relationship. Incorporate the eight simple practices into team discussions and make them a part of everyday conversation. You want your work group to see you as a leader who is actively concerned with the employee experience.

Manage the Workplace

1 Plain everyday work

2 Make human connections

3 Manage group meetings

4 Share good news with the group

5 Get the distance right

6 Sharpen your social awareness

7 Catch important personal events

8 Act like the Mayor

1 PLAIN EVERYDAY WORK

James Michener writes in *Centennial*, a panoramic story of the American West, about two fur trappers who work as partners isolated in the rugged western wilderness. These two men were dissimilar and in another life they would never be associates or friends. In this shared working experience in the uncharted wilderness, they developed a extremely close affinity for each other. Michener writes, "They had the unbreakable bonds of danger shared and work done."

Despite their personal differences, these two workers were close associates through plain, everyday work.

Shared work

We often feel closer to people with whom we have shared difficult and challenging experiences. For example, there are strong bonds of unity between software developers who worked together to build a now-popular software product. It is the *unbreakable bonds of danger shared and work done.*

You can build lasting connections and memories as you share hard work, risks and challenges. You feel closer by helping one another and contributing to a joint cause.

Working together is the best social glue.

Look for special all-team projects that you can use as unifiers for your group. Nothing unites a team like working together to solve a big hairy problem.

When assigning work, mix up the usual groupings so people can work with others outside their usual circle. This will require some facilitation on your part.

Special needs or emergencies that require an all-hands type effort are a great team-building opportunity. For example, in one technology startup, there was a big push to send out shipments on Friday afternoon. Every employee—the CEO, engineers, marketing and staff would migrate down to make the big 4:00 pm push. The stressful effort pulled people out of their cubes and united the group.

Make people feel like insiders

You break down walls through a common understanding of what is important in the business and what the team is working on. People may not be in a high-level position and sometimes need access to information to do their jobs. So they have to ask you for help—is that what you want?

You want everyone "in the know." Shared information will break up internal clubs and silos. There is nothing worse than hearing teammates talking about work matters and you feel like an outsider.

One practical thing you can do is to make sure everyone understands the words and lingo. "Let me just break in here to make sure everyone knows what EBITA is and why it is important to us."

Be aware, I've seen managers create insiders as they develop closer friendships with a favorite employee. Over coffee at Starbucks, you share news with your employee/friend and give them an edge over the team.

Bring more information to the group table. This creates a common narrative and strengthens the team bond.

Helpfulness

I rode my bicycle coast-to-coast with 60 or so riders who assembled from all over the world. The physical demands were extremely arduous. There is no way I could keep going alone. We rode spread out in small groups. Some choose to ride alone. But if you passed a fellow rider on the side of the road, you would always stop to see if they needed help. *Helpfulness was a shared norm.*

The essence of adult participation is sharing and staying mindful of the needs of others. This should come spontaneously, as an everyday way of doing work together. Your team will feel closer when they see coworkers paying attention to others. We know people have our back.

Look for ways to promote helpfulness. Make this a regular point of discussion at meetings and show value for people who step in to help others. Role model this yourself by stepping to help and support others.

Catch the right time and place

You may find that people will be more open for feedback, questions and sharing at certain places and times. As manager, the trick is to become skilled at sensing the right moment. I think if you get the right time and place, you will not need to worry so much about what you say.

An interesting book by a Seattle sports coach is written for parents involved with youth sports.[2] He writes about the enhanced communication that can occur with your teenager in the car ride home after a sports event. Bergstrom shares that teenagers may be in their own world much of the time but after a sports event they will be more likely to open up as you ride home together.

---

2   Bergstrom, Mike. *The Car Ride Home*. Seattle: Altri Prima Publishing, 2008.

I add, from my experience, that the principle is the same for drama or musical performances, taking the SAT or finishing final exams. These are events where you do not want to miss talking at the finish line.

I took this concept to heart and always drove to away volleyball games so that my daughter could choose to ride home with me. Tough to stay connected with teenagers? *Right place, right time.*

At work you can apply this insight by looking for the transitional moments where individuals will be more open to feedback or discussion. For example, be there when your people start or finish something like a large work project. Extra communication often happens at those junctures.

Look for "first time moments" for people, like their giving a group presentation to a meeting room packed with customers. Ask them in advance to stop by your office to tell you how it went.

Look for learning moments. Your group will be more open to feedback after finishing a major project. Hold a "postmortem" discussion to reflect on what happened.

2 MAKE HUMAN CONNECTIONS

The lost art of conversation

I was beginning a day of skiing at Vail Ski Resort. Forgive me, I am an incurable watcher of people.

There were two twenty-something guys riding up to the top of the mountain on the gondola to start their day of skiing together. They were chatting about their plans for the day. About halfway up the mountain one of them put on his ear buds and started listening to music. Of course this immediately quenched the conversation. His friend looked surprised and the ear bud guy said, "I got to have my tunes...if you have something to say, just let me know." Interesting, even when we share the same physical space, we may be barely there.

Important to note: You manage employees who are not always there in the room. There is a soundtrack running in their minds or they are carrying on multiple electronic conversations with people who are not in the room and who are not even a participant in present events.

This has created a rising generation of potential leaders who may lack the ability to hold an ordinary conversation...with real people.

When we have face-to-face conversations with real people, we get to hear what others think. We give the opportunity for follow-up questions.

We also have to take responsibility for our words and be ready to explain ourself. It's not so easy to get the last word or "dis" people when you face them.

Become exceptional at conversational skills

Public speaking is often not an area in which we feel successful. One-on-one conversation skills, even less.

However, anyone with aspirations to advance in the business world should endeavor to master the art of communicating with individuals and groups. The people who will move up in the organization will always be leaders with superior verbal communication skills.

Watch and learn from the best.

Become the promoter of human connections

You should take the lead to create more opportunities for human interaction within your work group. Bring more to the group table and ask for group input. Ask everyone in the room to comment on the agenda item. This shared conversation builds affinity and common threads.

When you think about employee development, we often think about job skills. Think about role modeling simple conversation skills. *You can teach conversation skills* by showing how it works in everyday discussions and team meetings.

> Human interaction is an important ingredient for workplace satisfaction.

Go talk to people. Often we send back hundreds of emails without talking to a live person. Take the lead to have human connections.

Get to know your employees, one person at a time

I worked one summer at a youth camp called Fort Wilderness in Northern Wisconsin. At first, it was overwhelming to see 250 teenagers moving in all directions at the camp. I wondered how I could make a positive impact on all these kids.

The wise camp director, with a hundred years of experience running the camp, gave the staff some wise advice. "Do not be overwhelmed with the large group. Each day pick one kid to get to know and influence. *You make connections and influence kids one at a time.*"

Make employee connections one at a time.

To apply this principle at work, everyday I would print out one or two emails and hand carry them to give a face-to-face reply. This gives you a human connection with at least one person every day. Imagine your impact across one year.

Schedule out in advance opportunities to make connections with the people in your work group. Make sure you do not miss people or play favorites.

Access to my boss

At the climatic moment in the *Wizard of Oz*, the dog Toto pulls back the curtain to expose how the Wizard runs the kingdom through smoke and noise.

Play Toto for your work group. Pull back the curtain on yourself and give people opportunity to see what you do. Not all of what management does needs be a mystery. Without monologuing or bragging, share updates on what you're doing and why it is important.

There is a distinction between doing for and doing with. Scott was my first boss and a true Managing Genius. He would invite his staff to a "with me" meeting, where we would join him as he did some aspect of his job or a drive to a business meeting. I learned later that if you got invited to a "with me" meeting it was a sign he thought you were worth the investment.

I have worked with senior managers who struggle in the relationship area. They are experts in the business and have all the right abilities to get work done but ask them to take one of their employees to lunch one-on-one and the conversation dries up after five minutes.

Try inviting employees to go with you to visit a customer. I remember one Managing Genius inviting me along with him to see a cell tower. While the tour was interesting, I really enjoyed our time together through which I developed a greater appreciation of his job and how he thought about business issues. I had the opportunity to pick up tidbits of advice from his experience.

One general manager of a manufacturing plant did a weekly safety walk-through. Each week he would ask a different employee to join him. As they walked, the GM would share updates and teach them how the business works.

It is fun to share stories about your memorable "muck-ups." These are "with me" moments where you give employees access to how work happens in different parts of the business.

Make your team feel important

"Love the One You're With" is classic oldie single by Stephen Stills.

> *"If you're down and confused,*
> *and you don't remember who you're talking to...*
> *Love the one you're with".*

I often use this song to remind myself that the people I am with deserve my full attention. It is interesting that when your phone buzzes, you momentarily forget about the person you are with and your mind has now gone down a path thinking about another person and interaction.

Make your direct reports feel special, like they have a unique connection with their boss and other team members.

I have been impressed with Holly Leach, a Managing Genius and Head administrator of a K-8 Academy near Seattle, Washington. Each year in the parent orientation meeting, she will individually introduce every one of the seventy-five teachers and staff. She knows where they went to school, their families, what they're working on and their hometown. She pulled this off through no small effort.

When we walk down the hall together at her school, Holly will stop teachers in the hallway to introduce them to me, like "You need to meet our awesome biology teacher." When she does this, I always get the feeling that I have just met her most favorite, exceptional teacher, until we meet the next teacher in the hall. This attitude is infectious.

"Andrea, are you aware that Steve completed his MBA last month?"

The key is to make your employees feel as if they are a high priority; show them that your team comes first. Read and reply to your employees' emails first. Make it easy for your employees to get on your schedule and give them the best part of your day. It will make them feel like you have given them a backstage pass.

Manage the electronic world

Electronic tools and Apps are a great benefit--scheduling, organizing group projects, sharing information across distance and speeding up decisions. It is just that the interface is blurred and tough to control. Just as important as the shared physical space, manage the electronic workspace to maintain professionalism, courtesy and focus.

It starts with you. I was in the corporate cafeteria meeting with a senior executive at his request. At no time during the lunch did he put down his smart phone. Apparently, my time was worth wasting. It was difficult to get him to focus on our reason for meeting.

How do you use your smart phone? Do you let yourself get interrupted during meetings? Do you break eye contact to check the screen? Your team is watching.

Act like the owner. Would an orchestra conductor allow the violin section to text on their cell phone during a section that only uses the horns and percussion?

This is your team, you own this workplace. Employees do not have some inherent personal right to do whatever they want at work. You should feel empowered to step in to redirect the use of email, texting and any other electronic communication on behalf of your group, to maintain professionalism and reduce the noise.

I remember one holiday season the parent company decided to cancel all holiday parties. What followed were a flurry of group-wide emails complaining and bantering. The senior leader of the group let it go for a while and then sent a friendly email closing down the discussion. It was appropriate and timely.

This will not just accidentally happen—are you directing the orchestra or just playing along?

Set team norms. The FX series, *Sons of Anarchy*, is a crime drama about the lives of a close-knit outlaw motorcycle club. Whenever the club has a group meeting, team members throws their cell phones into a shoe box at the door. Even the criminal clubs have team norms about cell phones that goes for everyone.

Do not create policy that you cannot control. When you put yourself into "surveillance mode" to watch wayward employees, you have diminished your power and authority to manage your group.

Instead, you should discuss with your team and develop eCulture team norms that everyone can readily support.

First, introduce a few norms that are important to you and seek mutual agreement. "Friendly reminder for everyone. Email is for exchanging information and schedule updates. We handle personal differences with face-to-face discussions."

Let the group add their own expectations to the list and refresh the norms to keep them relevant.

Of course, role model the behavior and let them call you on it when you mess up. Show value for face-to-face discussion by focusing on the people in the room. As you meet, are you looking at your phone and texting other people?

Open issues to consider concerning electronic communication:
- Anyone can raise an issue and make it today's agenda.
- People can skirt authority and sidestep protocol to share frustrations and problems. They can voice any opinion to literally anyone they want, whenever they want.

- Emails and phones have an illusion of power—they let you go wherever you want to go and as fast as you want. With email, it is too easy for one individual to pull the chord and stop the train, forcing you to respond to give an explanation.
- Smart phones, texting and email can easily digress into a "free-range" work style. That distracts people, minimizes your leadership of the group and fractures team accountability.
- Email allows unfettered discussion and third-party triangles that skirt personal responsibility. This can blow up issue and involve the wrong people in the discussion.
- Email allows the sender to get the "last word" without the accountability of a face-to-face encounter.
- Smart phones are valuable if they help get real work done and facilitate effective team relationships. However, electronic communication often becomes a dangling conversation that does not give closure. In the early days of the telephone this was what was called a "party line" where anyone could listen and join in the conversation.

3 MANAGE GROUP MEETINGS

In the early 90's, at the advent of the Internet culture, you may find it difficult to imagine that few people used or embraced email. Back then, I sat next to a senior software development director at a team-building workshop in downtown Seattle. As I got to know him, he shared that he was leading a subsidiary that packaged the software.

Interestingly, his chief complaint about the employees in his new organization was that they did not email him. He shared that he would walk through the operation and employees would come up to talk with him and he would stop them and say, "Email, I want you to email me!"

Today, the problem is that our digital culture has made it too easy to stay connected without a face-to-face encounter. Every day we find a new App that allows us to communicate with people without actually talking face-to-face. We can lose the art of talking to real people.

Master the art of facilitating group discussion

Bring more interaction to your whole group in the group setting. It fosters adult participation, sidesteps individual agendas and promotes mutual accountability. If people are in the room they can respond to your words and ask follow-up questions.

There is an art to managing group conversation. Without you stepping up to take the lead, the group can turn into a cacophony of personal opinion and individuals vying to be heard. It is like having an open mike on stage without anyone running the show. The extroverts will carry the conversation and some people will feel swept under.

How to manage the group discussion:
- The secret to success is how you start the meeting. Have a 10 minute "check-in" to give everyone a chance to speak up about what they are working on, a frustrating item or an interesting tidbit.
- Pull together ideas, like taking what Jeremy said and connecting it to what Sanjay said and highlighting what they both have in common?
- Writing main ideas on the white board will force the group to focus on what has already been agreed to or addressed. This makes it tough to ignore the group conversation.
- Take a minute at the start to ascertain why are we here and why it is important. (Sorry, you knew that was coming.)
- Manage the mic so the right people get opportunity to speak out and share their well-prepared ideas. Do not let the extroverts carry the meeting.
- Focus on a narrow agenda and find success fleshing out one topic.
- Keep the group on track. Make sure there is closure on issues.

Lead great meetings

Running effective team meetings will unify your group far more than any team building program. This is a must-have skill for your career.

People hate meetings because they are typically so poorly run. Every meeting needs a leader. Do it yourself or delegate to someone you know has the skills to enhance the opportunity for employees when they get together.

Once you create a sense of order and expectation for meetings, people will lighten up and relax. You may find spontaneity in the midst of structure.

Do people come to meetings prepared and ready? Do you ask meaty questions that get people engaged? Do you see dialogue and sharing?

Group norms and customs

Imagine a thirty-second speech describing your group: "Around here, we're ..."

For example, "Around here, we are always on time for meetings. People dress casual. We stop boring meetings. We drink lots of coffee and everyone makes a fresh pot when needed. We always help one another. We always keep our promises and tell the truth."

Now imagine you are hearing one of your team members describing the team culture for you. Group norms will create a predictable and safe "neighborhood," and create a strong social bond.

I suggest you bring 3-4 of your own "must have" norms. Then have your team discuss and agree to additional group norms that everyone can support. Here are a few examples:

- Do not speak about people who are not in the room.
- Always tell the truth.
- Openly share information that people need to do their jobs.
- Always on time for meetings.
- Leave your cell phone in your pocket for meetings with team members.

In the end, your group should have a list of mutually agreed-to practices that they will all adhere to. Then the group can apply friendly peer pressure and self-manage. This is a game-changer.

4 | SHARE GOOD NEWS WITH THE GROUP

The key point is to take advantage of any team meeting or gathering to build up your team. You want people to see you as a visible leader of team operations.

When the group is assembled, give recognition for individuals and teams. Look for every opportunity to say people's names for real and tangible results. Share news and information so everyone is in the know about the organization, the team and what you are doing.

> Make use of any group gathering to build community.

Two things are important. First, you should get involved with the planning yourself and not just your Admin or the group social butterfly. See this meeting as important as a key customer event. Show people that "this is your party".

Second, when your group is together, take front-and-center leadership for the event. Just be yourself and keep things light and casual. Show people that you are glad to be there. Do not "blow in and out" like the rock star who is too busy for your own employees.

Try this: be the first person to arrive and the last one to leave any group meeting that you lead.

5 GET THE DISTANCE RIGHT

With the workforce becoming more diverse, it is important to build an inclusive team culture. This is not as easy as it sounds. People bring different expectations to the workplace and could have unnamed desires or partially formed ideas, or even secret ambitions. They might also be bound by strong cultural traditions.

> Build a respectful culture where everybody gets heard.

It is great if you develop a closer affinity with coworkers but with some people you may hit walls. Make it everyone's responsibility to establish their own boundaries and share what they prefer. You don't want to be in the middle of everyone's relationships. This is a topic for an occasional group meeting.

Here are some talking points:

- Allow personal space and emotional distance—do not assume others want what you want. You can effectively work together, enjoy work and have fun without becoming "best buds." The problem usually stems from us—we share personal stories and this sets things in motion.

- Spread the attention: Spending extra time with certain employees can set up comparisons and jealousy. An extroverted person may choose to open up and share more of their personal thoughts.

- In our management role, we can unknowingly use our power to cause people to open up. If my boss asks me, I may feel compelled to share more due to perceived power and position. You control this through your questions and choosing to get involved.

- When you manage people, telling people what you feel or think can affect people's emotional temperament. Never pass to your people your own personal worries or fears. Your employees should not hear things they have no control over.

One last point on people going through personal issues. You can show empathy without getting involved. A colleague came to me deeply distressed about something in his home life. I was honored that he made a beeline to my office to vent. I listened to allow him to self-calm and encouraged him that I was sure he could solve this problem.

I have never been successful in trying to fix problems for employees. It can become awkward as you know more about personal issues than you prefer. Entering into private conversations will influence your ability to make neutral and unbiased decisions.

People who are going through personal trauma may need closer managing to help them focus on specific short term goals. You may need to pare down their work goals in the short term to allow them to focus.

6 SHARPEN YOUR SOCIAL AWARENESS

The Upper Peninsula of Michigan is a geographically separate space in America that lies north of Wisconsin on the south shore of Lake Superior. The Upper Peninsula contains 29 percent of the land area of Michigan but only three percent of its total population.

The populace is close-knit and it is a true small-town culture, with extremely harsh winters. Residents have a strong regional identity. Large numbers of Finnish, Swedish, Cornish and Italian immigrants came to the Upper Peninsula to work in the area's mines.

The open-pit mining operation where I worked, after engineering school, was near Ishpeming, Michigan (try finding that town on a map).

With all this said as an introduction, here is a small-town story. I was surprised when one of my close work colleagues did not invite me to his daughter's wedding. It seemed like everyone else at work was going to the party. I felt left out when I did not receive an invitation in the mail.

Later, this coworker acted hurt and disappointed that I did not show up. He eventually asked, "Where were you? I was expecting you to come to the wedding. I wanted you to meet my family and share the event." It turns out that in this small town, the local practice was to run an ad in the hometown newspaper announcing the wedding. Then everyone who feels close to the family knows to attend. I read the paper but did not realize that was the invitation.

How many times have you made social and cultural assumptions based on your upbringing and experiences? Ways to keep your social antenna sharp:

Stay in a learning mode. Be willing to humbly ask questions in order to understand the differences in the people on your team. If a coworker is expecting a baby, ask him or her how people celebrated a new baby when they were growing up. What are the wedding customs? Do not make assumptions and don't be afraid to ask.

> Do not make assumptions. Ask people to let you know what is important.

Be a great communicator. The biggest challenge in a diverse work-force is the potential language barrier. When we work with people for whom English is their second language, they may do well with formal or literal meanings. But the informal words and colloquial speech can be a significant problem. People may not pick up on idioms and nonverbal expressions. This is a great opportunity for you to take the lead and draw people out.

Times of crisis and time crunches. Everyone responds to stress differently and as leader you should step in to speak simply and clearly so that everyone understands the current situation. It's OK to micromanage in those moments as you may not have the time to ensure that everyone understands you. This is when relationships can break down. Demonstrate competence with a composed demeanor.

Be inclusive. It is as simple as making introductions. Manage the invited list for standing group meetings to make sure the right people are attending. Do what you can to make people feel like they belong. This involves opening doors so they can meet the right people. Not everyone is good at networking and making connections.

Numbers speak clearly. A bridge for a highly diverse workforce is to focus on facts and data. It is easier to communicate over a common set of information and reports.

Be a giving person. Always look for ways to help out or give a listening ear. Giving speaks well in any language.

Avoid engaging in office gossip and banter. You can negate all the positive good will you create through better workplace relationships. By your participation in gossip and chatter, you validate and promote this destructive workplace behavior.

You should stand ready to redirect conversation and even shut down banter that is disrespectful to people. "Hey guys, Joe is not here to defend himself" goes a long way to communicate to your team that you are a respecter of persons and gossip isn't OK in this environment. They will make the connection that you would you do the same for them.

7 CATCH IMPORTANT PERSONAL EVENTS

Show that you are personally aware and leading the team neighborhood. Managers often see social events as small details, not worthy of their time. They may just ask their Admins to handle the social stuff.

You will build respect for yourself when you show personal interest and stay in the middle of important team events. People will appreciate it when you catch that something big is happening outside of the workplace: graduation, new baby, marriage, new house or bereavement. If you don't, people may feel slighted.

Pull out your calendar right now and mark as many events as you can.

- People love to be recognized on their birthdays—it is as American as apple pie.
- Always celebrate education milestones: "I want everyone to know how proud we are of Dawn. She finished her degree in accounting last week, after attending night classes for several years."
- Recognize personal achievements like finishing a marathon, walking in the breast cancer 10K or winning an election to the local school board.
- Always remember babies, weddings and kids' graduations.
- As a former MBA evening program student, I know how important it is to always remember final exam time. People should not let their night education interfere with the team's business but you might send an employee to "work from home" the day before an important exam. This warms everyone's heart.

8 ACT LIKE THE MAYOR

Any community needs someone at the local level who can be counted on to look out for the needs of the community.

In most companies, HR serves as the de facto head of team culture. However, it is Managing Genius to take ownership for your own workplace neighborhood. See your role differently from the norm:

Communications Officer. You want your people to trust you and believe that you will keep them informed on what is important.

People have an insatiable need to "fill in the blanks." Human nature drives us to seek closure and we will look for answers from anyone, especially people whom we perceive to be on the inside. In the absence of up-to-date news, you can expect your employees to keep walking the halls until they satisfy their inner need for an answer for today's big questions.

If you choose to remain silent, people will ask around to get whatever facts and information they can find. The unofficial group communicator may step in on your behalf to fill in the blanks. If you avoid talking about the fired employee, someone will speak for you. With or without you, *communication always happens*.

Who speaks for you? Opinionated people often serve out the daily news—they love talking to people, they love drama and intrigue.

If you show distance and keep people in the dark, you lose trust and credibility as the manager of your work group. If you cannot share the full personal story, you can share your decision process and walk through the steps for making employee decisions.

It is important to ask, where do you want people go with questions? Do they go to coworkers, HR or your Admin? Do they know to bring questions to you or the team meeting? You do not need to immediately answer the question or make it today's priority. People just need a place where someone will at least hear and validate their concerns.

Just be sure that your group is not taking their questions purposely away from you. *You want to be their first phone call.*

Play a visible leadership role. You cannot hang out in your office. Your presence in the work area will build trust and assurance that things are under control.

Walk the neighborhood to personally connect with your employees. Go into their space whenever you can—have coffee or lunch in the employee break room. Walk the production floor or stop by their office. Ask your employees to show you what they are working on.

This speaks to your availability and access. This will help your team weather the peaks and valleys of workplace relationships. Your presence will build trust and assurance that things are under control.

Virtual employees: Many of us manage off-site workers. You need to pay particular attention to keeping virtual employees feeling connected and informed. The key is to stay disciplined in your communication processes. Set up standing meetings and adhere to that schedule. You cannot just shoot from hip with your communications like you do with employees who just work down the hall.

Use a set agenda and ensure clarity at the end of the meeting as you will not have the luxury of seeing non-verbal affirmation.

There will always be a crisis or changes that affect everyone. For the occasional tornado, you need an early warning system that reaches everyone.

Stressful times. Eventually your group will face a major storm or unexpected trauma. For example, suppose a senior leader leaves, a major reorganization is announced or the company hits financial problems.

> When news comes in "dribs and drabs" it creates suspense and drama.

See that there are times when your team will greatly benefit from a visible and engaged leader. People can become blinded by stress and pressure. Help people get through special times of stressful change, confusion or toxic worry:

1. **"He who rules must rule with calm."** There needs to be at least one person in the room who rises above the emotion of the moment. You set the tone for your group.

2. **Reset the team.** Freeway accidents can slow down traffic for hours. Likewise, bad news and unfortunate events can negatively affect your team. Help your work group reset and restart after a stressful event. For example, a basketball coach will call a timeout when the team is flustered. Then they call the next play so the team has a way to get restarted and move past the previous mistakes.

3. **Stay visible and give extra communication during stressful times.** People may need your help to shake things off, so walk around the "neighborhood." Do not monologue or give people too much to handle. No need to water down, sell or spin. In most cases, we are just delivering the news and it is what it is. Your presence should be enough to calm the nerves.

4. **Damage control.** Learn how to handle bad news. Toby Ziegler was the character playing the White House Communications Officer on the TV show *West Wing*. Toby shared these rules for damage control:
   - Get the information out early.
   - Get it out yourself.
   - Do it on your own terms.

Discover Your Managing Genius

- People come to work expecting to find social community. Social connections are a strong indicator of job satisfaction.

- A Managing Genius will take the lead to build and maintain a colleague-friendly work community.

- There are eight simple practices (page 283) that you can use to manage the employee experience for your team. This is how you create opportunities for team members to build effective working relationships and everyday rapport.

- Keep the right balance: stay *friendly* without focusing on *friendship*.

- Workplace community does not just happen—this is your team to manage. Do not delegate this to HR or your staff. Your employees need to see you in the center of the team culture.

APPENDIX

The Managing Genius 50

I sought to write this book based on real managers making real decisions concerning real people doing real work.

So I went back and identified fifty of the best of the best people managers whom I have worked with in my career.

Those interactions became the framework for this book. I then went back through my work journals and wrote of real life examples that captured their composite actions and collective mastery.

These people were the heart and inspiration for Managing Genius. A few people may be surprised to receive this recognition. To them I say, you were role modeling Managing Genius before I had a name for it.

Bob Beckert	Eric Hertz	Matthew Moore
Christine Martin	Dan Hesse	Scott Morton
Richard Brockman	Steve Hooper	Rod Nelson
Alan Caplan	Chaz Immendorf	Karen Noller
Lewis Carpenter	Najmi Jarwala	Scott Peabody
Doug Carter	Mary Jesse	Matthew Price
Vikram Chalana	Nick Kauser	Bob Ruhlman
Stacy Cheuvront	Doug King	Ed Salley
Dennis Davenport	Kerry Larson	John Saw
Ginny Eagle	Holly Leach	Toby Seay
Mark Fanning	Dave Lindstrom	Larry Seifert
Rob Frasene	Bob Mahlik	John Song
Dave Gibbons	Margaret Marino	Tom Van Wie
Lon Gentry	Jane Marvin	Kendra VanderMeulen
Jim Grams	Ed McCahill	Gerry Vanderwel
Julie Halfaday	Lynn Mellantine	John Vlastelica
Lois Hedg-peth	Tucker Moodey	

Acknowledgments

The Managing Genius project spans across five years. The scope of this endeavor is so immense that I need to give credit to many people. I wish to thank the following colleagues for stepping in at the right time and place to make contributions, share ideas and stories, edit material and provide the encouragement that writing the story about Managing Genius was worth the effort.

Holly Leach	Bill Kersey	Lee Gessner
Lon Gentry	Ann Richardson	Tom Deyonker
Dan Laurenzo	Clyde Dildine	Scott Morton
Julie Halfaday	Robert G. Fong	Craig Thompson
Richard Brockman	Carolyn Sherwood	Alan Cleland
Matt Jackson	Jeff Steinke	Tim Trosvig
Marjorie James	Don Wolfe	Jennifer Barnes
Mary Sanford	Shannon Zastrow	Dave Dibble
Ed McCahill	Tom Deyonker	Debbie Cleland
Matthew Price	Mike Vander Wel	Bob Ruhlman
Rick Allen	Matthew Moore	Scott Swick
Brad Turcott	Lewis Carpenter